Architecture and design for the family

IN BRITAIN, 1900–70

MANCHESTER
UNIVERSITY PRESS

general editor:
CHRISTOPHER BREWARD

already published in the series

Utility reassessed
JUDY ATTFIELD

The culture of fashion
A new history of fashionable dress
CHRISTOPHER BREWARD

The hidden consumer
Masculinities, fashion and city life, 1860–1914
CHRISTOPHER BREWARD

The British country house in the eighteenth century
CHRISTOPHER CHRISTIE

Pioneers of modern craft
Twelve essays profiling key figures in the history of contemporary crafts
EDITED BY MARGOT COATTS

Defining dress
Dress as object, meaning and identity
AMY DE LA HAYE AND ELIZABETH WILSON

The culture of craft
Status and future
EDITED BY PETER DORMER

Eighteenth-century furniture
CLIVE D. EDWARDS

Graphic design
Reproduction and representation since 1800
PAUL JOBLING AND DAVID CROWLEY

The Edwardian house
The middle-class home in Britain 1880–1914
HELEN C. LONG

The birth of modern London
The development and design of the city
ELIZABETH MCKELLAR

Eighteenth-century ceramics
SARAH RICHARDS

Women and ceramics
Gendered vessels
MOIRA VINCENTELLI

American design in the twentieth century
Personality and performance
GREGORY VOTOLATO

Architecture and design for the family

IN BRITAIN, 1900–70

David Jeremiah

Manchester University Press
Manchester and New York

distributed exclusively in the USA by St. Martin's Press

Published by Manchester University Press
Oxford Road, Manchester M13 9NR, UK
and Room 400, 175 Fifth Avenue, New York, NY 10010, USA
http://www.man.ac.uk/mup

Distributed exclusively in the USA by
St. Martin's Press, Inc., 175 Fifth Avenue, New York,
NY 10010, USA

Distributed exclusively in Canada by
UBC Press, University of British Columbia, 2029 West Mall,
Vancouver, BC, Canada V6T 1Z2

British Library Cataloguing-in-Publication Data
A catalogue record for this book is available from the British Library

Library of Congress Cataloging-in-Publication Data applied for

ISBN 0 7190 4928 8 *hardback*
0 7190 5889 9 *paperback*

First published 2000

07 06 05 04 03 02 01 00 10 9 8 7 6 5 4 3 2 1

Typeset in ITC Giovanni
by Carnegie Publishing, Lancaster
Printed in Great Britain
by Alden Press, Oxford

Contents

Illustrations

Acknowledgements

I am extremely grateful for all the help from libraries and archives that I have used, making extended use of the British Architectural Library, and Library of the National Motor Museum, and I greatly appreciate the assistance of Mrs J. Faraday, archivist, John Lewis Partnership; Mrs D. G. Stobbs, Pilkington Brothers PLC; Mrs Linda Walkden, CWS Library and Information Unit. I value all the help that I have received in obtaining illustrations, particularly that provided by Tony Rowe, and the invitation from Mr and Mrs Tailby to view their 'all-electric' home. To Sam Smiles and my research colleagues in art and design history my thanks for their interest and encouragment, and to Christopher Breward and John Hewitt for their invaluable advice and suggestions on the manuscript.

To my wife Maureen for her support and critical advice at every stage of the project.

✧ Introduction

MODERN and modernisation are the two central issues of an inquiry intent on developing an increased awareness of the social function of architecture and design in Britain during a time that was dominated by two periods of national reconstruction. The study begins with an acknowledgement of the importance of the nineteenth-century legacy, and the defining of the social purpose of architecture and design for the family as the provision of 'Health, Comfort and Happiness'. Drawing substantially on official and professional publications it is a history that brings together the ideas and practices motivated by a desire to raise standards of everyday life. Attention is directed towards the models, texts and demonstrations that cultivated ideas of the practical and the ideal for a loosely defined consumer group that embraced 'the people' and those of 'moderate means', and which through government legislation, local authority intervention and commercial speculation was widened to include the poor and those living in poverty. By bringing together what sometimes appear to be disparate initiatives it is intended to show the importance of an overriding agenda to provide a better life, sustained by a belief in the objectives of progress and improvement, which through planning and technical change would put in place a modern Britain.

The three key areas for consideration are: family homes and new neighbourhoods, the products and schemes for everyday life, and the housewife and family lifestyle. For the purposes of understanding the emerging patterns of change, a chronological framework has been employed and, in terms of class, the contemporary conventions of working- and middle-class groupings have been used. The documentation shows how, for commercial and planning purposes, the ideal family was simplified as being mother, father and children of both sexes, and the responsible family was rarely if ever portrayed as having more than three children. The imaging of the family in the context of home and as a consumer of products directs attention to the representation of social order and values, and the manner in which this association was used as an indicator of national characteristics and taste. Involving the construction of models of the ideal as an attainable dream, consideration has been given to ways in which the welfare and happiness of the family was identified as the barometer of the nation's fortunes and social stability. The emphasis placed on the work and management responsibilities attached to the role of the housewife are a recurring feature of the debate, critical moments are highlighted and while gender is not dealt with as a separate issue it is anticipated that the work will add to recent collections of essays, *A View from the Interior. Women and Design,*[1] and *Women Designing. Redefining Design in Britain between the Wars.*[2]

The study draws on the traditions of architectural and design history, town planning, sociology, history and local history. Much use has been made of contemporary journals: *Illustrated London News, Builder, Art Journal, Architects' Journal* and *Graphic* of the nineteenth century; the *Studio, Country Life, Municipal Journal, Autocar* and *Architectural Review* from the turn of the century. The important new journals of the post-First World War, such as *Homes and Gardens, Good Housekeeping, Ideal Home, The Listener* and *Picture Post,* have been essential sources in identifying the topical and social mood of architectural and design change. Government reports and guides have been constant reminders of the political intervention in matters of taste and social priorities, while *Design* acts as a reminder of the establishment dominance of professional opinion from 1949 onwards. Exhibitions on national and regional scale have provided defining moments in consumer values, and those displays arranged through the collaboration of retail trade and professional organisations have been essential conduits of new ideas, conspiring to raise public expectations. In this respect it was a difficult decision to stand back from a detailed study of patterns of consumption and the studies that have dealt with social habits and preferences, yet defining and assessing the significance of what might be described as an official line this choice had to be made. This means that there are lines of inquiry on popular taste, poverty and the economics of taste, which could be pursued further through the use of oral histories, and examined in detail within the framework of local history and family histories, including the social inquiries and visual documenting assembled by the work of Mass-Observation from 1937 onwards, and the findings presented in studies such as B. Seebohm Rowntree and G. R. Lavers, *English Life and Leisure,*[3] and Geoffrey Gover, *Exploring English Character.*[4] Equally the family as represented in children's books and novels, or women's magazines, are important yet distinct subjects in their own right for future consideration.

In its breadth of understanding the historical narrative of Peter Clarke's

Hope and Glory Britain 1900–1990[5] provides an invaluable backdrop, as do social histories such as Jose Harris, *Private Lives – Public Spirit,*[6] Patrick Joyce, *Visions of the People,*[7] John Stevenson, *British Society, 1914–1945,*[8] and Arthur Marwick, *British Society Since 1945.*[9] Similarly I recognise the importance of the growing number of publications that are adding to works on twentieth-century British culture, including the recent *Design and Cultural Politics in Post-War Britain,* edited by Patrick J. Maguire and Jonathan M. Woodham,[10] and Ross McKibbin's *Classes and Cultures, England 1918–1951.*[11]

Style and taste are an integral part of this history, in which the representations of products, homes and landscapes were used to establish new ideologies, and on which the writings of Nikolaus Pevsner on British architecture and design as a regular contributor to *Studio* and *Architectural Review,*[12] and his *Pioneers of the Modern Movement* and *An Inquiry into Industrial Art in England*[13] played a formative role. Taking social purpose as the primary interest provides a new opportunity to re-examine work on the everyday as pioneering and by formulating an inclusive agenda should make a contribution to the debate opened by Adrian Forty in *Objects of Desire: Design and Society 1750–1980,*[14] and recently developed by Jonathan M. Woodham in *Twentieth-Century Design.*[15] In addition it is anticipated that it will provide an added dimension to the important studies of decades, amongst which the exhibition catalogues *Thirties,*[16] and *1966 and All That,*[17] are good examples, and to the publications on major exhibitions, such as 'Britain Can Make It' and the 'Festival of Britain'.

Planning, whether it was of landscapes, towns, homes, interiors or lives, became a national preoccupation. Order and new orders, through architecture and design, dominated professional, social and political thinking and actions, and in this respect the study makes recurring reference to the understanding of minimum standards, economy of space, services and amenities required by the family. The importance of land as a national resource, is well illustrated by the reports which went towards L. Dudley Stamp's *The Land of Britain. Its Use and Misuse.*[18] The published literature on housing and schemes, both on type and place, is overwhelming. I have drawn on histories of model housing and the garden city movement, and in terms of the approach of this study, useful alternatives are provided by publications such as A. A. Jackson's *Semi-Detached London,*[19] Alison Rowetz with Richard Turkington, *The Place of Home. English Domestic Environments 1914–2000,*[20] *Rebuilding Scotland,* edited by Miles Glendinning,[21] and the comprehensive work *Tower Blocks* by Miles Glendinning and Stefan Muthesius.[22] Having visited a wide range of new settlements, particularly those generated by company and government intervention, I am aware that there remains much research which could be carried out on the processes of change through the personalisation of the domestic landscape, notably by the introduction of applied architectural features, while in the case of the land settlement schemes there is an opportunity to follow through the design consequences of recent social and commercial changes.

Medical Officer of Health reports played an important part in drawing attention to a whole range of social problems connected with housing, diet and general considerations of community health care. These made a significant contribution to local policy and opinions on housing and amenities, increasingly so in the early decades of the twentieth century. Integral to the social histories of health and, as shown by Annmarie Adams, *Architecture in the Family Way. Doctors, Houses and Women 1870–1900.*[23] this source provides an additional dimension to the established architectural and design histories.

Diverse in its interests, extensive use has been made of primary material establishing the sequences in which the social purposes of architecture and design for the family addressed questions of replacement and renewal. Constrained by politics and commerce on one hand, and technology and manufacture on the other, it becomes possible to identify how architecture and design policies and practices responded to the desire for a new social order, tracking the professional optimism through to the fading confidence in the technological dream of the 1960s.

Notes

1 J. Atfield and P. Kirkham, *A View from the Interior. Women and Design*, London, 1989.

2 J. Seddon and S. Worden (eds), *Women Designing. Redefining Design in Britain Between the Wars*, Brighton, 1994.

3 B. Seebohm Rowntree and G. R. Lavers, *English Life and Leisure*, London, 1951.

4 G. Gover, *Exploring English Character*, London, 1955.

5 P. Clarke, *Hope and Glory, Britain 1900–1990*, London, 1996.

6 J. Harris, *Private Lives – Public Spirit*, Oxford, 1993.

7 P. Joyce, *Visions of the People*, Cambridge, 1991.

8 J. Stevenson, *British Society 1914–1945*, London, 1984.

9 A. Marwick, *British Society Since 1945*, London 1996.

10 P. Maguire and J. M. Woodham (eds), *Design and Cultural Politics in Post-War Britain*, London, 1997.

11 R. McKibbin, *Classes and Cultures, England 1918–1951*, Oxford 1998.

12 N. Pevsner, *Pioneers of the Modern Movement*, London, 1936.

13 N. Pevsner, *An Inquiry into Industrial Art in England*, Cambridge, 1937.

14 A. Forty, *Objects of Desire: Design and Society 1750–1980*, London, 1986.

15 J. M. Woodham, *Twentieth-Century Design*, Oxford 1997.

16 *Thirties*, exhibition catalogue, London, 1979.

17 *1996 and All That*, exhibition catalogue, London, 1986.

18 L. D. Stamp, *The Land of Britain. Its Use and Misuse*, 3rd edn, London, 1962; 1st pub. 1948.

19 A. A. Jackson, *Semi-Detached London*, London, 1973.

20 A. Rowetz with R. Turkington, *The Place of Home. English Domestic Environments 1914–2000*, London, 1995.

21 M. Glendinning (ed.), *Rebuilding Scotland*, East Linton, 1997.

22 M. Glendinning and S. Muthesius, *Tower Blocks*, New Haven, 1994.

23 A. Adams, *Architecture in the Family Way. Doctors, Houses and Women 1870–1900*, Quebec, 1996.

1 ✧ Health, comfort and happiness

The legacy

Health and home

As Britain's first phase of post-war reconstruction approached the end of the 1920s, the lack of progress in urban renewal could not be ignored. There was a growing feeling that rather than improving, the social and environmental problems were getting worse and beginning to undermine the plans for modern life in Britain. A scapegoat had to be found, and the nineteenth century proved to be a convenient all-embracing villain. It was, as John Gloag put it, a generation that had 'bequeathed us the Black Country, the slums, and the Albert Memorial'.[1] At a stroke he had dismissed the nineteenth century as an age of smoke, disease and bad taste, yet it was its legislation against the ills of industrial society that substantially shaped the twentieth-century agenda of architecture and design for the family.

Over the nineteenth century homelife and homelessness remained a national preoccupation, and was to remain so in twentieth-century Britain. Increasing access to education, culture and leisure retained a similar importance in national planning, as did the overriding ambitions to turn the privileges of the minority into the pleasures of the masses. Health was the key issue to the programme of social improvement. In celebration of Queen Victoria's Jubilee of 1887, Captain Douglas Galton had devoted his opening address as Chairman of the Society of Arts Council to the subject of sanitation. Reflecting on the Society's long involvement in campaigns to improve the plight of the poor and labouring classes, including education, moral and social welfare, health and housing, he identified the progress in sanitation and housing for the poorer classes as being the greatest achievement of the previous fifty years.[2]

The *Builder*'s Jubilee review supported this view: 'The many blocks of healthy dwellings which have been built during later years, not indeed beautiful architecturally, but representing the possibility of decent, comfortable and healthy housing for the poor, are as important architectural works in their way as cathedrals and churches.'[3] At the same time the *Journal of Decorative Art* ran an article on 'The homes of the working classes: how to make them sweet, clean and beautiful'.[4] The remarks were directed at those who had the capabilities to improve the general living conditions, the landlords. The ideal model for the artisan's family was a parlour, kitchen, scullery and three bedrooms. The reality for the poor and labouring classes was more likely to be one room acting for all functions, and with no sanitary facilities.

In the years leading up to the Queen's accession in 1837 there had been a growing recognition of the need to take action over national poverty and disease. The 1832 cholera epidemic had demonstrated that these problems were not restricted to the large urban conurbations. Fevers were rife among the poor, food was expensive and the level of poverty was overwhelming. It prompted the inquiries of the Poor Law Commissioners whose findings led to the influential *Report on the Sanitary Condition of the labouring population of Great Britain*, by Edwin Chadwick, published in 1842, and with the further threat of a cholera outbreak in 1848, the introduction of a General Board of Health Act to improve the sanitary conditions of towns. With the 1846 Act to Encourage the Establishment of Public Baths and Wash-houses, legislation was in place for boroughs to raise a rate to provide the necessary funds to construct and run such establishments. It meant that for the first time the labouring classes were to be offered the opportunity to wash themselves and their clothes in purpose-built premises. The privilege was not cheap, costing twice as much to have a hot, rather than cold, bath, although up to four children under the age of eight could have a bath for the same price.[5] Washdays remained a major event; the new facilities were slow to appear, and serving large districts were far from convenient for women with young children. Consequently, even the sharing of a copper by tenement families, with dangers of spreading disease, was often a preferred option.

Providing for the basic family needs, and agreeing on the minimum living standards was established on the national agenda, as was utility, and the economics of production and marketing things for everyday use. In the 1840s the Society of Arts played a radical role through its revised premium lists in encouraging the development of design that combined 'art with objects strictly useful'. The demand was for elegance and economy, plain and inexpensive items relating to everyday life, which in turn would lead to improvements in personal hygiene and domestic comfort. Its annual Exhibitions of Invention, started in 1849, featured many designs which sought to answer such demands. Design was seen as technical invention, resulting in products described as 'mechanical contrivances for simplifying and diminishing the labour required in the preparation of articles of daily use, and for domestic purposes'.[6]

The local Boards of Health reports continued to present a picture of disease and complacency, with a high mortality rate amongst the poor classes. Success was only slowly gained. Outbreaks of cholera in 1854 and 1866 showed that water pollution was the root cause, having 'transferred our beautiful rivers into foul sewers, from which we still, after a more or less imperfect filtration, draw our water supply, not only for manufacturing and ablutionary purposes, but to drink'.[7] The picture was often as bad in rural communities as the new industrial villages,[8] although the conditions in the pit villages built without drains, water or any form of sanitation were the most extreme.[9] A continuing frustration over the pollution of rivers and streams, sewer gas and the disposal of household refuse in 1873 eventually brought about a new professional association for the sanitary engineer and architect. It embraced both moral and scientific considerations, with the better classes being encouraged to take it on themselves to improve the lives of the lower classes.[10] Three years later the Society of Arts held a major conference on the 'Health and sewage of towns' which in its comments and resolutions, particularly on the recently introduced Public Health Act (1875), stressed the need for legislation which would give an overall authority to local boards and compel house owners to comply with the development of a co-ordinated sanitation system for the district. Public inspections, and the role of Sanitary Inspector was established. So, at the time of the 1887 Jubilee, pollution of rivers, bad housing and treatment of diseases remained major causes for concern. Even so, the published statistical surveys showed that by the 1870s there were positive signs of a reduction in the mortality rate, and it was with justification that Galton could relate the triumphs of the previous fifty years as the lives which had been saved from disease and the education which had been developed.[11]

Public taste and self-improvement

Alongside the concern over matters of health and sanitation, educating the public in matters of taste was one of the great nineteenth-century achievements. Development of the social well-being of the nation, and the working classes in particular, was a key part of the movement to establish public museums and galleries. Out of the 1834 Select Committee set up to inquire into 'the prevailing vice of intoxication among the labouring classes' came a recommendation for the joint action of the government, local authority and residents to create public walks and gardens, open spaces for athletic and healthy exercises, and establish district and parish libraries, museums and reading rooms, that would be accessible at the lowest possible rate of admission. It was envisaged that the new buildings would also include meeting halls, a schoolroom for infants and classroom for older pupils, rooms for societies and local associations, and a lecture theatre.

The scheme was designed to bring opportunities for learning and self-improvement to the general public, but the proposed Act did not get beyond the committee stage. However, the investigation of the 1836 Select Committee on Arts and Manufacture and its successful launching of what became a national art school system ensured that the momentum was not entirely lost. With this in mind, on 6 March 1845 Parliament agreed to introduce a 'Bill to enable town councils to establish Museums of Art in corporate towns'. This Bill, and its effect, marked a significant stage in the development of the gallery system, taking it outside the limitations of private or institutional galleries, and placing it within the reach of the general public.[12] There was much enthusiasm for the proposal, with general support for the museums to be opened at times and under such regulations as would make it possible for the working classes to use them. Social improvement was at the centre of the legislation, and brought to the forefront the questions of free entry and Sunday opening.

The Bill received its royal assent on 21 July 1845, but it was soon discovered that as it was restricted to towns with populations over 10,000, and councils could levy an entrance charge, few authorities took advantage of the scheme. Of the handful who did, Salford and Warrington made the most significant start. Five years later the Bill was modified through its incorporation into a new Bill for Public Libraries and Museums. This new legislation, with further revisions in 1853, encouraged a building programme that linked libraries and museums in schemes throughout the country. The government offered some assistance, but never to the extent that the proposals could be totally viable without the generosity of individuals or some other form of subscription.

All of this was to be overshadowed by the determined planning and vision, inspired by the efforts of the Society of Arts and regional associations and institutes, which secured the construction of the Exhibition of the Industry of All Nations, London, 1851.[13] A landmark in the recognition of mass consumption, it confirmed the view that the working classes were deserving of better entertainment, education and homes. Closely associated with the movements of the previous twenty years to improve the housing of the labouring classes,[14] and standards of design, the successes of the Great Exhibition, as it was known, were proof that substantial economic as well as social gains could be made from enabling the working classes to share in the commercial revolution.

Organisationally the Great Exhibition was an extraordinary venture. The preoccupation with the representation of national taste was integral to the work displayed. Introducing the concept of friendly competition, with its medals for outstanding achievements, these ideals remained part of the design culture, that was to lead ultimately to the Council of Industrial Design (CoID) awards in the 1950s for good design.

The construction of the exhibition building and assembling all the exhibits in London were huge achievements in planning, but the mobilising of the whole country to visit the exhibition was the most audacious and revolutionary part of the enterprise. Nationalism and consumerism had been blended into one. In the space of one summer the world had been reduced to human proportions, and the possibilities of all classes eventually becoming consumers took on an air of reality.

Although never officially recognised, it was the Working Classes Committee,[15] which held its first meeting on 6 May 1850 at the Society of Arts, that provided invaluable assistance to the local area committees that had been set up to collect subscriptions, arrange cheap travel and negotiate for suitable accommodation for the working classes during their visit to London. A register of approved accommodation was prepared, and guides organised to meet the trains from the provinces. Considering the estimated influx of visitors, there were numerous anxious moments over issues of law and order, and at one stage the authorities seriously considered barring the public from the opening ceremony in case it provided the opportunity for revolutionary activity. Such anxieties proved unfounded, and once the cheap entry days had been introduced, it was quite clear that the artisan classes had made a substantial contribution to a final profit that was in excess of £150,000.[16]

Not unexpectedly, attitudes, as well as dress, were visibly different on the 'shilling' days. Contemporary reports noted that there was an overall greater sense of urgency amongst the visitors, not only interested in products of manufacture, but the range of musical instruments being demonstrated, the display of stuffed animals and the machine section with all its noise and activity. It was the mixing of noise and bustle, and families picnicking in the aisles which made a lasting impression.

The exhibitors, although initially forbidden to display the details of the price and availability of goods, in the end were allowed to distribute their own pamphlets and price lists. It was as consumers rather than connoisseurs that the public approached the objects of art and industry.

The highly decorated pieces of furniture, utensils and general domestic furnishings and ornaments received much publicity and subsequent criticism, but the more practical and utilitarian basic household appliances were equally important and innovative. For example, in the cottage range, the Victorians had perfected a machine for cooking, heating a room and warming water, that was still to be fitted into new workers' houses in the

1930s. The advertising language remained the same: 'for durability, economy and real efficiency ... for large and small families'.[17]

Functional aesthetics and convenience were part of the model home:

> This machine, which for simplicity of mechanism, durability of construction, and beauty of form, stands unrivalled – is well worthy of the attention of private families and of public institutions. Performing its functions with ease and efficiency; never damaging the linen; diminishing labor; economising fuel, soap, &c, and obviating much of the proverbial discomfort of the washing day, it has invariably secured the approbation of those parties who have had it in use.[18]

The expression was nineteenth-century, but the sentiments describing Taskers Washing, Wringing and Mangling Machine could just as readily be applied to a 1950s automatic washing machine.

Preoccupied with all things useful, the nineteenth century continued to develop a culture in which even much of the nation's leisure time was expected to be devoted to useful pursuits and self-improvement. For example, in September 1852, a Factory Operatives Exhibition and Bazaar was held in the Temperance Hall, Bolton. The intention was to show that since the introduction of the Ten Hours Bill, the factory workers had made good use of their increased leisure. Work on show included plain sewing, specimens of good mending, patching and well-darned stockings, knitting, netting and crochet work, fancy needlework, specimens of penmanship, drawings and paintings, and garden produce. Confirming the benefits of the well-run home, and the ability of the working classes to take advantage of opportunities for social improvement, it ultimately played a part in the arts and crafts movement at the end of the nineteenth century, with its promotion of home arts and industries.

Economic design and social purpose

Design was providing British society with a new set of objectives. In June 1857 Thomas Twining opened the new Economic Museum in London, formed out of his own collection that had been stimulated by the display of articles and appliances for improving the physical and intellectual conditions of the working classes in the Economic Gallery at the Paris 1855 International Exhibition and the Brussels Economic Exhibition, August 1856. Its purpose was to teach the working classes 'the knowledge of common things, and to show them how they may promote the health, comfort and happiness of themselves and their families'.[19] Reporting on his visit to the Paris Exhibition in the *Journal of the Society of Arts* a number of key issues were identified for incorporation into the museum, amongst which cheapness was a primary objective, allied with good quality and durability, which together would give value for money. It was expected to work closely with the retail trade, and hoped that it would show architects, builders and speculators how they could get a good return for their investments in raising 'improved habitations for the working classes in town or country' and renovating existing dwellings.[20] In proposing to establish a library, and publish catalogues and handbooks, Twining was also much influenced by the Commercial Museum, Brussels, which produced a weekly information sheet on foreign and domestic developments in commerce and industry, ran an information bureau and devoted a special room to the study of the packaging of merchandising.

Able to convince the Society of Arts of the merits of his argument, for the interim the Society accepted responsibility for his collection. Shortly afterwards Twining negotiated its relocation to the developing museum at South Kensington,[21] but its tenure only lasted two years. Transferring briefly to the Regent Street Polytechnic, it eventually ended up in Twining's own house in Twickenham, and subsequent obscurity. But the idea was not forgotten, and exhibitions both permanent and temporary kept the latest inventions for domestic efficiency and comfort in the public eye.[22]

With the publication of the *Builder* in 1843 and the *Art Journal* in 1848 the professions and upper classes were being kept informed on the history and contemporary practices and principles of art, architecture and decorative arts, and information on taste was readily available. When Richard Redgrave published his *Supplementary Report on Design* in 1852, he established the model for the official report on design at the international exhibitions, but it was Charles Lock Eastlake's *Hints on Household Taste,* 1868, that set in place the popular culture of taste. First he demolished the idea that you could not question the taste of a lady, and then advised that if you had to buy from a shop, it would be sensible not to trust the recommendations of a shopman, as 'his business is simply to sell'.[23] What the reader needed was Eastlake's advice, 'to encourage a discrimination between good and bad design in those articles of daily use we are accustomed to see around us'.[24] A hundred years later such sentiments were still at the core of the consumer culture. Similarly, the affluence of some families was edged by the poverty of others. Luke Fildes' powerful image of 'Houseless and hungry' on the page of the first issue of *Graphic,* 4 December 1869, was another reminder to Victorian society of the plight of the destitute families huddled together, freezing and ill-clothed, no home and no possessions, a forerunner of the 1960s 'Cathy come home'.

Appearances and language changed over the years, but the nineteenth and twentieth centuries were bound together with the same determination for improvement of society and the provision of an acceptable minimum standard of living. It was in this context that model dwellings remained a matter of public interest, and played a major role in defining these standards. Following on from the 1850s they were a prominent feature at the Paris Exhibition of 1867 when Edwin Chadwick, in his report on the exhibition, reiterated the continuing concern for ventilation, sound and damp insulation, and the problems created by the use of inferior materials. Household appliances attracted similar attention. At the Annual International Exhibition of 1873 in South Kensington, Yapp carried out a review of the cooking apparatus, showing special interest in pressure cookers and the continuing efficiency problems of gas cookers. He saw nothing new, but felt that the quality of workmanship had improved. The International Health Exhibitions, London, the first in 1884, underlined the broadening concern over the social and moral implications of national health and, as well as providing a general public entertainment, were 'expressly designed for practical instruction, more especially with regard to the actual improvements in Food, in Dress, and in Dwellings'.[25]

From the 1830s various Acts had been formulated to demolish slum property and build new houses. Public interest was maintained through the Housing Acts of 1851, Artisans and Labourers 'Dwellings Improvement Act', 1875, and the Royal Commission on the Housing of the Poor of 1885 which led to the 1890 Housing of the Working Classes Act. It was Luke Fildes who again put this legislation into its human context and captured the imagination of the nation with his painting of 'The Doctor', 1891, and published as a photogravure by Thomas Agnew & Sons in 1892 (Figure 1).

A picture of the workman's home, a cottage, the scene was of a tragedy as the father stood helplessly in the background, comforting hand on the distraught mother, watching the doctor, equally helpless, patiently observing a young sick child lying on pillows stretched across two chairs. The oil lamp was burning on the table, it had been a long night, and at that stage the outcome was dependent on nature. The hard-working and dependable family, the precariousness of life, the caring doctor, the limits of science, were all brought together, an imagined yet believable drama that could have been repeated in many homes. The picture was of the heroic family, and the caring face of society, of a family that had furnished its home with pieces of vernacular work, and a miscellaneous collection of second-hand chairs, a print on the wall, and plants on the window sill. These were the everyday details of the workman's family whose aspirations were self-improvement and deserving of support.

Well received at the Royal Academy Exhibition, its realism a marked contrast to the idealised scenes offered by Sir Frederick Leighton, the representation caused some critical disquiet: 'the whole is pathetic from its truth, as the real scene would be pathetic: but is it in the true sense a

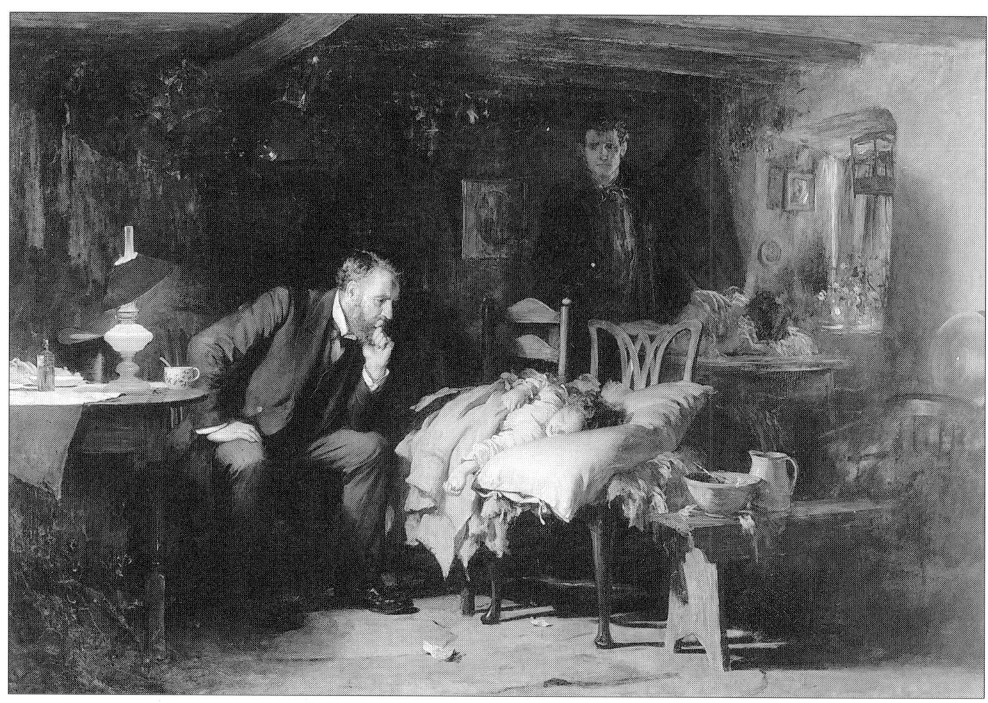

1 Luke Fildes, *The Doctor*, 1891

"picture"? We think not; the moral interest overrides the artistic'.[26] Despite these doubts, the message was unmistakable, a paradigm of all that was honourable about the British worker and his family, their simplicity and integrity, and yet it was threatened by death.

Home and neighbourhood

Health and housing of the family as the cornerstone of the well-being of the nation was now well established, and it was the type of family portrayed by Fildes that municipal authorities sought to help in their new housing programmes. How far such families would be able to benefit from the advances of medicine, science and technology was a difficult question to answer, but how to define the minimum standards for home life was even more problematic. It was in this context that the creation of Port Sunlight, from 1889 onwards, changed the perceptions of workers' housing, with its cottage-style comfort and convenience, and having gardens back and front. The cottage was also being talked about as the antidote to the forest of suburban villas, the former with its garden which created the true spirit of home with its rest, quiet and simplicity.

It does not matter how small it is, it can always be treated in a broad and

> simple manner, and have a quiet dignity of its own. A glance at any country cottage is sufficient to convince us of this. I don't mean to say that a house must necessarily be bare and simple in every part, but simplicity must be the keynote.[27]

The same values of the 'plain cottage' were used by Barry Parker in *Our Homes*; its truth and honesty contrasted with 'the artificiality, falsity, pretension, and sham of the modern drawing-room'.[28] Parker had no intention of living in or designing homes with the frugality of the workman's cottage, but his argument was for principles of design on matters of beauty and economy that would satisfy all classes of society.

Although the cottage was now established as the ideal home for the working- and middle-class family alike, for the programmes of city slum clearance the building of new tenement dwellings remained the only realistic solution to the acres of insanitary, dilapidated and overcrowded houses.

> Some of the inhabitants are Italians – organ-grinders and penny-ice dealers. What the condition of ices made in such courts must be had best be left to the imagination. Other inhabitants are very poor labourers, and of course the habits of this class of tenants do not tend to improve the property. The scenes of misery, of squalor and of dirt to be witnessed within these small, rickety houses are truly appalling. The dirt and despair of the one discourages the other, and these tenants will never be raised from their present abject condition till they are removed to better surroundings.[29]

A description of Manchester that could be replicated by scenes from any major British city, planners and architects were now confronted by questions of minimum space, services and which of the facilities should be established as a communal provision. One of the most effective schemes, and yet revealing of the uncertain transition taking place, was the LCC housing scheme at Boundary Street, started in 1891, of which the last block officially opened on 3 March 1900. Replacing one of London's worst slum areas, it had concentrated on housing the better class of artisan rather than the very poor.

Set out with a central raised garden area from which the streets radiated, existing schools were retained and a central laundry, with bathhouses and clubrooms constructed in 1895. Showing a mix of Queen Anne and arts and crafts influences, the domestic accommodation was a curious mixture. The 1,069 flats were evidence of an obvious attempt to meet the different needs of the community, sizes ranged from one room to six rooms, with the majority having two or three rooms. The surprise came from the scullery and WC arrangements. Only 601 were fully self-contained flats, some had private lavatories and sculleries on the landing, 142 had to share a scullery, and 35 shared lavatories and sculleries. The mix of services showed an indecisiveness over what should be standard and minimum. In future lavatories and sculleries would be included, but opinion over the provision of a bathroom remained deeply divided and was to remain so through to the late 1930s.

As neighbourhood schemes, these new housing developments were able to take advantage of the services that had come to be accepted as an integral part of urban life. New market halls had given a permanence to the weekly traders, and the steady expansion of the Cooperative movement not only brought a range of shops to new housing schemes and high streets, but eventually resulted in large-scale stores that incorporated libraries, reading rooms, assembly halls and restaurants.[30] The multi-purpose cultural centres of library, art school and museums of the 1860s, such as the Royal Albert Memorial Museum at Exeter and the similar model at Dundee, were difficult examples to follow, but, later in the century, a range of towns benefited from substantial gifts from trusts such as Carnegie and Pasmore-Edwards. At the same time towns that had missed out on the early stages of the art school movement were being brought into the national frame through the technical education legislation of the 1880s, with a new phase of institutional building and the expanding culture of evening class education. Nonconformist chapels and Sunday schools also continued to play a significant role within working- and middle-class communities by providing educational as well as social programmes of light entertainment, children's parties and days' outings. While not being strictly identified with the family as a unit, clubs for working men, cycling, athletics and cricket completed the framework of community life of the Victorian town. Families living in slums, while unlikely to be enjoying the benefits of much of these local amenities, had expectations of new housing that would still enable them to draw on the established services and provide convenient access to work.[31] The eventual preoccupation with images of bad taste, the perceived decay and uncontrolled expansion of the nineteenth-century urban legacy obscured the importance of these relationships and resources to the twentieth-century rebuilding programmes.

Electricity was the final piece of this undervalued inheritance. While it was identified with the culture of the modern interior of the 1920s, and modernist expression of the 1930s, the technological advances were already well understood. With electric lighting used for the exhibition halls at the International Exhibition, Edinburgh, 1886, and the following year at the Royal Jubilee Exhibition, Manchester, its reliability and safety was confirmed, although costs remained high and supplies were severely limited. Electrical and industrial exhibitions directed at industrial and municipal uses became regular events,[32] but it was opening up the domestic market that was a primary objective of the new industry. Although cautious in setting out a projected timetable, R. E. Crompton in his paper, 'The use of electricity for cooking and heating', to the Society of Arts was in no doubt that ways would be found to extend the use of electricity from lighting to cooking and heating.[33] Illustrated by a range of kitchen utensils, such as a kettle, saucepan and frying pan, his arguments were those of economy, efficiency and cleanliness, simplifying tasks and guaranteeing quality. The electrically worked kitchen was to be the ideal model of the future.

So it was that the nineteenth century could offer images of the well-furnished appliance-filled home, as well as of the destitute and homeless, overcrowded tenements and workhouses. It had popularised taste and promoted ideals on the health, comfort and happiness of the family. Most importantly of all it had framed the concepts of Useful, Economy and Improvement as the parameters of the social purpose of architecture and design.

National welfare and the home

Services

In its architectural style, taste and commercial ambitions the Glasgow International Exhibition, opened on 2 May 1901, had little to add to the established nineteenth-century exhibition culture. But, by coincidence, it gave a glimpse of two movements that were to play a dominant role in the shaping of family life over the next fifty years. It gave a clear indication of a growing public transport network with the modernisation of the tramway systems, and with the display and demonstration of motor cars, although still only available to the very rich, a future of new freedoms was on public show. Less obvious, but just as important, were the 'Sunlight' workers' cottages shown by Lever Bros. As exemplars of the development at Port Sunlight, they introduced to a wider audience a model of domestic comfort that challenged the contemporary standards and perceptions of working-class housing (Figure 2).

The year 1901 also saw the publication of B. Seebohm Rowntree's *Poverty. A Study in Town Life*. In its analytical approach, it gave a new dimension to the national responsibility and failure to understand the scale of the social problems generated through the poverty of life and environment endured by the urban poor. Food, clothing and sanitation were on the agenda, but it was the home and its setting that was perceived to be at the core of the problem, and its solution. Concern for the health and welfare of mothers and children of working-class families was beginning to influence national policy and legislation. In 1890 the London

2 'Sunlight' cottages, International Exhibition, Glasgow, 1901

School Board had been the first authority to appoint a school doctor, Bradford followed three years later, and by the time that the School Medical Service was set up as a national system in 1905, eighty-five authorities had appointed a school doctor. This legislation was concerned with the personal health as well as the environment of the child, and supported by school nurses who could visit the homes of the children.

By the early 1900s, more attention was being given to the possibility of building open-air swimming pools as part of the inner city recreation grounds, and designed to provide more suitable accommodation for schoolchildren to receive swimming lessons. For family health there was a move towards building the smaller cottage or people's baths,[34] the intention being to introduce them into the slum districts of the cities. Brighton and Liverpool made the first moves, and were soon to be followed by Birmingham, Bradford, Manchester and Leeds. Located in either converted or purpose-built premises, the scale was domestic, and arranged around separate men's and women's facilities. Slipper baths rather than the douche were the popular choice, increasingly so as mothers could bring their children for the same price, and a 'little mother' would superintend 'the bathing of her little brothers and sisters'.[35] This still left large sections of the urban and rural homes without adequate provision, and at best dependent on the tub filled from the range or copper. An unresolved question, it was to dominate the new housing projects throughout the 1920s and 1930s.

3 1,001 uses for gas, 1915

Hot water for the nation was how the gas industry portrayed its contribution to modern society:

> There is one luxury shared alike by peer and commoner which wealth cannot by any chance monopolise, and that is a generous and economical hot water supply in the home. Whether it be in workman's tenement, artisan's cottage, tradesman's villa, or ducal mansion, the pleasures derivable from a copious and unlimited flow of hot water in any part of the house, and at any hour of the day or night, can only be adequately measured by actual experience.[36]

The illustrations were predominantly of the middle-class life, introduced with the pleasures of a soak in a hot steaming bath (Figure 3). Helping the servants, catering for the needs of the sports girls and married life in general, gas was also presented as the 'working woman's friend'. For the wife who had everything to do herself, it was gas that brought convenience and economy to the demands of cooking, house-cleaning, mending and washing, and still allowed her to have a hot bath ready for her husband coming home from work in the factory or the fields. Combination appliances were being developed. Having argued against the unreliability and demands of the kitchen range, the principle of an all-in-one cooker, fire and water heater was transferred to the gas appliance. For most it was all still very much a dream, but on the new municipal cottage estates, the all-gas house was beginning to make its appearance.

Electricity still had to convince the consumer of its reliability and economy in the home. By the time of the Manchester Electrical Exhibition, 1908, the 'model' house had appliances working throughout the house, that would 'clean the knives in the kitchen, play the piano in the drawing room, provide heat for warming pans in the bedrooms, and in a score of other ways add to domestic comfort'.[37] Demonstrations at every opportunity were the key to the success with which the advantages of electricity were kept in the public domain, but with the opening of Tricity House, Oxford Street, in December 1912, persuasion had taken on a new dimension. It was a new restaurant in which all the cooking was done by the latest 'Tricity' appliances, and the benefits then put to the test.[38]

Ingenuity and labour-saving were the values represented by the electrical appliance, and with the 1913 Ideal Home Exhibition they had been grouped together to form the 'Maison Electrique'. Three months later, the Electric House was made the centrepiece of the Birmingham & Midland Institute Conversazione, January 1914. Constructed as a series of room settings for the study, dining room, kitchen, scullery, bathroom and bedroom, electricity was presented as 'the new servant in the home'.[39] A record of inventiveness in its range of appliances, both luxury and practical, its obsession with solving the servant problem by reducing the manual labour and the number of servants required, at times tilted the designing into the eccentric. The star attraction was the 'King Arthur' Electric Dining Table.

> The whole of the operations of the Table are carried out electrically, and are of so simple a nature that the mere pressing of a button is sufficient to rotate the top portion in either direction or to cause it to rise and fall, acting as a lift for the bearing of plates and dishes, etc., to or from a serving room below.[40]

It was a fantasy world, in which the housewife was surrounded by a range of new appliances from 'Ozonair', supplying pure health-giving ozone, a cooking stove providing 'cheap, clean, cool and comfortable cooking',[41] a washing machine that saved your laundry bills, and a vacuum cleaner that removed 'dust and dirt once for all, quickly and thoroughly'.[42] It was the representation of a futuristic home, with 'the Electric Servant ... ready to give instant response to your wishes day or night, all the year round'.[43]

Minimum and the cottage ideal

The National Health Exhibition, London, 1913, focused on the latest scientific and hygienic principles of home management, showing the usual range of appliances and furniture, as well as a suite of model rooms and a kitchen. The home, its physical, mental and moral role, was the basis of the nation's greatness and its 'greatest hope for the future of the Empire'.[44] In this climate, the debate repeatedly returned to the lack of planning control and inadequate housing. In a contribution to a lecture series organised by Manchester University in 1914, B. S. Rowntree reminded his audience that there were in the region of 3,000,000 people living in conditions that were deficient in light, space, ventilation, warmth, dryness and water supply. Acceptance of minimum standards, state aid and increased municipal control were seen as the only solution to the dilemma.

The provision of child welfare was accepted as being integral to this problem. For the mother the problems started with childbirth: 'She was cleaning, scrubbing, and washing right up to the time of her confinement, and then had to lay up in the one single room in which the whole family lived.'[45] For the child it continued with years of neglect of diet, care and education, aggravated by housing that made it impossible 'for babies and young children to be assured of the proper amount of quietness and sleep'.[46] Any progress had been dependent on voluntary organisations, but with the Notification of Births (Extension) Act, 1915, that made the local authorities directly responsible for child welfare, and with powers further extended by the Maternity and Child Welfare Act of 1918 change was about to take place. It was to bring about a greater awareness of the links between health and housing, environment and diet, and most significantly it brought the welfare centre and clinic into the remit of a community facility.

The demand for a minimum standard of living space and services also extended to the values of home furnishing. It set the simplicity and integrity of craft furniture against a continuing retail commitment to reproduction furnishings, used to represent national taste at international exhibitions. For example, at the Louisiana Purchase Exposition, 1904, the British Pavilion was a reproduction of the Kensington Palace Banqueting Hall, and its main features were a series of rooms furnished with originals and reproduction. There was the Elizabethan Breakfast Room, the Georgian Dining Room, an Adams English Tea Room and a Queen Anne Reception Room. Four years later at the Franco-British Exhibition at the White City, London, national identity was aligned with the greatness of the Empire, dominated by the pinnacles and minarets, pavilions and bridges of the Court of Honour, an extravagant Edwardian interpretation of Indian architecture.[47] Alongside the baroque confection covering the various pavilions, the exhibition was also memorable for its picturesque cottage architecture. There was John Knight's, soapmakers to the King, 'Primrose Cottage', with leaded bay windows, climbing plants and a rustic bench; Schweppes' reconstruction of the old shop of Jacob Schweppes; and the furnishers Oetzmann's bungalow cottage that captured the popular taste with its three bedrooms, living room, hall and kitchen, built for £230, economically heated, and artistically furnished for 45 guineas, the ideal and for many the attainable model.[48]

Although, since its introduction in 1893, *The Studio* had provided the forum for the craftsmanship values of the plain and simple style, and struggled against the antiquated, it also had continued to do its part for the cottage style and the romance of the village.[49] A view that was more English than British, it was reinforced by *The Cottage Homes of England* by Stewart Dick and Helen Allingham and *The Village Homes of England* by Sydney R. Jones. They were, as Jones explained in his introduction, unpretentious examples of homely taste, symbols of order, security, comfort and a stable intellectual life. Characteristically English, they appealed to the imagination and sentiment and, along with the cottage exhibitions, encouraged a national interest in the home and its setting, and the enduring qualities of village England. It was these qualities of taste that were to permeate the first 'Ideal Home' exhibition in October 1908.

Receiving a mixed and generally critical reception, it was the *Builder* that recognised 'a stroke of what may be called journalistic genius in giving so attractive a title as "the ideal home" to the exhibition'.[50] It meant that 'the ideal' was associated with Englishness, not only through the popular cottage style, but in the display of decorative and furnishing styles of different periods, and the latest products for cooking, lighting, heating and sanitation. The ideal had become the everyday, and homelife the ideal. Room settings were used to represent the competing tastes, and in the following years arts and crafts furnishers competed with the trade for public attention. The garden suburb movement played an influential role, and it was hardly surprising that the 1912 Ideal House competition was won by a design for a garden suburb-type cottage.

Alongside the furnishings and decorations was the growing range of household equipment. Increasingly the attention was directed to the needs of the average housewife and, by 1913, with the steady reduction in the prices of household appliances, their availability to the 'average small household'.[51] It was further confirmation of the continuing importance of the home and home-making, showing that 'comfort is the keynote of the British home, and ... how recent inventions make that ideal more possible'.[52]

The Ideal Home Exhibition was not alone in promoting this new home world. In October 1909, The International Trade Exhibitions Ltd held the first 'Everything for the Home Exhibition' in Birmingham, exhibiting 'many appliances for saving time in cleaning and cooking', the latest on lighting, and demonstrations on food and diet. Model cottages were on show as were models from Birmingham Corporation on homes for the poor. The project was repeated the following year, and also arranged for Manchester, and again in 1911, with one in Cardiff in 1912. The Chronicle Home Exhibition, May–June 1910, Manchester, included a model home, furnished for £100, appliances and fashion, a model of Letchworth Garden City, and a lecture programme on holidays, cookery, housewifery, modern day nurseries, garden cities and 'How to make the best of a backyard'.

Art and industry

Arts and crafts practices, ideologies and personalities continued to dominate the work of the British art schools, and whatever the changes in commerce and industry, the schools resolutely paraded the virtues of the handmade. But as had happened at regular intervals since the art school system had been set up in the late 1830s, as British manufacture and commerce felt the cold winds of economic recession, attention turned to the failure of the art schools to provide for the design needs of the nation. Pivotal to this disquiet was the continuing dissatisfaction with the effectiveness of the Royal College of Art which, since its reorganisation in 1901, had failed to break with its preoccupation with the crafts, or improve its relationship to regional art schools. The subject of a Parliamentary Committee inspection in 1910, its report and recommendations placed great emphasis on the needs of design for industry, with a policy of specialisation through decentralisation to regional centres, and the Royal College of Art becoming a centre for advanced study. In reality the report had put in place a policy of art for industry that was to dominate the next twenty years, reinforcing the divisions between the 'popular' and the 'cultivated', for even though craft production continued to be marginalised in the commercial market, the values and principles derived from the arts and crafts arena remained the dominant art school influence. The remit centred on the decorative arts, cultivating the crafts as an art form and an enlightened hobby for the substantially middle-class audience.

This culture reworked the opposition to mass-production and popular taste, and encouraged Roger Fry to establish his Omega Workshop.[53] He sought to counter the pretentious elegance of the machine-made, but ended up producing pretentious interpretations of the primitive and peasant. Even so, it was good fun. He was invited to show at the Ideal Home Exhibition, October 1913, and his post-impressionist 'cubist' room provided an amusing diversion, joining the 'Moonlight sonata' room, an Adam drawing room, and a series of rooms constituting 'the perfect room'.

There were no immediate benefits for industry in these educational and artistic developments, but what they did was to generate an increased interest in the role of government in matters of public taste. There was a growing clamour for a Ministry of Fine Arts, which in July 1914 led to the setting up of the Parliamentary Committee on Fine Art. This left the original question of design for industry unanswered, and in a somewhat surprising move in 1915, the Board of Trade put on an exhibition of German and Austrian articles typifying successful design for British manufacturers. The lesson to be learnt was that arts and crafts production, with all its quality, was only available to the well-off, in contrast to the work of German designers who had come to terms with designing for machine production, and had recognised the importance of cooperation with the retail industry. This relationship had ensured that progressive design was commercially viable.

It was these responsibilities that the 'Design and Industries Association' (DIA) sought to meet. Launched in May 1915, and followed two months later with the publication of its aims and ambitions, it set out to promote the role of the designer in the process of manufacture, and to influence national taste through exhibitions of the best current examples of commercial products. Its activities were initially restricted by the First World War, but independently, and in collaboration with municipal authorities and retail outlets, the Association was to add its weight to the post-war attention to the beauty of the common object and the art of everyday things in the home.

New domestic landscapes

The model village

With the passing of the Small Holdings & Allotments Act, 1908, County Councils were given the responsibility for settling families on the land, and helping the urban family to achieve a level of self-sufficiency. This required County Councils to appoint land agents and set up departments to administer the schemes, which relied heavily on the dividing and adapting of existing farms. Some new cottages were built, but it was an ad hoc development, and there were even suggestions that the smaller the holding, then the smaller the dwelling.[54] However, it was not an insignificant movement, with 13,112 smallholdings being established.[55] An indication of the growing concern over the decline of agriculture and the rural exodus, it inspired a renewed interest in the values of the arts and crafts escape into a rural retreat.

Linked to a belief in the pioneer spirit of the homestead, it was ironic that these moves should coincide with the economic failure of the Guild of Handicraft's experiment to build a new life in the countryside five years after moving into rural England. An escape from cities 'like London, or Birmingham, with their horrible workshop associations and dreary confinement of their grey streets and houses',[56] there were others prepared to search out the new simple self-sufficient life. There was, for example, The Homesteads, on the outskirts of Stirling, *c.* 1910, by James Chalmers. The outcome of the combined efforts of the Independent Labour Party, the Scottish Branch of the Garden Cities Association and the Scottish Guild of Handicraft, the settlement was made up of a collection of detached and semi-detached houses and cottages, of garden city style, each with its own smallholding, and linked to a farm, operating as a self-sufficient agricultural cooperative.

It was, though, the model village with its cottage architecture, serving new industries and established urban developments, that became the hope for the future for the working classes and middle classes. The vision was for villages and townships that would be 'healthy, comfortable and picturesque'.[57] Recognising that it was not possible to replicate the beauty of the village that had grown over the centuries, planners set out to 'give to the working miner and the "Sunlight" soap manufacturer a home, which, without aping a suburban villa, shall be admirable and even enviable to his neighbours, and to secure for the public something pleasant to look upon in the place of the landscape he is bound to destroy'.[58] Port Sunlight, Bourneville and Cresswell, the mining village near Bolsover, were obvious examples. New Earswick, started in 1904, became an immediately influential model appearing on any list for new settlements.

At a time when the concept of the garden village more than dominated thinking on the house and neighbourhood, it encouraged a missionary zeal, a message 'to promote the spread of a new civilising and uplifting influence'.[59] The artisan and lower middle classes were joining the exodus from the city, with the homeward bound worker greeted by an elegant wife and lively well-dressed children (Figure 4).

Alongside company and cooperative ventures were the municipal initiatives. Stimulated by the National Housing Reform Council, the development of collective municipal values on issues of housing and planning began to emerge, and the cottage became the ideal home.

The tone and ambitions of the debate were well illustrated by the Conference on the Development of Suburban Areas, October 1905, Sheffield. Promoted by the City Housing Sub-Committee, in conjunction with all the leading housing associations, it attracted over 200 delegates. In part the conference was set on influencing government opinion on the need for improved legislation that would allow municipalities to acquire land in the suburbs for houses, restrict building developments that were not in the interests of the community, and relax the current building regulations. W. H. Lever, inspired by his Port Sunlight initiative, set the tone of the conference in its opposition to the tenement block and preference for garden homes that would produce 'Englishmen and Englishwomen, boys and girls, and young children that would be able to uphold the prestige of our race the world over'.[60] The backdrop to the debate was the 1890 Housing of the Working Classes Act, the vision was for a life of fresh air and sunlight, 'a cottage with a small garden plot, where the children could learn to love the flowers and enjoy the pure fresh air'.[61]

The practical success of some ventures produced sharp divisions of opinion, particularly in response to the lessons to be learnt from Letchworth. For those trying to help families living on 18*s.* or 20*s.* a week, such as Councillor Fildes in Manchester, it was felt that there was little that could be applied to local authority initiatives struggling to set up economic schemes, supported by the introduction of cheap transit systems from the suburbs to places of work. None of these cottage schemes were directly linked to slum clearance, and there was a clear indication of a belief that slum dwellers would turn new housing into a slum, and therefore should be left in the poor city areas vacated by the upwardly mobile

4 'For those of moderate means', Garden Village prospectus, 1913

workers. It was the worthy family as previously portrayed by Fildes that was destined for the municipal garden estates, the type that could be found in the city art gallery on a Saturday evening, the well-dressed, well-behaved family with three children (Figure 5).

Sheffield, having made a positive commitment to build its own garden city on the current city boundary, decided that it should form the basis of a national competition and exhibition of cottages costing £200. This was to take place from August to October 1907, to coincide with a similar one in Newcastle upon Tyne, which did not in fact take place until the following year. There were to be three classes of cottages, all with a bath: there was (A) with two bedrooms, living room and scullery; (B) with three bedrooms, living room and scullery; and (C) with three bedrooms, parlour, living room and scullery.

Alongside the competition entries, Sheffield laid out a group of municipal houses, in categories A and B, designed by Percy Houfton of Chesterfield, who had won first prize in the 1905 Letchworth Exhibition for a cottage not exceeding £150. The exhibition catalogue gave great prominence to the model villages of the Rowntrees, Cadburys and Levers, populated by children whose 'bright, smiling, chubby faces proved beyond

5 Art for the man on Saturday night. The working-man's playtime: a visit to Manchester City Art Gallery, 1909

question that the model village properly planned is a success from the point of view of humanity'.[62] The North of England Cottage Exhibition, Newcastle, 1908, maintained public interest, which was further enhanced by the South Wales Cottage Exhibition, Swansea, in 1910.

Hartley's in Liverpool and Rickett's on the edge of Hull were other examples of company housing, but it was Woodlands, a model village about four miles out of Doncaster, begun in 1907 for the new Brodsworth Main Colliery, that attracted most attention, primarily because its Voysey design associations and garden city aspirations broke with the conventions of the poor standard of housing associated with mining villages. Great emphasis was placed on the preservation of the natural landscape, including woodland and a fishing lake, and the provision of community facilities, including churches, a school and cooperative store. In the first phase the houses had vegetable gardens, but in the second phase this facility was dropped in favour of the houses opening directly on to an open green. While making a range of design variations to meet the different family needs, the houses were in two basic standard types: a three-bedroom living room house, or a parlour house that also had a bath; all houses had an attached WC, fitted cupboards, dressers and wardrobes. The intention was to re-create a clean old English village, with houses positioned to maximise light, air and sunshine to all rooms.[63]

Garden suburbs

For the affluent, Hampstead Garden Suburb offered a similar environment, uniting 'modern standards of comfort and hygiene with old-world standards of proportion and refinement, to bring together the best that the English village and English city have to give'.[64] The illustrated map offered a picture of pastoral England, a blend of the artistic and practical, 'an old-fashioned country town in the shires'[65] whose charm and beauty, with the Golders Green Tube Station just 20 minutes from Charing Cross, was an ideal retreat from London. Work began in March 1908, offering large houses at one end for between £3,000 and £4,000, and cottages at the other for £350–£1,500, that not only had 'beauty of line and harmony of light and shade, but an ample supply of cupboards in the right positions'.[66] The Metropolitan Railway exploited a similar strategy in brochures that offered the picture of living in the countryside of Buckinghamshire, Hertfordshire and Middlesex, and using its services into central London from the 'beautiful' Wembley Park suburb, the 'delightful' village of Eastcote, and rural charm of Pinner.

Landowners found the idea of developing a garden suburb extremely appealing. They could speculate with good intentions, satisfying commercial needs and generating local interest and national publicity through competitions and exhibitions. The Fallings Park Estate on Sir Arthur Paget's land, about a mile from the centre of Wolverhampton, was one such enterprise. First announced in early 1907, the initial architectural interest was disappointing, and the competition was relaunched later in the year. The first houses were finished in February 1908, and the exhibition finally opened in September 1908. The plan was to develop 400 acres, with private houses on the more attractive parkland, and artisan cottages on sites nearest to existing factories. Reworking ideas shown at Letchworth and Sheffield, prize-winning cottages at those exhibitions were included in the Wolverhampton exhibition. The three-bedroom parlour house was the preferred design, with separate bathroom or bath in the scullery. Much was made of the provision of kitchen gardens, recreation space for play-grounds, tennis and bowls.[67]

An increasingly popular development model, there were, for example, developments at Coryndon on the edge of Cardiff, Harborne in suburban Birmingham and Knebworth in Hertfordshire. The language of the garden suburbs was that of the 'cheerful- comfortable- beautiful homes', satisfying all tastes 'from the happy beginners in life to the busy cityman seeking rest after toil and a healthy home for his family, and to the good friends who are looking for a nice quiet spot wherein to spend the eventide of life'.[68] It was a home for life, furnished in a comfortable and dignified manner, in a neighbourhood that offered a range of recreational and sports activities.[69]

The attraction of the cottage estate was its adaptability to artisan and middle-class economics. Letchworth's orientation was middle class, Sheffield's was artisan, Fallings Park had hoped to capture both markets. The Town Planning and Modern House and Cottage Exhibition, 1911, at Gidea Park, Romford, was unmistakably middle class, and arts and crafts in taste, with interesting houses and interiors by Parker and Unwin, and Baillie Scott, but also, with its £500 houses, it was perceived to interest a wide audience, including 'people of small means who want an inexpensive permanent home, and also those town-dwellers of larger income who dream of a week-end cottage in the country or by the sea'.[70]

Planning matters

The National Housing Congress, held in London during May 1908, and organised by the National Housing Reform Council, had brought together more than 300 delegates to discuss the Housing and Town Planning Bill which, as the 1909 Act, ensured that planning and civic design were the primary topics of professional debate. The 1910 competition for a new town at Ruislip Manor, Middlesex, promoted by Ruislip-Northwood Urban District Council gave substance to the debate, directing attention to questions of travel, and the extent to which the new neighbourhood would need its own community services or could rely on ready access to other local facilities. It was widely accepted that it was the social class that would define the character of the town: 'Motor garages, for example, will not be required in very large numbers if the houses are all of £30 a year rental or less, while public baths and wash-houses need scarcely be provided for the inhabitants of houses at £100 a year rental'.[71]

The scale of municipal influence on the domestic landscape, with an extraordinary list of responsibilities for planning and the provision of services, was given widespread publicity by the first Municipal Building and Public Health Exhibition, at the Agricultural Hall, London, in the first two weeks of May 1908. Matters of sanitation, highways, including tram systems, building materials and lighting were prominent. Two years later, the second of these exhibitions was held on even more ambitious lines, including the construction of the 'Model Municipal Cottage'. It was official recognition of the three-bedroom cottage, that had a living room with a cottager range that also heated the water for the copper in the scullery, and which housed the bath under a table-top. A larder, coal cupboard and WC completed the internal arrangements, a model of economy in space and cost (Figure 6).

Tenements continued to be a popular solution for working-class housing, and slum clearance schemes, but steadily municipal housing programmes began to incorporate variations of the cottage model as an experiment in social improvement. For example, in its Beavington Street scheme, 1910, for the first time Liverpool introduced the cottage type, 'the

6 The Municipal Cottage, Municipal & Health Exhibition, 1910

desire being to enable the dispossessed to have more the idea of an Englishman's home than sentiment can give in the large blocks of tenement dwellings'.[72]

The Housing and Town Planning Act of 1909 had given local authorities new powers to oversee development of buildings and land, and in the process gave a new dimension to civic awareness. Municipalities had control over the shape, type and scale of any changes.

> Town planning is the mapping out by Local Authorities of their new districts as a whole, instead of allowing them to grow up in a haphazard piecemeal manner. A town plan settles the direction, width, and nature of the proposed streets, the situation of open spaces, and in some cases defines the class of buildings to be erected in particular districts.[73]

Adapting the principles of the garden city movement to the needs of the city was how J. S. Nettleford saw Birmingham providing 'cheap, cheerful and healthy' neighbourhoods for the poorer of the working classes.

The Town Planning Conference and Exhibition of October 1910, arranged by the Royal Institute of British Architects (RIBA), gave substance to the significance of municipal legislation. A further exhibition, Cities and Town Planning, developed out of it and was shown in Edinburgh, 13 March–1 April 1911. It reinforced the importance attached to the garden city and suburb movement, but gave much more attention to the questions of city planning, showing both historic and contemporary international examples. The emerging picture was of a clean and socially responsible urban life. Architects and planners alike saw the coming age of gas and electricity as displacing the evils of the age of coal and steam.

Attached to the exhibition catalogue was the opening address by Lord Pentland on town planning. The underlying theme was one of the minimum standards for a decent life for a family of husband, wife, and children of both sexes and all ages. For this, the requirement was a three-bedroom house with kitchen or living room, in a neighbourhood that provided fresh air and sunshine, and access to playing fields or parks for the children. It was further confirmation of the demand for order and the importance attached to the home as the key element.

Raising the capital to fund the housing initiatives was demanding, and one important development to the spread of the garden village movement was the formation of The Welsh Town-Planning and Housing Trust Ltd in 1913. It not only financed some important schemes across Wales, such as Barry and Rhiwbina, but in the post-war period supported the creation of a range of garden suburbs and estates, of which those for the Great Western Railway, following the line from London to Penzance and Swansea reinforced the link between cottage life and industry. Offering a blueprint for the post-war reconstruction, even though there had been concerns over the social isolation and increased costs of living in the new villages, no one believed that it could fail to meet the demands of the building programme. No one could foresee the impact of the post-war economic depression, or the consequences of failing to answer the slum problem, and so the confidence in the picturesque model of a new Britain remained high.

Motor car and landscape

Enjoying the new-found freedoms of rural Britain by motor car was still a luxury, but the social changes were well understood:[74] 'In ten short years the motorcar has revolutionised travel. To the owner of one or more motor vehicles distance does not matter, and country and town are linked together.'[75] A new social life was being enjoyed by the rich in town, while country house life had changed, with the installation of fully equipped garages for storing and maintaining a range of motor cars, bringing a new dimension to the weekend in the country. Suburban life was also changing. No longer dependent on the railway, ladies from Horsham or 'such places as Sunningdale, Leatherhead, Slough, Crawley, Haslemere, and Wargrave' could be driven into London's West End, and taken from shop to shop in Oxford Street and Regent Street (figure 7). The car could take the family to the theatre and other social events, to race meetings, an excursion in the country and, if really determined, afternoon tea in Brighton.[76] Convenience and comfort were the primary values associated with motoring, but it was at this stage that speed, real and imagined, and streamlining, added new meanings to motoring and the structure of everyday life.

As the freedoms associated with motoring became more apparent, so the demand for cheaper motor cars increased. The £100 family car, the one big enough for the men who 'want to take their wives, their sisters, their cousins, their aunts and all the family out for a drive', was the dream.[77] Small two-seater light cars were available, but the real need was for a medium-priced family car for the middle-class owner-driver.

The demand for a weekend cottage was increasing, now complete with garage.[78] For example, the Country Life Competition, 1912, for a holiday cottage and garden, placed great emphasis on the inclusion of a motor house, and a siting close to the road. T. Brice Philips in a paper to the Royal Society of Arts drew attention to the social significance of these changes:

> the movement from town to country is one that apparently is materially affecting the face of the countryside. It is a movement, too, which is likely to grow in magnitude. At present it is confined for the greater part to the

7 Shopping the modern way, 1909

> upper and middle classes, but it is expected that as transit becomes easier and cheaper, and labour is thus made more mobile, the working classes will also avail themselves to a great extent, of the privilege of living away from the scenes of their labour.[79]

Commuting by car was not yet a serious proposition, but no one could doubt that it was not far away, just as motorised transport would be taking men to war. An extraordinary exercise took place on 17 March 1909, the day chosen to reconstruct a modern Battle of Hastings, when a battalion of Guards was transported by car from London. It was imagined that Hastings had been invaded, and the railway line was out of action, so the 'experiment with mechanical transport' was arranged.[80] Organised by the AA, it attracted widespread publicity as 286 cars were used to carry troops, while 28 London taxis were stripped down to their chassis, and boarded over to carry guns, ammunition and general supplies.

For pleasure and emergency, the motor car was now integral to the life of the nation. Although still only available for the rich, it was redefining the general understanding of communication systems, increasing the demand for through roads and new roads. Getting into, out of, and between big cities was the prime concern, and the volume of London traffic was setting the pace. Having been recognised as a problem since the 1905 Royal Commission Report, and a preoccupation of the London Traffic Branch of the Board of Trade, it was the latter's 1911 report that gave a glimpse of things to come, with proposals for new roads that included the Great Western Avenue, the Brentford By-Pass and the beginnings of the North Circular Road. The markings of a new suburban life had been drawn on the greater London map, an example to be followed across the country, a key part of national planning.

Already there was alarm at the impact on the landscape and quality of rural life. By December 1907, the spread of advertisements to country lanes and entrances to villages was attracting public criticism.[81] Immediately supported by the motoring journals, it developed into a prolonged campaign that reached a peak of activity in 1913, before being picked up again in the early 1920s. Traffic and roads were now established as a key part of the visions for a new domestic and city landscape, as was the architecture demanded by the new car trade.

The artistic garage was designed for the gentleman's house, while prefabricated garages were available for the middle classes. Both demanded space and for those families living in the inner cities, new commercial garages were constructed offering a 24-hour service, with lock-up and open space garaging. In 1907 London's theatreland had its first multi-storey car park, on six floors, moving cars by lifts and turntables. The final confirmation that the motor age had irrevocably changed the British townscape came in 1915, when Legge and Chamier put Britain's first kerbside petrol pump outside their Shrewsbury premises. The expansion was brought to a halt by the war years, but it was to become the single most dominant influence on planning policies and ideological arguments that were to affect family life in Britain.

Set alongside the services and technologies that were reshaping homelife, the continuing support for the cottage home movement, and the growing range of competitions and exhibitions for the home, the dreams of a new affluent society inclusive of all classes was gaining credibility. Such possibilities were still set sufficiently far enough in the future, but there was a growing belief that the conveniences and lifestyle currently restricted to the rich would one day be enjoyed by the people.[82] It was a vision that ensured that homes and health would continue to dominate the future debates on the social purposes of architecture and design.

Notes

1 J. Gloag, Introduction, *The Face of the Land*, DIA Year Book, London, 1929/30.

2 D. Galton, 'Address A Retrospect', *Journal of the Society of Arts*, vol. 35, 19 November 1886.

3 *Builder*, 25 June 1887, p. 928. Industrialists and manufacturers had known for some time that they had much to gain from a controlled well-housed workforce at the factory gate. Gregs at Styal or Titus Salt at Saltaire are the often quoted examples to set alongside the speculative developments of terraced communities or the growing number of philanthropic ventures such as the Peabody Trust in London,

Iveagh Trust in Dublin or the Talbot Village erected by two sisters, Georgina and Marianne Talbot, on the edge of Bournemouth with its homesteads extended over 465 acres, created to generate self-support amongst the working classes.

4 *Journal of Decorative Art*, March 1887, pp. 33–5.

5 There were minor amendments over the next fifty years. For example, in 1878 emphasis was placed on the provision of covered swimming baths and gymnasiums, then, following the Local Government Act, 1894, in 1896 London was allowed to use the premises for music or dancing, a clause which three years later was extended to the rest of the country.

6 It was a project to make available cheap, well-designed products for the poorer classes, with aspirations similar to those chosen by the Society for Improving the Conditions of the Labouring Classes and promoted through their published plans for model housing. Prince Albert's Model Dwellings at the Great Exhibition kept these developments in the public view.

7 *Builder*, 11 August 1866, p. 599.

8 *Ibid.*, 10 October 1863, p. 721.

9 *Ibid.*, 22 April 1865, p.269.

10 'at last the public mind was awakened to the great truth that all classes of society, including the very lowest, were bound together with the ties of a common interest; and that what affected and injured any one class, in some and often in great and painful measure injured all other classes': *The Industrial Self-Instructor and Technical Journal*, vol. 1, London, n.d. p. 129.

11 Galton, 'Address A Retrospect', p. 23.

12 As with the new art schools, the intention was to establish direct links between the museums and the local trade and manufacturers. In 1840 the Central School of Design, London, had been allocated a £10,000 government grant to form a museum of ornamental art as a teaching college for the students. This was augmented in 1844 with an additional £1,400 grant. It was this collection that was seen as the model for the regional centres, possibly forming the core of a loan collection, but now introducing good taste to the public.

13 There are really far too many books on Victorian taste and architecture to make a sensible list, but by way of locating it within a general context S. Allwood, *The Great Exhibitions*, London, 1977 and N. Pevsner, *Studies in Art Architecture and Design*, vol. 2, London, 1968 are useful.

14 For discussion of the Prince Consort's Model Houses see S. M. Gaskell, Model Housing. *From the Great Exhibition to the Festival of Britain*, London, 1987.

15 Henry Cole had taken responsibility for this part of the project.

16 For the first month of the exhibition access was restricted through the cost of entry; on the first two days there was a £1 entrance charge and for the following three weeks it was 5*s*. The first 1*s*. day was not introduced until 26 May, and from then on £20,000 a week was being taken at the turnstiles.

17 Edwards Improved Family Kitchen Range, trade pamphlet, 1851.

18 1851 trade pamphlet.

19 T. Twining, The Proposed Economic Museum', *Journal of the Society of Arts*, 5 June 1857, p. 422.

20 *Ibid.*

21 Discussions on a new site and institution had followed on from the Great Exhibition, but it was 1856 before work on a purpose-built exhibition building was started. See J. Physick, *The Victoria and Albert Museum*, London, 1982.

22 Henry Cole was in no doubt that museums, and the South Kensington Museum in particular, was for all the people. There were still doubts on the ability of the working classes to behave themselves, but Cole had no such reservations. 'It is simple savage ignorance, and priggish pedantry, not to recognise the absolute necessity of examples of art, easily consultable by the public, who are *consumers*, by the manufacturers, who are *producers*; and by artists and artisans as *students*': Henry Cole, Address to students at the Haney School of Art, *Journal of the Society of Arts*, 1873, p. 913. South Kensington was open free on Monday, Tuesday and Saturday and between 7.00 pm and 10.00 pm on Monday and Tuesday evenings.

23 C. L. Eastlake, *Hints on Household Taste*, London, 1868, reprint 1872, p. 159. These ideas and other objects of Victorian taste and culture are extensively dealt with in A. Briggs, *Victorian Things*, London, 1988.

24 *Ibid.*, p. 8.

25 *Illustrated London News*, 2 August 1884, p. 94.

26 *Builder*, 9 May 1891, p. 363.

27 E. Newton, 'Homelike Houses', *The Architect*, 29 May 1891, p. 330.

28 R. B. Parker, *Our Homes*, Buxton, 1895, p. 3.

29 'Rehousing the Poor in Manchester', *The Architect*, 24 July 1891, p. 61.

30 See J. Birchall, *Coop: the People's Business*, Manchester, 1994. An essential part of local history, there is much more work that needs to be done on its contribution to consumer products and domestic life, through its stores and cottage building departments. The commercial architecture deserves research, and of the range of sites that I have visited one particularly good example of the progressive high street development from the 1880s onwards can be found at Ipswich.

31 See J. Harris, *Private Lives-Public Spirit*, Oxford, 1993.

32 Two early ones were at Bingley Hall, Birmingham, 1889, and Edinburgh, 1890.

33 'The Use of Electricity for Cooking and Heating', *Journal of the Society of Arts*, 26 April 1895.

34 These had first been seen at the 1883 Exposition of Hygiene, Berlin.

35 *The Municipal Journal*, 30 October 1908, p. 889.

36 'Domestic Hot Water from the Cottage to the Mansion', *A Thousand and One Uses for Gas*, vol. 111, September 1915, p. 3.

37 *The Municipal Journal*, 4 September 1908, p. 729.

38 *Illustrated London News*, 7 December 1912, p. 868.

39 *The Electric House*, exhibition catalogue, Birmingham, 1914, p. 10.

40 *Ibid.*, p. 17.

41 *Ibid.*, p. 19.

42 *Ibid.*, p. 21.

43 *Ibid.*, p. 20.

44 *National Health Exhibition*, catalogue London, 1913, p. 9.

45 Mrs R Reeves, 'Provision for Maternity', *The Needs of Little Children Conference*, Women's Labour League, London, 1912, p. 3.

46 Mrs Salter, *The Needs of Little Children Conference*, Women's Labour League, London, 1912, p. 7. A few months earlier the London branch of the Women's Labour League had opened the first baby clinic.

47 The exhibition also gave the Empire a new form of architectural expression with the construction of a major new sports stadium built specially for the Olympic Games, providing a 150,000 capacity for what could be claimed as the first of the modern Olympics.

48 These shows were also linked to a declared customer policy. For example, Waring & Gillow offered 'good design and good taste in everything, even the most insignificant article; good materials and good workmanship, and an undertaking to exchange anything that does not give satisfaction; the lowest price possible consistent with good quality, and every price marked in plain figures': *Illustrated London News*, 29 May 1909, p. 791.

49 In the first issue of the *Studio Decorative Year Book*, 1906, there was a renewed declaration of an editorial policy that, in its articles and selection of objects and interiors, would reflect a design philosophy based on the suitability for purpose, moderation of styles and truth in principles of decoration.

50 *Builder*, 17 October 1908, p. 395.

51 *Journal of the Royal Society of Arts*, vol. 61, 31 October 1913, p. 1077.

52 *Ibid.*

53 Registered in May 1913, closed 1919.

54 *Builder*, 20 February 1914, p. 218.

55 See unpublished report, George Herbert, *Land Settlement Report*, York, 1934.

56 C. R. Ashbee, *Craftsmanship in Competitive Industry*, London, 1908, p. 20.

57 E. Wood, 'Modern Industry and the Village', *The Builders Journal and Architectural Record*, 23 May 1900, p. 279.

58 *Ibid.*

59 Cardiff Worker's Cooperative Garden Village Society, *Prospectus*, 1913, p. 3. The Garden City Association was established 1899 and the National Housing Reform Council formed in 1900.

60 *Report of Proceedings*, Sheffield, 1905, p. 13.

61 *Ibid.*, p. 14. The family garden was a subject for much discussion, and not just for the working classes. In Mrs Waldemar Leverton's *Small Homes and How to Furnish Them*, 1903, a guide for the young middle-class wife, there was surprise that the husband should want a garden, 'but as it seems to be utterly essential to their happiness, by all means let them have it; they may not do much digging, but still it is well to humour them' (p. 16).

62 *Official Illustrated Catalogue of the Yorkshire and North Midlands Model Cottage Exhibition Sheffield*, London, 1907, p. 26.

63 A. & J. Soutar, architects of London, had won the original competition, but this scheme was abandoned, and the new scheme developed by Percy Houfton.

64 Raymond Unwin and M. H. Baillie Scott, *Town Planning and Modern Architecture at the Hampstead Garden Suburb*, London, 1909, p. 2.

65 *Ibid.*, p. 67.

66 *Ibid.*, p. 87.

67 A pattern replicated by Tenants Associations in many other sites, most were unfinished, and many, such as Fallings Park, are now obscured by later developments and idiosyncratic modernisation.

68 *Souvenir*, Chorltonville, 1911, p. 10.

69 E. W. Gregory, *The Art and Craft of Home-Making*, London, 1913: an essay on taste in decoration and furniture, in praise of the common object and common sense.

70 L. Weaver, *The Country Life Book of Cottages*, London, 1913, p. 81.

71 Editorial, *The Architect & Contract Reporter*, 13 January 1911, p. 25.

72 *The Municipal Journal*, 19 November 1910, p. 913. Plans were also made to provide children's playgrounds with swings and see-saws, and bandstand and garden.

73 J. S. Nettleford, *Slum Reform and Town Planning*, Birmingham, 1910, p. 2.

74 Although it was the 1896 Motor Act that marked the beginning of motoring on British roads, it was the 1903 Act, that came into effect on 1 January 1904, that introduced the legislation which laid the foundation for the culture and ethics of motoring. Registration of cars, driving licences, minimum driving age, codes, signs and speed limits were all defined. These were further developed in the 1906 Report of the Royal Commission on Motor Cars, published July 1906.

75 'Shopping by Motorcar', *Motor*, 5 November 1907, p. 385.

76 *Motor*, 11 May 1909.

77 H. Sturmey, 'That £100 Car', *Motor*, 6 July 1909, p. 774.

78 *Autocar*, 17 April 1909, p. 536.

79 T. Brice Philips, 'The Rural Housing Question', *Journal of the Royal Society of Arts*, vol. 62, 1913–14, p. 327.

80 *Illustrated London News*, 20 March 1909.

81 Letter, *Times*, 24 December 1907.

82 Prof. H. Stanley Jevons, 'A Century Hence', *The Housing Reformer*, vol. 1, no. 6, 15 June 1912, p. 82.

2 ✧ Reconstruction and the ideal, 1918–30

The housing question

Women's viewpoint

'NATIONAL Housing and National Life' was the subject of an informal conference at the RIBA on 13 March 1918.[1] Introduced by Professor S. D. Adshead, it confirmed the widespread support for cottage building programmes and planning schemes as the basis of post-war planning. Fuelled by the sense of debt to the war heroes, principles were being shaped by patriotism, emphasising the needs of women and children, and including the previously derided slum dwellers in the post-war reconstruction. It was left to Adshead to introduce a note of caution on the limitations of cottage schemes in being able to provide the whole solution.

> I think that our slum areas will be gradually cleared and the inmates of the worst of them accommodated in well-controlled flats. We have yet a type of town building to erect which shall consist of a huge quadrangle of flats arranged around a square laid out with cobbles or gravel and decorated with flowers, and where the communal kitchen, central heating, and central lighting, and all the so-much discussed advantages of communal and common sharing could be tried.[2]

No one developed this suggestion, even though it became apparent from the debate that housing was seen as part of a much larger problem that included the efficiency of the city, the social changes in rural life and the welfare of the family. Of particular interest was the rural question, not only the appalling conditions of the labourers' cottages, but that as the rich had built houses in the country, and were paying their employees good wages, 'they have been able to outbid the ordinary day labourer when a house in the village becomes vacant',[3] leaving an even greater shortage of decent housing.

In this nationalistic climate, two seemingly unrelated pieces of legislation of 1918 were to have a significant effect on the planning for the family in the post-war reconstruction. There was the creation of the Ministry of Health, which with its direct responsibility for housing, reinforced the direct link between housing and health, and the Reform Act that extended housewife suffrage. This meant that the established links between moral welfare, bad housing and particularly the needs of children, were joined by new arguments directly associated with the needs of the housewife. Considered to have been unable to participate in social and political activities through the endless cycle of housework, unaided by even the most basic services, the efficient house as a representation of modern living came to be seen as an important part of the increased emancipation of women. Of comparable importance was the growing recognition of the value of part-time education, and the need for quiet and space for home studies, an argument which was to be much used to defend the parlour house.[4]

These were important developments, but getting women heard on matters of national housing policy and programmes was more problematic. In 1916 the Welsh Housing and Development Association had established a sub-committee on housing, with a majority of women members, under the chairmanship of Miss E. P. Hughes, who in an article 'Housing Problems from the Standpoint of a Woman', 1918, wrote

> The tremendous importance of housing problems arises from the fact that almost every house is a home; that is, it is inhabited by the little community of a family, the natural unit of society, and that element in a nation's organisation on which depends more than anything else its health, comfort, morality and economic prosperity; and not only for the present but also profoundly for the future, for the embryo citizens of our country are growing up in our homes, and in the centre of this community of the family, is a woman home-maker, to whom housing problems are of profound and special importance for two reasons. She spends far more time in the home than her husband or sons. Also her chief contribution to the work of the world is the management of her home, and as her home-making is carried on in a house it matters profoundly to her that that house should be so planned and fitted up that she is able to carry on her work effectively, and with the least expenditure of time and energy.[5]

The conclusion was that working-class houses were inadequate for family needs. They were badly ventilated, with services in the wrong place, shelves too high, a shortage of cupboard space, and impractical bedrooms. It was argued that to produce improvements the only way forward was to consult women in the design of new houses by forming local advisory committees.

In autumn 1917 the Women's Labour League had approached the same question and were to reach very similar conclusions through a questionnaire on two specimen house layouts, circulated and discussed through a series of regional conferences, and the findings made public in the following June.[6] Modern fitments, services and space were the core demands in a cottage of three bedrooms, with kitchen-scullery, living room and parlour. Viewed as the practicalities of managing a home, cooking, washing, drying, storage, communal and private space were the priorities, with considerable emphasis placed on a constant supply of hot water. Unanimous in its opposition to the scullery-bath, in favour of separate bathroom with basin and heated linen cupboard, dismayed by the attack on the parlour, which with central heating would be an essential space for 'rest, recreation, and study',[7] and aware of the need to provide facilities for light laundry work it was an optimistic yet realistic list of requirements. With the gas stove beginning to replace the kitchen range it was also expected that cooking would increasingly be carried out in the scullery, and that in time electric labour-saving devices would be made available.

Reporting in March 1919, the Women's Housing Sub-Committee of the Ministry of Reconstruction re-emphasised these recommendations, underlining the need for increased living space, including a through room that increased light, sun and ventilation, the retention of the parlour and a separate bathroom. Services were expected to include good drainage, hot and cold water, electricity, and the construction carried out with better quality materials and workmanship. Central heating was favoured, and again there were strong objections against the continued use of communal wash-houses. The neighbourhood and its social amenities completed the list of concerns. There were demands for children's playgrounds, social centres for community activities, public houses converted into cheap restaurants, and communal holiday homes at the seaside or in the country, instead of the usual 'lodging' accommodation.

Tudor Walters and the cottage solution

It was an agenda that was well served by the 1918 report on the construction and provision of working-class dwellings, known as the Tudor Walters Report, which provided a comprehensive introduction to the scale of the contemporary housing problem. The housing shortage was estimated at 600,000 and little time was spent arguing the case for state aid, and the coordination of municipal and private developments. It was assumed that the strength of the case for national intervention, including the compulsory purchase of land, would be self-evident. The majority of the report was spent describing minimum standards for health, comfort and convenience, and setting out the priorities and values that would shape the homes and neighbourhoods of the inter-war years. More advisory than authoritarian in its style, Raymond Unwin ensured that the garden city and town planning movement ideals were well represented in the report. The ideal was for family dwellings, suitable for a sixty-year life. Unwin's vision was for a return to the traditions broken by the industrial revolution,

> remember that if our people are many, and their houses congregated into vast cities, still each family is as valuable, as human, and as much worthy of a home adapted to its life and its individuality as were their forefathers who dwelt in the beautiful small houses with which our country is still dotted.[8]

Regional planning came into the frame, as did edge of town development linked by new transport networks. The national objective was to provide 'spacious suburbs with convenient and attractive houses designed by competent architects, with districts planned so as to provide the amenities of healthy social communities'.[9] The sense of community, its social, educational and recreational needs, was a recurring theme, alongside the preservation and development of the beauty of the site.

Double-flatted houses and tenements were considered, but the preference, wherever possible, was for the two-storey cottage. Again time was spent considering the most effective internal arrangement, with the committee coming out strongly in favour of the parlour house, believing that it was the most effective way of catering for home study, visitors, and illness in the family. While recognising that there would always be exceptions to the recommendations, considerable emphasis was placed on the urgent need for the three-bedroom family house, with a back garden for children to play in. Three basic house types were adopted, each illustrated with a number of internal variations. They were small houses, varying from a total ground floor space of 25ft× 16.5ft, to 25ft× 22ft, and so it was suggested that the municipal authorities should ensure that such details as the positioning of doors did not interfere with the most effective use of the living space. All had a larder, an internal WC and coal store, and some had a cycle store. Despite some reservations, there was a preference for the cooking range to be located in an enlarged scullery, and more contentiously that it would also accommodate the bath and washing facilities. Any problems arising from this arrangement were believed to be offset by the provision of a communal wash-house, and the possible introduction of a centrally provided hot water system. Coal was used for heating and cooking, gas for lighting and cooking. Although the electric age was dawning, it did not yet feature in working-class housing.

The report was both pragmatic and optimistic. Whilst setting minimum standards it was hoped that these would not inhibit more generous provision. Economies were essential, but there were a number of reminders that these should not be gained at the expense of design. It was thought desirable to have a living room that had an 'attractive outlook' and 'sunny aspect', while

> Good exterior design in harmony with the site and surroundings should be secured by the choice of suitable local materials, by adopting good proportion in the mass and in the openings, by careful grouping of the parts of each house, by suitable grouping, and by well-considered variations of design to suit the position, site and materials.[10]

Mr Hayes Fisher, President of the Local Government Board, speaking at a public meeting on 25 September 1918, at Exeter, outlined the growing responsibility of local authorities in solving the 'Housing Question'.

> They aimed at a better standard of house, to contain a living room with a sunny aspect, a parlour, three bedrooms, a scullery, a bathroom, and so on. He urged local authorities to take into counsel some practical working women in their districts to suggest the best place for the fittings. Six million women were being enfranchised, and they were going to have something to say as to the domestic policy of this country, and he hoped and believed they were going to take an interest in this housing question, which was part of the great health question.[11]

The underlying theme was one of houses that were for 'the savings of labour for the wife and the convenience and health of the family'.[12] Unfortunately most authorities had little opportunity to make considered responses, and insufficient attention was being given to the distinction between density and overcrowding, between personal and communal space, and between quiet and noisy activities. Regarded as a national problem, many of the ideals had to be submerged in the act of rescuing the destitute slum dweller.[13] The perception of problems in Scotland was no different. The Report of the Royal Commission on the Housing of the Industrial Population of Scotland, 1917, covering rural and tenement areas of large cities, estimated that 235,990 houses would be needed to overcome the problems of overcrowded, ill-ventilated, damp dwellings.

The cottage was the preferred solution, chosen by the *Builder* for a series 'Housing for the people' that began on 3 January 1919, and for municipal housing competitions and the ongoing government and company housing schemes (figure 8). In spring 1919 the *Daily Express* ran a competition offering prizes to professionals and amateurs for three categories of cottage designs along class lines, providing houses for the unskilled labourer, the skilled artisan and the clerical worker. Included in the Model Homes Exhibition that was held at the Central Hall, Westminster, in May 1919, it was the *Daily Mail* Ideal (Workers') Homes Architects' Competition, with its published books of prize-winning designs of 1919, that was the most effective of these initiatives. With its range of cottage

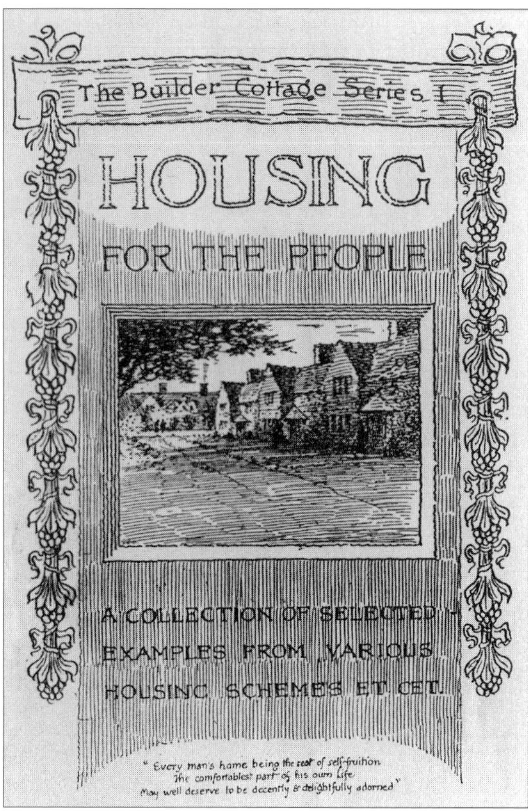

The Builder Cottage Series I
HOUSING
FOR THE PEOPLE
A COLLECTION OF SELECTED EXAMPLES FROM VARIOUS HOUSING SCHEMES ET CET.
" Every man's home being the seat of self-fruition the comfortablest part of his own life May well deserve to be decently & delightfully adorned "

8 Housing for the people, *Builder*, 3 January 1919

architecture, the purpose was to raise the awareness of good design and the need to set housing standards that would still be ideal in fifty years' time. General design principles were being made even though for both architectural and political reasons, the competition was targeted at the needs of four regions: Northern, Midland and Welsh Industrial Areas, and a Southern and Midland Counties Rural Area. The introduction to the published designs drew attention to the involvement of men and women as assessors, who had viewed the social implications of house design, alongside the professional architects, ensuring that the 'appearance of the house, the health of the inhabitants, the convenience of the housewife, and the purse of the taxpayer'[14] had been taken into account in providing houses that were 'homely and bright ... the centre of a happy family life'.[15] They were homes with maximum sunshine, parlour and bathroom, and equipped to meet the practical needs of the tenants.

The understanding of the relationship between the home and quality of life had been effectively rehearsed in debates on housing and planning over the previous twenty years, but it was the *Illustrated London News* with its graphically illustrated article on 'London Housing Problems' that reminded the nation of the scale of the housing problem, with its picture of family life in Shoreditch and Whitechapel, where 'one little room is frequently the complete abode – the kitchen, parlour and bedroom in one – for two families with their children'. There was no provision for cooking or washing, so that 'most of the meals are taken at a fried-fish shop'.[16] A snapshot of slum life, it could have been duplicated with illustrations from any British town, city, or rural slums. Faced with the realities of the slum dweller, in a landscape of poverty, it was understandable that municipal authorities should grasp at any proposal that appeared to offer a quick and cheap solution. The difficulty was deciding on the minimum acceptable standards, and making sure that the short-term relief did not turn itself into a long-term problem. One much visited and discussed initiative, was the Logie municipal housing scheme in Dundee, introduced by the City Architect, James Thomson, in 1918, and opened on 27 May 1920, when about half of the 250 houses had been completed. Conventional in layout and setting, it was the services that made it unique, with a communal central heating system that fed radiators in each room and supplied hot water for the scullery and bathroom. But it was expensive to run, and the experiment was not repeated.

Prefabrication

The urgent demand for new houses turned attention to the benefits of factory constructed houses and use of cheaper materials. Temporary structures for the army and navy, at home and on the battlefields, were now seen to offer both immediate and long-term solutions to domestic problems. Vacated camps across the country were converted to meet emergency housing needs, and new prefabricated houses, using steel, cast-iron, concrete and wood constructions, came under consideration. The 'Winget' system of concrete block construction, had been the popular choice of government departments for housing schemes and camps, at home and in the colonies, and valued for the building economies and practicality it retained its popularity in the post-war reconstruction, playing a dominant role in the range of experimental and model houses being undertaken by local authorities and companies. A topic that figured prominently in the 1920 International Housing Congress, London, delegates visited new estates being built on the 'Winget' principle by private enterprise at Wembley Hill, and by the Metropolitan Railway Company at Wembley Park and Neasden, as well as established estates at Wrotham and Otford in Kent. The three-bedroomed, parlour semi-detached house was the model home of the West London developments, and much was made of the new suburbs being created out of the ashes from the neighbouring electricity works.[17]

Interest in steel frame housing was stimulated by the initiative of Dorman, Long and Co., the iron and steel manufacturers in Middlesbrough. The firm had established a workers' garden village, Dormanstown, designed by Adshead and Abercrombie, which in the first phase had used brick and timber for the construction of the houses. Now they were developing a steel frame structure, in which the sections were bolted together, with a metal-lathing finished in concrete for the external walls and breeze blocks for the interior. Although adopting Georgian style, it was emphasised that the steel frame structure could be used with any architectural style and building material.

In October 1919, Glasgow Corporation held the first of what was to become its annual 'Housing and Health Exhibition'. The exhibition included the expected range of furnishings and sanitary fittings, and dealt with questions of heating, lighting and labour-saving appliances. But, with its attention to housing and health reform, and child care, the emphasis was on houses for the artisan class.[18] Four model cottages were on show, three of which were prefabricated structures. Messrs Cowleson had a timber cottage that could be delivered in sections and bolted together on site. The 'St Mungo' cottage, had a living room, scullery, two bedrooms and bathroom, with gas cooker and boiler, coal-fire that also heated water and electric lighting. Built of concrete blocks on the 'Winget' system, it could be dismantled after the exhibition for erection on a site of the purchaser's choice. The 'Spieresque' cottage used an almost identical layout, except that it was equipped with an electric cooker. This was a timber frame construction, externally finished with a metal lath and cement rendering, and internally with fibre-board. It claimed to be erected complete in twenty-one days, built to last a lifetime, and was romantically imaged as the perfect home for the small family (figure 9).

Glasgow Corporation had already considered timber frame houses as a realistic solution to its more urgent housing problems, even considering buying ready-made houses from British Columbia. By the time of the opening of the exhibition, the city had decided to build 500 temporary homes, costing £325 each, with an expected five years life. Two years later, the Glasgow Housing and Health Exhibition had another concrete cottage on display, and a much more ambitious timber framed house. The timber house attracted the greater attention, with its potential to be used as a five-bedroom house, and promotion of home-grown timber. The structure and floors were of larch, windows, doors and mouldings of Scots fir, and tiles and shingles of spruce.

The adaptation of army camps as temporary housing was being considered by a number of local authorities as a possible short-term solution. In May 1920, on the Town Moor, Newcastle, the corporation exhibited

9 'Spieresque': prefabricated cottage, Housing & Health Exhibition, Glasgow, 1919

an army hut that had been converted into a three-bedroom parlour house, as a possible solution. Bristol Housing Committee came up with its own bungalow, based on the hut structure, at an estimated cost of £195. Consisting of a steel frame, covered with corrugated galvanised iron sheets and tarred, interior walls of breeze blocks, and rooms without ceilings, heating them would have been difficult and, with an appearance little different from the huts on which they were modelled, they had limited appeal.[19] With the housing shortage unresolved families started taking matters into their own hands, either squatting, or, as in one reported instance in Sheffield, purchasing ex-army huts for erection as homes on allotments. Local authorities were also finding themselves overtaken by the construction of timber framed houses and bungalows on a scale that could not be met by the existing drainage and water-supply. One such scheme was the Lawnswood development on the edge of Leeds. The building costs and the increasing realisation that under current practices the shortfall in housing would never be satisfied brought attention to methods of construction and the organisation of labour.

The possibilities of using new constructional techniques and materials for middle-class housing were introduced by the show houses that formed the 1922 *Daily Mail* Model Village, built at Welwyn Garden City to coincide with the Ideal Home Exhibition at Olympia. The 'Dorlonco' concrete system used in the workers' housing at Dormanstown was on display with houses in neo-Georgian style, and an extraordinary flat-roofed house with neo-Georgian windows by Louis de Soissons, painted Indian yellow walls, vermilion window frames, and yellow, indigo blue and green pergolas. There were timber frame houses, as well as the traditional constructions, two of which had been built by disabled ex-servicemen trained by the Ministry of Labour. Back at Olympia, the exhibition visitor was reminded of what the nation was trying to replace with a full-size replica of a miner's hovel from a Lanarkshire colliery district. The following year the Ideal Home Exhibition created 'Bungalow Town', putting the emphasis on different types of timber construction.

Organising an adequate workforce was as much a problem as construction. In his paper 'National Housing and a National Municipal House-building Service', presented to the RIBA, Major Harry Barnes outlined his proposal for a national 'public cottage-building service', with its own labour of 200,000 men and supplies, that would have the older men settled in specific districts, with the workforce supplemented by itinerant young craftspeople as the need arose.[20] The nation was not ready for such a radical proposal and finding alternative building techniques, while retaining the traditional styles and appearance of the English cottage was the more acceptable solution. At the 1925 Glasgow Health and Housing Exhibition, a four-apartment steel house was on display, the same year in which Lord Weir's steel house and bungalow began to attract attention.[21] Timber framed, with interior walls of composite board and plywood, and asbestos roofing tiles, steel was only used in the exterior sheeting. Not all reports were favourable, but encouraged by the Ministry of Health grant for specimen steel houses to be constructed around the country,[22] it was part of a growing movement to counter the perceived failures of the building trade, and was made a major feature of the Palace of Housing and Transport at the 1925 British Empire Exhibition, Wembley. The concrete houses, 'The Universal', 'Easiform' and 'Corolite', all used a similar process of shuttering in their construction. There was a timber framed house, with asbestos panels sandwiched between concrete and breeze block, an all-slate cottage, a cedar shingle type, a 'gunite' process, which involved spraying cement on to a felt base, reinforced with expanded metal, and a 'Dennis-Wild' cottage that had a steel frame finished in traditional building methods of brick and tile, which was to be widely used by municipal authorities. There was little variation in the interior layout, with three bedrooms, living room, and either scullery with bath, or scullery leading into bathroom.[23] Exaggerated claims of the benefits of the different systems were being made, but as the new methods of construction were still trying to replicate the appearance and layout of the traditional small working-class house, or modify the wartime 'hut' structures they either failed to reduce housing costs or overcome prejudice against the appearance and temporary nature of the buildings.[24]

Radical or conservative, style was essential to the introduction. Accepting that materials more frequently associated with engineering structures were a possible answer to the production of cheap mass-produced houses for working-class families, by the middle of the 1920s moves were being made to promote their uses in the provision of the professional middle-class house. There were for example, the two prize-winning designs in the Portland Cement architectural competition that were shown at the 1928 Ideal Home Exhibition: the Thomas S. Tait modernist design for a £1,750 house, and the £750 neo-Georgian house by Frank J. Brown and J. H. Peck, which brought concrete into the mainstream. The Tait house had four bedrooms, a maid's bedroom and garage, while the Brown/Peck house was three bedroomed. There were interesting differences of terminology, in that the Tait had a kitchen, the Brown/Peck a scullery; the Tait had a sitting room and dining room, whereas the Brown/Peck had a sitting room and a living room, which meant that it was used for dining. The Welcome House at the 1929 Ideal Home Exhibition was strongly criticised for being a concrete version of a middle-class neo-Georgian suburban house, but the whole point of its design had been to show that it could be used to do what had been traditionally carried out in brick and timber.

While searching out solutions to the housing problem, the experiments with prefabricated structures had produced another significant development, albeit for the middle-class family. The house with a garage, or at least space for one, was in demand. There was an ever-growing choice of prefabricated ready-made garages, in wood, concrete, asbestos and galvanised steel sheets, ranging in size and facilities, which in 1920 were at prices from £33 to £110. Prices steadily came down, and by the mid-1920s garages could be acquired for as little as £10 5*s*., by which time Morris Motors Ltd was anticipating the demand with two garages of its own, one to fit the Morris-Cowley, the other for the Morris-Oxford, at £15 15*s*. and £17 respectively. The new suburban house with attached or integrated garage if not yet standard was visible in all parts of the country, because of the belief that every new house owner was an actual or potential motoring family.

> Some builders of small villas to-day do not seem to have rid themselves of the outdated idea that the occupants will be artisans with incomes insufficient to own cars, whereas, of course, the whole trend of the industry is to bring them within the purse range of these classes, too.[25]

With the nation unable to satisfy the demand for homes for its people, finding homes for cars was not perceived with any sense of urgency. It was, though, an underestimated environmental problem that future planners would have to try to unravel.

New neighbourhoods and lifestyles

Boundary changes

The problem for cities was overcrowding. The question was whether this was best answered by a programme of relocation or rebuilding. The 1920 Interim Report of the Housing Committee of the Ministry of Health understood this as a choice between building horizontally or vertically. Although it was recognised that the vertical building would create recreational space for children, and room for new parks and gardens, within the existing urban areas, it was felt that this was an unsuitable solution for those families who did their own housework and were responsible for their own children. Consequently the cottage estate continued to be recommended as the preferred solution for rehousing, and cities moved their boundaries and acquired more rural land for the new estates.

This pattern of large-scale cottage house estates began with the LCC Becontree estate in the autumn of 1920. It was planned with arterial roads, civic centre, shopping centres, public buildings and open spaces, and like many similar developments that followed, the transport and service needs were slow to arrive. Municipal housing schemes became a study in their own right. An exhibition first shown at the 1920 Ideal Home Exhibition, and then rehung at the RIBA provided a public summary of the work being undertaken by the large provincial cities, alongside schemes being developed for small towns and districts of London. The influence of the garden suburb movement was much in evidence, and it also provided a glimpse of future problems with the lack of attention to neighbourhood centres and limited understanding of the future road systems.

There was an increasing concern that the historical and the natural features of the rural landscape should be protected within the new city plans, while making sure that the new developments included all the necessary community facilities, and the new road systems to anticipate effectively the long-term traffic needs. The formation of the Birmingham Civic Society on 10 June 1918, and its response to the new city plan encapsulated the mood of these concerns. Actively supported and funded by George Cadbury, the ideas behind the creation of Bourneville were influential. Over a period of time the Society was to purchase land and give it to the city for public open space and parks, but it was the proposals for the road schemes and expansion of the village of Northfield that effectively illustrated the thinking behind this movement. Involving the construction of new roads and the widening of existing roads, there was a limited awareness of the scale of the impending expansion of motoring and increase of traffic. Illustrated with a pictorial map of the new neighbourhood, with its public buildings, schools, institutes, recreation grounds and public gardens, in a language and typeface that replicated its medieval associations, it was the portrait of a modern society that had kept faith with the values of old-world England. It was not nostalgia, but an argument for a policy of preservation to be integral to a process of modernisation.[26]

It was similar unease that resulted in the first regional planning scheme. The dramatic expansion of the South Yorkshire coalfield in the years leading up to the First World War had begun to alarm Doncaster. Having developed as a railway town, the engineering centre for the Great Northern Railway, it seemed that a new phase of industrial development might engulf the surrounding agricultural land. In the post-war climate of reconstruction Doncaster could see its boundaries and identity threatened. Such was the concern that on 16 January 1920 a meeting, convened by the Ministry of Health, was held in Doncaster, from which came the first meeting of the Joint Town Planning Committee on 31 May 1920, when P. Abercrombie and T. H. Johnson, the local architect, were invited to prepare a report. The outcome was the Doncaster Regional Planning Scheme of 1922, important not only for Doncaster but as a landmark in setting the national pattern of regional planning. Outlining a regional development of ten or more communities, the expectation was that the villages would in time become new towns ringing a modern metropolitan city created out of Doncaster. Designated as the proposed centre for finance, higher education and the arts, the ambition was to provide Doncaster with a civic centre that followed the Cardiff model, and rivalled the grandeur of other northern cities. For the region, land was identified for industrial development, housing and preservation, and road systems of radial, bypass, and parkways were indicated.[27]

The anticipated expansion of the Doncaster regional plan never came. Despite the plans for new towns of between 15,000 and 20,000, with their own industries and community facilities for shopping and recreation, the villages remained as such, modified and unfinished, and Doncaster continued life as a town of indeterminate character. A story repeated time and again across the country, the idealism behind these plans continued to dominate the ideological base of town planning and its concepts of community life. Imagination was a key part of planning, but in visualising the plausible, it was frequently difficult to separate out the fantasy from the reality of the representation. Nevertheless, the successful beginnings of the garden city and suburb movement meant that it was the preferred choice of the post-war housing schemes. Company, municipal and speculative projects were as one, believing that it offered the best of the past and the present. With the village the preferred national module, the quality of provision in materials, space and services was only separated by economy and purpose, not principles of design. It did not provide an answer to the rehabilitation of cities, only adding the working classes to the continuing middle-class exodus, but it raised questions on the social implications of this pattern of migration.

The use of land and traditions of rural life were primary concerns, but so were the expected services for homes in areas were the established public utilities of urban communities had yet to reach the countryside, and the expectations for recreational, welfare and educational provision were similarly formed by the municipal and commercial facilities of townlife. For the middle classes these problems were less acute, having elected for the garden suburb lifestyle based on commuting and the separation of home from work. The popular representation was of an old-world setting, accommodating recreation, relaxation and hobbies; a safe place for children, it offered a dream life, as shown by a 1922 advertisement for a new estate planned for Hillingdon, where 'Every day's a holiday in a Halden garden'. With its publication *Homes in Metro-land* in 1923, the Metropolitan Railway Co. was confirming the success of its plans to open up new residential areas. With six estates of its own, the principal one in Ricksmanworth and others in Wembley, Pinner and Kingsbury, since 1919 more than 400 houses had been built, available on long-term mortgages, in what seemed a country setting, but with direct travel into Baker Street. It was confirmation that commuting into town by car was not yet a realistic choice, but driving to the local railway station was a convenient alternative. Station garages with petrol filling facilities became a common sight as cars were left in the station forecourt. Soon the picture of the wife with the family car, usually accompanied by healthy happy children, meeting the homecoming husband at the station, became a familiar part of motor car advertising. For the working-class family tempted to the new villages by the prospect of acquiring work and a new home, and a healthy life for the children, the aspirations were little different from the ideals set out for the middle-class family, except in one key factor, the quality of local amenities and public transport links were far more critical to an everyday lifestyle.

Company estates and villages

The clearest indication of what Abercrombie and Johnson had envisaged as the format for the embryo communities of the Doncaster regional plan was laid out in their own plans for the new village at Kirk Sandall. Designed for the new Pilkington's Glass factory that had been developed since August 1919, in its scale it was more new town than village. With its central square, and radiating avenues, it was garden city rather than suburb in its aspirations. By the time that the Regional Report was published about 250 houses had been completed at Kirk Sandall, which was about one-fifth of the projected number. A further 80 houses were completed by 1925, but nothing else of significance until a small development in the 1930s. An assembly hall, nursery and boys' club were built, a bowling green and tennis courts laid out. The Cooperative opened a shop in temporary accommodation, otherwise residents were dependent on the local bus services into Doncaster which ran on Fridays and Saturdays. As with all of these types of settlement, there was a pioneering concept attached to the venture, and in the houses, a mixture of parlour and non-parlour, with at least three bedrooms and bathroom, families were being offered quality accommodation. Construction was either a conventional brick and part-rendered houses, or in the more experimental Dormon Long steel framed method. In its amenities and layout it was no better or worse than a range of company and municipal developments, but as elsewhere it was to fall short of the ideal represented by the claims and illustrations generated by the architects and planners, remaining isolated and incomplete.

When in October 1925, the manufacturers Crittall's alighted on farm land for a new factory site, with space to build houses for the workers, the attraction of Silver End was its location, near enough to Braintree and Witham for it not to be too isolated, while allowing the company to build 'a village with all the advantages of a town'.[28] The intention had been to provide houses with hot and cold water, gas or electric light, proper sanitation and a garden, 'a friendly spot where a man might well choose to set his home and make a garden'.[29] Learning from the Welwyn Garden City development, the first phase followed a conventional cottage style by C. H. B. Quennell, differentiating in its provision and layout between managers, staff and workers. F. H. Crittall had an imposing manor house approached along a tree-lined walkway from the village hall. The feudal spirit was alive, and was maintained in the modernist development by Thomas Tait. In its public buildings, it showed the extent to which it was an embryo town, the village hall was positively municipal in scale and concept, as were the public house and department store. It offered a landscape of domestic security, but was not immune to the changes in the national economy and as economic depression brought redundancies so the plan as envisaged came to an end. An almost identical approach and similar outcome can be found at the Kemsley Garden Village, Sittingbourne, Kent, designed by Thomas Adams and Langstreth Thompson in

1924 for the new paper mill of Edward Lloyd Ltd. By the end of 1926, 176 of the 750 houses planned for the village had been completed, in four grades according to the class of tenant: the highest grade had a separate kitchen, instead of the kitchen-living room, and four rather than the standard three bedrooms.

The concept of the village green, surrounded by small modern houses, sometimes the home for cricket, tennis, and even country dancing, was the much favoured representation of the garden village lifestyle. Integral to the countrification of the English suburbs, it was a model even transposed to the heart of Perthshire. James Miller's design of 1925, to replace existing cottages on the Forteviot estate, about seven miles out of Perth, comprised ten cottages grouped around an open square facing the village hall and smithy. Finished in a rough white rendering, with white woodwork and olive green doors, the interchange of gables and dormer windows reworked the arts and crafts proportions and details, emphasising the attention to ventilation and sunshine. They were parlour houses, with an entrance porch, two bedrooms and bathroom on the first floor, and a kitchen garden. Their quality was of the highest standard. The village hall had a reading room, and was equipped for social functions, including a cinema projection room. A school was to be built, and a bowling green was being laid.

In *The Building of Twelve Thousand Houses* (1927), Tudor Walters described the running of a scheme that extended similar values to twenty-six villages across the Yorkshire, Derbyshire and Nottingham coalfields. Costs and restrictions of the building trade were still a problem, but with some standardisation of construction, economies had been made. The underlying design principles were based on the three-bedroom parlour and non-parlour houses, with a bathroom, ample cupboards, space for prams, cycles, motor cycles, and in a few cases, even for a motor car. With a ready local supply, brick construction was favoured. Gardens were provided, but because of a pattern of neglect, it was felt that these should be smaller, with allotments nearby for those who wanted them. It was determined that there would be

> plenty of open spaces, no monotonous lines of dreary houses, no barrack blocks, and no 'jerry' building, but that the layout of the land should in each case be carefully considered with a view to preserving any natural beauties that the site might possess, and that the frontage line should be broken up into well-designed groups of houses with plenty of variety in the elevations.[30]

The representation of the 'typical' was of a fashionable neighbourhood, the cottages with neo-Georgian details, spacious and ordered, and arranged with arts and crafts interiors. Plans identified sites for social facilities, shopping centres, sports fields and children's playgrounds, but in general these were for future development and, in the first instance, if there was any provision at all, it survived in temporary accommodation. The building of public houses was more successful, as the brewers took on the financial responsibility. The high cost of living in these new villages, particularly the everyday cost of shopping, was a concern that remained unresolved. There were problems of bad tenants, but the majority were good, and rumours of unsocial behaviour, such as using the bath for storage were disputed.

The prospect of the industrialisation of Kent, particularly through the expansion of its coalfield, prompted the production of the East Kent Regional Planning Scheme, preliminary report 1925, final report 1928. It was interesting for its consideration of communication network and housing densities, and an analysis that led to proposals for eight new towns as the core of the regional development. Similar to ideas expressed in the Doncaster plan, in this instance the preference was for new towns serving more than one industry, which from the outset would include plans for civic centres, shopping areas, schools and open spaces, making 'the most artistic and economical use of their beautiful sites'.[31] Opting for a density of twelve houses per acre, the growth was seen as developing over a thirty-year period, with 10,000 houses for new development, and 4,000 houses for slum clearance in the first five years. Accepting a formality of layout, the suggested architectural style was 'a simple Georgian, modified into a provincial touch with the somewhat high-pitched roofs, and with a further local flavour of the Flemish influence in its brickwork'.[32] Garden city in its idealism, it rejected the application of the self-sufficiency ideas of 'homecrofting', in favour of setting out designated areas for allotments.

As a whole the coalfield did not live up to its expectations, and within two years of its start, development projections were being rapidly scaled down. At the same time the mines achieved a reputation for being difficult to work, with intense heat and problems with water. There was also considerable suspicion and at times opposition towards the immigrant families. Collectively it produced very unsettled communities. The grand civic plans remained on paper, as both social and architectural problems achieved a monumental scale (figure 10). There had been insufficient funding to build the houses in the materials and styles first described by Abercrombie. Some were brick, while others were the concrete/steel structures developed by Dormon Lond & Co. The most serious problem was the indecision over whether to include bathrooms or rely on the miners being provided with baths at the pithead.

As the plans suffered from a lack of investment, it required great

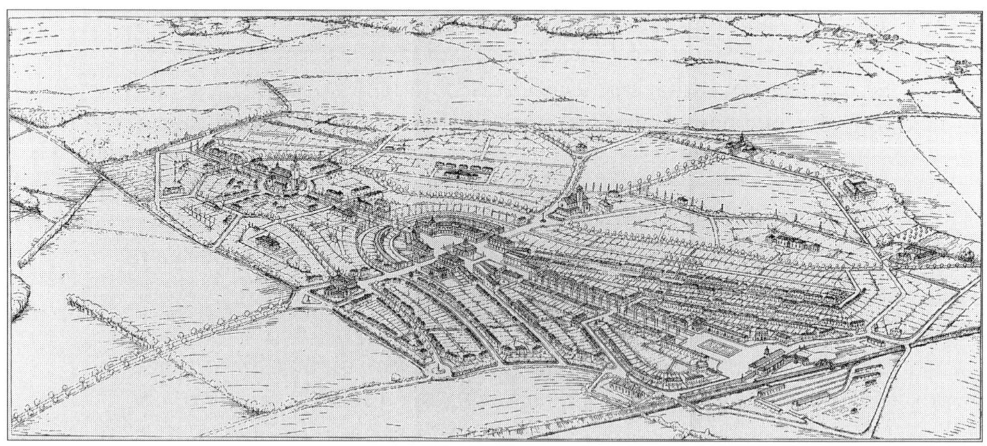

10 P. Abercrombie, Plan for Aylesham, 1927

imagination to envisage anything ideal rising from the mud. Describing his plans for Aylesham in a paper given to the RIBA, Abercrombie remained optimistic, despite the immediate planning difficulties: 'Anyone, indeed, visiting the site at the moment would unless possessed of the prophetic eye, consider this an extreme act of rural desecration. But behind this churned up welter there is a method, and eventually, we hope, something will emerge'.[33] Soon afterwards Aylesham had acquired four church halls, a public house, two small shops and a temporary school building, but the hopes for the grand plan with its boulevard, crescents, civic and church architecture and commercial grandeur of a new railway station were fading fast. In its first two years it was estimated that about 300 families had left Aylesham. The basic mechanics of everyday life had not been satisfied: costs of living were high, social amenities lacking and public transport was infrequent. The vision had not matched reality. Being isolated, and with little prospect of any improvement, it remained an unstable community, and any pretence that it could achieve new town status slowly disappeared.

Far from being an exception, from the mid-1920s it was a pattern of hardship that was affecting most of those living in the garden villages. House building that had stopped during the war years had recommenced, but it had turned out to be a short-lived revival. Community facilities had been slow to materialise, and those that existed were surviving in temporary arrangements. Because they were suburban estates rather than new villages, the railway housing schemes developed by Great Western avoided many of these problems of isolation, and were socially more manageable.[34] Others such as at Rhubina, in 1928, fifteen years after the first houses were built, although the first phase of the school was opened, by then tenancies were being given up as the economic depression forced families back into Cardiff. At Kirk Sandall, families that had chosen to buy their house were unable to maintain the purchase payments, and had to revert to tenancy agreements.

Rural reconstruction

As this pattern of urban settlements had sought to satisfy industrial needs the Land Settlement (Facilities) Act, 1919, introduced legislation designed to rescue rural Britain. It was responsible for land acquisition, its division into smallholdings, and the adaptation or provision of new houses and farm buildings. Picking up the work started by the 1908 Act, at the outset the scheme was restricted to ex-servicemen. Describing its operation in England and Wales, Lawrence Weaver explained how in its first two years they had received 48,340 applications, and settled 13,314 families.[35] The holdings varied greatly in size and type, from market gardening or fruit growing to dairy holdings, but averaged 13½ acres. Training programmes were established, and much thought was given to the grouping of the holdings, in order to facilitate cooperative marketing and overcome the general difficulties of rural transport. Costs of setting up settlements continued to rise, particularly because of building costs, and developments began to be restricted to estates near to the applicants' homes, or where existing property could be modified to provide the necessary dwellings. Despite these changes the scheme continued to prove difficult to manage. There were reports of families having to camp in tents or shacks, and use had to be made of temporary wooden huts. Faced with these emergencies Weaver was of the opinion that while they needed architects with artistic talent, they should 'be even more an organiser and economist'.[36] Using a farm settlement at Amesbury, Wiltshire, an experimental scheme was set up to evaluate the benefits of different types of house plan and materials, including cobb, concrete, timber and brick. Building thirty-two cottages, they found brick to be the most versatile, but accepted that the building programmes would have to be adapted to take advantage of the local conditions and resources. Starting optimistically with building standards that 'would justify our desires for a new world',[37] it was a short-lived dream as the national guidelines were changed twice in quick succession, reducing the accommodation to a minimum, and removing the parlour cottage as an option.

In the early 1920s there had been a revived interest in the concept of 'Homecrofting', a scheme part way between a smallholding and an allotment, with the house on a ½–⅔ acre plot to grow food for the family. In 1927 a demonstration unit of ten houses was built at Cheltenham. Each family was supplied with ten laying fowls, six pairs of rabbits and two goats, and the backs of the gardens were kept open to allow for communal tilling of the potato ground. But as with British agriculture in general, the economic depression was leaving its mark, and many of those running smallholdings and allotments did not have the finance to plant any crops. It was at this stage that the Society of Friends played an active role in supporting programmes of self-help through its 'Small Holdings for the Unemployed Committee'. This scheme had started with help for the destitute miners in the South Wales valleys, providing seeds and seed potatoes, and had rapidly taken on a national dimension with the Society providing much of the organisational input, working alongside local societies and the National Allotments Society. Times were difficult, yet, since the introduction of the first Small Holdings & Allotments Act, 1908, 30,905 holdings had been established by the beginning of the 1930s[38] It was a major responsibility for County Councils, but the experiences gained from areas of high unemployment suggested that by settling unemployed men and their families on the land, providing training programmes and group settlements, it might be possible simultaneously to solve urban and rural social and economic problems. As the plans to rejuvenate the decline of rural Britain took shape, so the concerns over the erosion of the countryside by uncontrolled development came to the fore.

New landscapes

In 1922, the future of the British car and motoring was to be redefined with the launch of the Austin Seven. It was the first opportunity for those families previously restricted to the motor bike and sidecar, or cyclecar, to enjoy owning a motor car. With new filling-stations, roadside tearooms, and garages lining the new roads, motoring became confident in the importance of its contribution to modern life, opening up rural Britain to the middle classes. It was the age of the great escape and, with the caravan, the illustrated articles and advertising projected images of middle-class suburban life transferred to a quiet corner of the unspoilt countryside (figure 11).

The rich had long had their country house garages filled with cars to meet every occasion, but with the introduction of the small family car, the idea of the two-car family becoming both normal and expedient was presented to the motoring public.

> Once regarded as extravagant luxury, the ownership of two cars by one family to-day is not merely convenient but it is also an economical convenience. For £500 you can now obtain a Morris Six Saloon and a Morris Minor Tourer. There is the big car for every important occasion. For short

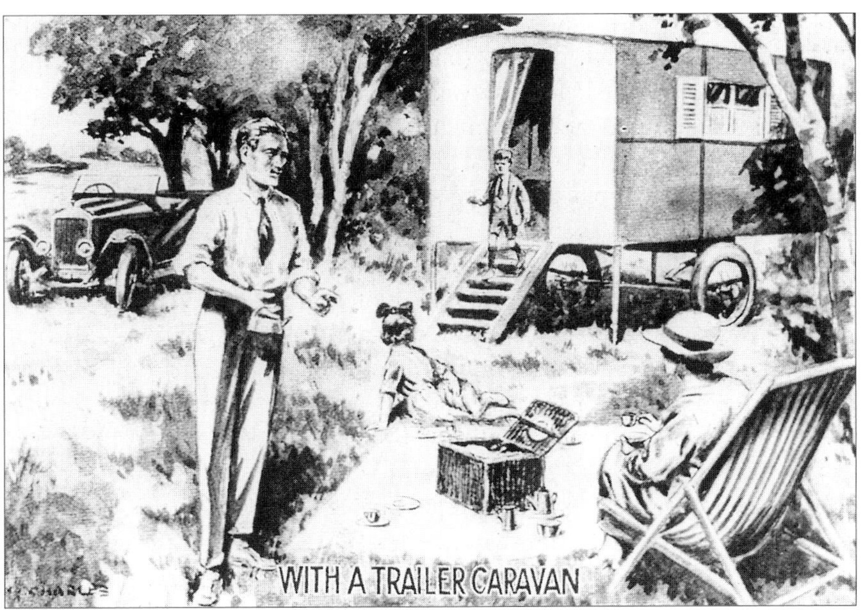

11 The caravan boom. The light-weight caravan for the family, 1920

runs and for the young people there is the sturdy Minor, economical and handy.

Modern domestic conditions demand greatest possible availability of transport.[39]

It was two-car convenience at one-car cost. The future of popular family motoring was being redefined. When the Road Traffic Act received the Royal Assent in August 1930, abolishing the speed limit, introducing new driving licence regulations, and leading to the publication of the first highway code, the framework of modern motoring was in place. But this new freedom generated great anxiety over the potential commercial destruction of rural tranquillity and village life. As the motor cars and charabancs flocked for their weekend outing to some 'beauty spot', professional and upper classes became increasingly alarmed that what had been an exclusive pleasure was now being overrun by commerce and the lower orders (figure 12).

Yet even as these changes were being absorbed, a futuristic technological landscape was attracting attention. New World fantasies constructed around the future of road and air transport, with multi-functional vehicles and streamlined cars, aircraft landing on the roofs of tower blocks and motorways cutting through the city and rural landscape, were promoting the

12 Cuningham, 'Save England's beauty spots. The village as it might be – and as it is likely to be', *Motor*, July 1923

idea of new neighbourhoods based on speed. The full page illustration of a curiously oriental futuristic world of 2922, drawn by Cuningham for *Motor* in 1922, which he remodelled for the 1928 *Daily Mail* Ideal Home Exhibition of the Sun-Ray Town of 2000 popularised the exotic vision of a technological future. Le Corbusier's essays were hardly less futuristic, but in their manipulation of past and plausible renderings challenged the cottage solution. That they might eventually offer an alternative could not be dismissed, but given the immediacy of the housing problem it was not unexpected that initially they failed to be taken too seriously.

> Eventually we may construct our bungalows on scientific lines, to give the inhabitants the maximum supplies of health-bearing sunlight and fresh air, with a minimum of surface to harbour bacilli and dust. Life may become so rational and organised that we all have to live in machines as perfectly disciplined and as communal as hospitals or ships. The week-end withdrawal to the country will then be devoted to absorbing a prescribed percentage of rays and calories, with appropriate scents (hay, violets, or wet earth) turned on by tap, and the restful sounds of the countryside (gurgling water, bleatings and mooings) administered at certain hours in accordance with ascertained formulae . . . A brilliant, but slightly unbalanced, French architect has already made out designs and plans for communal living-machines of a kind with the one suggested above, and goes so far as to say that they are aesthetically beautiful.[40]

A perceptive critique of Le Corbusier's influential 'Vers une architecture' of 1923, Britain confined much of its future to the cottage and the village module, and left many of its working-class families to worry about bus services into the nearest town.

There were good reasons to increase the public perception of the dangers of uncontrolled development of rural Britain. New arterial roads, road widening, ribbon development and building threatened the picturesque village and created a climate which, after twelve months of planning, led to the inaugural meeting of the Council for the Preservation of Rural England (CPRE), at the RIBA, on 7 December 1926. 'Ugliness' and 'Disfigurement' became the slogans, the architects became the missionaries, and the suburbs the darklands of cultural savages.[41] The preservation of buildings and landscapes became a dominant movement, motivated by thoughts of beautiful scenery and pastoral England.

No one was more vigorous in campaigning for the protection of 'ancient loveliness' for the nation's children than Clough Williams-Ellis,[42] and no one did more to ridicule the 'pink asbestos villas',[43] or frighten his readers with descriptions of the macabre beauty of smoky northern towns.[44] He wanted to return to a pre-industrial world that was beautiful and unspoilt, constructed from traditional values. His was a vision of a town 'in which to be born, pushed out in a perambulator, be educated, play, court your sweetheart, and conduct your business, healthily, agreeably, and with a minimum of friction'.[45] Planning for basic human needs, the question was how could this idyll be achieved. Provided with the opportunity to construct his dream, from 1925 he built his romantic fantasy at Portmeirion. It was a coastal pleasureland which, at the time of its construction, rather than offering an alternative to the flow of speculative dreamlands, only added to them.[46]

Some new amenities

There was no grand plan for Britain, but in an ad hoc incremental manner the luxuries of the few were being adapted and made available to a mass audience. Out of a mixture of good business practice and local authority benevolence, family lifestyles were changing. In May 1924 it was announced to Parliament that the telephone service was going public.[47] 40,000 kiosks were to be erected on Britains streets. The first design, constructed in concrete, met with general disfavour, and following a competition, in April 1925, the design by Sir Giles Gilbert Scott was announced as the winner. It had a cast-iron structure, with teak door, and was neo-Georgian in its details and proportions.[48] Emergencies could be reported, orders and queries made, and with careful pre-planning the public could use the kiosk for receiving personal calls.

In terms of consumer products it is impossible to overestimate the importance of the role of the CWS in providing everything for the working-class family. Houses, furnishing, clothing, food, insurance, transport, nothing was excluded. When the Scottish Cooperative Wholesale Society held an exhibition in Glasgow in March 1928, it claimed to be supplying 690,176 families through its 268 affiliated retail societies, with

£17.7 million sales for 1927. At a time when economic depression was being felt, this was a remarkable record, and similar stories could be told for England and Wales. New department stores were being built in all major provincial centres and London's expanding suburbs, and new local stores were being provided for municipal estates, as well as for the Coops' own housing estates. Renaissance or classical were the preferred architectural styles for the redeveloped high streets, providing the framework for the modern store. Good examples can be found in Bristol and Reading. The Tudor style was not ignored either, this being the choice of Shrewsbury and Chesterfield. Just as important was the widespread programme of shop modernisation, remodelling both shop fronts and interiors. The horse-drawn travelling shop was an established part of the service of urban communities, and throughout the 1920s motorisation radically changed the operation of the mobile shop and home delivery as new services were developed and new districts were reached. A commercial lifeline for many new housing estates, it also changed the service and working life of the family business in rural districts.

The health of the family was primarily taken up through the child welfare and maternity provision. Being a major part of public health programmes and a key feature of urban regeneration, the building of the child welfare centres was to play a significant role, not only on medical matters, for they were also designed to provide meals, day nursery facilities and play areas. They took on an important social role and educational role, in responding to the need for mothers to be taught matters of general hygiene and 'how to make clothes properly, how to cook food correctly, and how to prepare special diets for infants'.[49] Most municipal authorities had begun to develop well-established welfare programmes before the First World War, but it was in the 1920s that they were steadily expanded, providing routes of escape for poor children and their families. Left behind in the earlier migrations from inner cities, the idea that the poor were undeserving, the victims of their own social and moral inadequacies, was beginning to be questioned. The failure to develop effectively many of the new estates and villages had also exposed the difficulties of establishing self-supporting neighbourhoods, and although there was no clear view of how these difficulties should be overcome, at least the poor had joined the middle classes and working classes in the revised plans being made at local and national level for buildings for a new nation.

Home comforts

Efficiency

Two new publications were to have a profound influence on the redefining of homes and the role of the housewife in post-war society. In June 1919 the first issue of *Our Homes and Gardens* was published, the middle-class version of *Country Life*.

> Everyone desires to make his home as comfortable, as tasteful and as convenient as means will allow; and it will be the endeavour of this magazine to help continuously towards that end ... Always we shall strive to avoid the extreme, devoting ourselves instead to what is within the compass of those who think that good taste, expressed in a moderate way, is far more to be desired than what is bizarre and extravagant.[50]

Furnishing, labour-saving, gardens and home management provided the substance of the regular features that secured the representation and expectations of middle-class life and values. Articles devoted to the house without a servant, dealing with questions of convenience and efficiency, and published in 1920 as *The Servantless House and How to Equip It*,[51] confirmed the determination that the established lifestyle and routines of the middle-class home would not be undermined by the social changes of post-war Britain. In effect the message was that with well-arranged rooms, good management of time and resources, and a liberal supply of labour-saving appliances, the middle-class housewife could take on all of the tasks previously done by at least one servant without any lowering of standards or diminishing of her social commitments. At the same time, with the help of new products, the young mother could still be expected to look beautiful, and play with the children (figure 13). The launch of *Good Housekeeping* in March 1922 secured this ideal model. Each month issues of management, taste and leisure were dealt with in a manner that safeguarded home values and comforts, while articles on art, music and drama encouraged the readers to enjoy an informed cultured life. Two years later the Good Housekeeping Institute was created, 'primarily to form a connecting link between the manufacturer and the woman who wishes to have the best equipment in her home'.[52] Whether through taste or efficiency, the desired quality was 'homeliness', a home where 'wise, civilised and refined people' lived.[53]

It was already recognised that the one-room living of the working-class house was not only desirable because the kitchen range was for cooking and heating, but because 'the housewife has to simultaneously discharge the duties of cook, nursemaid, housemaid, stoker, wife and washerwoman'.[54] Intriguingly, as hints were being made that the working-class

OUR HOMES AND GARDENS, September, 1921
Joy in the Garden
A HAPPY ILLUSTRATION
IN the language of Cricket, efficiency might be described as "keeping one's end up." Mothers have to be efficient every day of the week and doubly efficient on wash-day. Children are delightfully exacting on wash-days as on other days, but the Purity and Efficiency of Sunlight Soap enables Mother to "keep her end up" without fatigue.
NO RUBBING—NO SCRUBBING.
The name LEVER on Soap is a Guarantee of Purity and Excellence.
SUNLIGHT SOAP
SUNLIGHT SOAP
LEVER BROTHERS LIMITED, PORT SUNLIGHT.
£1,000 GUARANTEE OF PURITY ON EVERY BAR.

13 Joy in the garden, advertisement, *Our Homes & Gardens*, September 1921

housewife might be about to enjoy more of the equipment and services currently available to the middle class, the middle classes were being reminded of the values of the simple life.

> The house we ought to live in will here be taken to mean a house where work is simplified, cleaning reduced, and convenience increased. It will not contain an unmanageable museum of labour-saving mechanism, nor will it be a costly and spacious palace. The purpose of this book is to examine certain principles that may be applied not only to the planning and building of new houses, but to the rooms and features of existing houses which may be adapted and altered to make life in them simpler and more practical for the houseworker.[55]

Although written for the household that could still afford at least a cook and a maid, the principles of *The House We Ought to Live in*, were accepted as being equally applicable to the small servantless house. It was the design response to social change as housework was being redefined and reallocated, and running a home was taking on a range of new meanings.

In her opening remarks for the 1921 Glasgow Health and Housing Exhibition, Lady Blythswood explained how

> The success of the Empire lay in its home life, and the more facilities that were offered for satisfactorily coping with the domestic problems, the better it would be for the country at large. Within recent years a new appreciation had arisen of the potentialities of home life and the value of hygienic and sanitary appointments, combined with the introduction of labour-saving methods in heating, cleansing and lighting.[56]

The design and equipment of the kitchen was now accepted as fundamental to these objectives. There was a greater awareness of the importance of a layout that made an effective grouping of activities, and the value of introducing built-in cupboards and all-purpose kitchen cabinets. The principles of planning were the same whatever the social class, but in terms of size, equipment and services there was a significant difference between the provision made for working-class and middle-class families. Even so the service industries were planning for expansion, anticipating that the working classes would become willing 'to spend a little extra in their homes for the provision of greater comfort and freedom from drudgery'.[57] The concept that housework could be a pleasure rather than a chore was now central to the equipping and furnishing of the home, so that while the acceptance that these tasks were 'duties' remained unchanged, the language of the advertisements and articles, and the purpose of exhibitions was to make them appear attractive.

As first the gas and then the electric cooker increased its hold on the market, there began a period of experimentation in the grouping of services and furnishing of what was considered to be the key to a well-organised home. This included a reappraisal of the ideas behind the kitchen range. For example, Sparke's Kitchen and Scullery Cabinet which had won a gold medal at the 1919 Bristol Home Life Exhibition, included airing cupboard, towel rail, shelves, sink, draining board, plate racks, gas stove, cylinder, and hot and cold water that could supply the sink and also the bathroom. The whole unit could be closed up to look like a piece of furniture, allowing it to be fixed in the living room, thereby replacing the kitchen and scullery, and making savings in space and labour.

More attention was given to accommodating the increasing range of appliances and utensils in the kitchen, but as yet it had not extended to the design of a totally integrated kitchen-scullery. A transitionary period, as gas and electric cooking began to supersede the kitchen range, the established working-class family lifestyle was challenged. The new services removed the necessity of family living taking place in one room, and positive efforts were made to persuade working-class families that it was more civilised for the meal to be taken from the kitchen-scullery, and consumed in the living-dining room. For the moment the dining hatch remained a luxury for the middle classes. Similar cultural differences were created by the location of the bath in the kitchen of the working-class house. Creating a bathroom adjacent to the kitchen made good economic sense, because of the centralisation of the water heating, and the possibility of taking off dirty work clothes before entering the house. However, the common practice of putting the bath under a table top in the kitchen-scullery was far from satisfactory, and showed the social gap that still existed between working-class and the new middle-class housing.

Going electric

Electricity associations, departments and manufacturers lost no time in labelling the 1920s as the Electric Age, but gas with its slogan '1001 Uses' proved to be a resolute competitor. Over the decade gas lost out to electric lighting, but at the outset there were still many new municipal all-gas estates, and gas more than held its own in the provision of cooking and heating appliances. Costs of electricity and appliances meant that at the beginning of the 1920s few families could afford to enjoy their benefits, but it was becoming a popular dream. With the General Electric Co. Ltd's three-bedroomed 'All-Electric House' at the 1920 Ideal Home Exhibition, evidence that this would be the future for those families of moderate means was on display. Although it was a family house with a maid, it was the labour-saving appliance house in which the housewife could happily take on more of the household chores such as vacuuming and ironing. The house could be equipped with washing machine and dish-washer, vacuum cleaner and sewing machine, milk-warmer for the nursery, electric towel rail in the bathroom, but it was the constant supply of hot water and electric radiators in each room providing instant heat that signified the qualities of the new home life. It was the ideal model of the 'Electric Age', 'a home of modern magic; fire is produced at a touch, water is heated without flame, and work of all kinds is done so easily that leisure becomes the rule not the exception'.[58] The picture of the family seated round the dining table laden with appliances, portrayed an era of the clean, comfortable home, in which routine housework had been reduced to a minimum, and the occasional use of rooms had become a realistic possibility.

Through the work of the recently formed Electrical Development Association, the drive was to supply electricity and this lifestyle to every home in Britain, and although the all-electric house was to remain a distant dream for working-class families, in 1921 the Association published a report by the architects, G. Blair Imrie and T. G. Angell on its use in working-class dwellings, outlining the advantages of the flexibility of use, the portability of appliances, constant hot water, instant power and clean operation. The 1921 *Daily Mail* Labour-Saving House Competition was for the design of a one-servant house, with five or six bedrooms, suitable for a professional family living in the suburbs of a large town or city, with a similar emphasis on the bright dust-free home, courtesy of good planning and electricity. Associated with the construction of the *Daily Mail* Model Village at Welwyn Garden City that coincided with the 1922 Ideal Home Exhibition, it was ideal homes in the ideal modern town offering a working solution to the housing and unhealthy city problems.[59]

Municipal authorities began to exercise an increasing influence both as producers and consumers of electricity. Birmingham, for example, decided in December 1923 that all its municipal schemes should be equipped with electric light. At the same time it opened its own showrooms in the centre of the city, with an 'Adam' room, 'Oak' room, 'Georgian' room, model kitchen and a variety of displays to demonstrate the electrical equipment. Two years later they introduced a rental scheme for three sizes of cookers, at 10*s*., 6*s*., and 3*s*. per quarter. A spectacular confirmation of this municipal involvement was provided by the 'Seven-Day House' built on the forecourt of St George's Hall, Liverpool, for the Civic Week celebrations in November 1926. Georgian revival in style, with three bedrooms, bathroom, parlour and living room, it was similar to the 250 houses being built by the Corporation. The structure of the house deservedly attracted attention because of its timber frame and outer skin of bricks, but it was the fact that it was an all-electric house that roused the greatest interest, demonstrating that the electric age was about to embrace the working-class homes.

Brighter Homes Exhibitions in a range of regional centres kept the new appliances in public view, encouraging homeowners to see the new products as a necessity rather than a luxury, and promoting the benefits of converting an existing house into an all-electric home. Typical was the Better Housing and Housekeeping Exhibition, Sheffield, October 1927, with its homes 'for real rest, comfort and recreation'[60] and the All-Electric House contributed by the City Electric Supply Department.[61] The following month the new headquarters of the Electrical Association for Women (EAW) in Kensington Court, London, was formally opened by Lady Astor. The centre consisted of offices, a clubroom and kitchen (figure 14) that

> presented a fairy-land of delight to the home-maker. Here was a washing machine which could also be used to mince meat, clean knives and perform many other useful but uncongenial household tasks. The electric cooker claimed its share of attention, as also did the water heaters, refrigerator and that most useful of all appliances, the suction cleaner. A dainty electric silver grill came in for much admiration and the electric jug, saucepan, and coffee percolator were coveted by many housewives present.[62]

14 Electrical Association for Women, Model electric kitchen, 1928

There was a significant change of emphasis following on from the Electricity (Supply) Act, 1926, with the recognition that in time electricity would become a national service. At the beginning of 1928, the EAW launched the nationwide 'Electrical Outlet Campaign', designed to raise the awareness of architects, builders and developers of the need for an adequate electrical system in all new houses. Intent on emphasising the woman's point of view the EAW also drew up a 'National Woman's Specification' listing the number and position of electrical outlets, concentrating on issues of convenience and safety. Hints on how to carry out simple maintenance tasks, such as change a fuse, were added to the list for the efficient housewife.

The emphasis throughout the 1920s was to ensure that new houses were adequately wired, with a liberal supply of power points, and that old houses could be converted to electricity without causing disruption or involving high costs. Interestingly the Elthorne Heights estate in Ealing, a three-bedroom semi-detached development by 'Tricity', made provision for the new owners to incorporate the costs of all the equipment and appliances into the purchase price of the house. From standard and table lamps to wall lights and diffused lights, the widening range of attachments for the electric cleaner, the electric sewing machine and the multi-purpose food-mixer, the mechanisation of the home had gathered pace. It was in the provision for what was widely understood to be the drudgery of family laundering that the differences distinguishing working-class and middle-class homelife were at their most extreme. The task being hard work and time-consuming, the answer was to have a home laundry equipped with washer, dryer and iron,[63] but for many working-class homes washing continued to be done in the communal laundry, with the ironing done at home.

Even allowing for some exaggeration in the claims being made for the labour-saving benefits, and the efficient standardisation of housework, the fact was that electricity brought about the remodelling of the house and restructuring of housework. The kitchen and home laundry were pivotal to the developing culture of housework as a branch of science and management.

> In short, the present reconstructed kitchen has taken its proper modern place as a cheerful sanitary food laboratory. There is no smell, smoke, or soot, because electricity has superseded coal and ashes; and other portable electric utilities, such as the electrical chopper, mixer, and beater, the electric tea machine or toaster, etc., enable the worker to remain neat and tidy while she does her work with step-saving and convenience.[64]

An ideal view of efficiency, it was part of the saving time philosophy that was being introduced from the models of commerce and industry, and much influenced by developments imported from America. The work ethic was further reinforced by Corbusier's influential *Towards a new architecture,* with its view of family life constructed around the father. The time when the father had his own workshop teaching his son the secrets of his trade was past, but with a romantic view of industry and commerce Corbusier imposed the qualities of men's work on the home, making it into a place of specialisation and precision. It was a man's world: the house as a tool, with human labour replaced by machines, supported by a communal servant class and restaurant service, that would replace the existing diseased anachronistic homes.

Good taste and the everyday

It was a period when the Design and Industries Association (DIA) played an influential role in defining for the nation what was good and bad in home furnishing and equipment. Its 'Fitness in Everyday Things' at the 1920 Ideal Home Exhibition, followed in October–December with the Exhibition of Household Things, including eight model rooms and display of artifacts, appliances and utensils, at the Whitechapel Art Gallery, October–December 1920, and a similar show at the South London Art Gallery, in May 1921, set the pattern. They coincided with the 'Art in Common Life' campaign launched by *The Times* and moves by a number of Royal Academicians to see a National Committee of Taste established to be responsible for buildings, public art and street furniture. As the working classes were being brought more into the frame, and anticipating the post-war municipal housing programme the DIA engaged in a number of collaborative ventures, particularly through its regional branches. Early in 1921, the Association worked with Manchester City Council to decorate and furnish a cottage on its new Anson estate, as a practical example of good taste, demonstrating the relationship of colour and contentment. In

May 1921, this became the 'Cottage Interior and Decoration' exhibition at the Manchester City Art Gallery. Displaying a simplicity of design, much of it handmade, using natural materials, priced at £160 for the furnished cottage, good taste did not come cheaply for their imaginary family. It was the representation of the puritan ethic that underpinned these design principles, continuing the campaign started by the arts and crafts movement.

The British Institute of Industrial Art Exhibition at the V&A, September 1923, showed a similar adherence to the arts and crafts ideals, but the debate on the relationship between art and industry was being moved on by the efforts of the Royal Society of Arts. Interest was sustained throughout 1922 and 1923, leading to the first student competition for Industrial Design, which was exhibited at the V&A, 26 July–30 August 1924.[65] What was being formulated at this time was the concept of national taste as the appreciation of 'beauty and distinction' without 'extravagance in expenditure'. It was the basis of the *Country Life* competition for a dining room and hall and a bedroom,[66] to be shown in the Palace of Arts at the British Empire Exhibition, 1924, and of the 1926 *Daily Mail* Ideal Houses Competition for houses costing £1,500 and £850. The *Daily Mail* competition in its call for designs that embraced beauty and utility, value for money, good materials and workmanship, confirmed the growing popularity of neo-Georgian taste.[67] Published alongside the houses exhibited at the 1927 Ideal Home Exhibition, with their determined Tudor features, it was believed to confirm a national commitment to traditional British styles that were compatible with the sensitivities of the developing movement for the protection of rural England. Modern thatch was also gaining popularity, and enthusiastically designed by young British architects such as Kenneth Dalgleish, Alan Fortescue and Oliver Hill, as well as by established traditionalists like Clough Williams-Ellis.

Exhibitions, showrooms and showhouses continued to offer new ideas on the decoration, furnishing and equipping of the home; as important changes were taking place in attitudes towards the objects of everyday and the decorative arts a closer association with the gallery culture began to emerge. In the high street the crafts moved from shops into galleries,[68] while the retail trade converted showrooms into galleries. The importance of the in-store gallery was well illustrated by the Basnett Gallery, opened by the department store Bon Marche, Liverpool, in 1926, for showing arts and crafts, and contemporary decorative arts.[69] At a time when expression and efficiency marked the extremes of the conceptual division of the house as home or machine, these developments re-emphasised the arts and crafts values based on the idea of the soul of the house, its magic and personality being much more than the conveniences of hot-water taps and kitchen ranges.[70] A core value of the cottage home movement, it was this spirit of the house as home that was picked up in *Architecture and Home Organisation*, 1926, published by the Association of Teachers of Domestic Subjects, as a guide for municipal authorities. Houses were perceived as 'a place where people may live healthy and happy lives; where children may grow up strong in mind and body; and where the tired may find peace and rest'.[71] It was the cottage home that could adapt to the changing needs of family life, catering for the emotional and practical demands, accommodating relationships as much as activities. In contrast R. A. Duncan's 'House of the Future' for the 1928 Ideal Home Exhibition, although remarkably conventional in its layout, envisaged a future home that would be packed with appliances, electronically operated services, and constructed of an imaginary synthetic material that would enable it to be mass-produced and disposed of like any other industrially designed product. It was a model of future home life as an exact science, replacing the popular blend of period style and labour-saving appliances.

At the 1930 Monza Exhibition of Industrial and Decorative Art, it was the lifestyle of the professional cultured family that was taken as representative of national taste. Arranged as eleven room settings it emphasised the role of the applied arts in modern life, its refinement and good taste, displaying the 'livableness' of the average interior of the upper middle-class reader of *The Studio*. Yet, as principles of design on the rightness and economy of form and materials, these were not exclusively middle-class values. Taking, for example, the breakfast room arranged for Monza (figure 15) and the typical non-parlour house outlined for a miner's cottage (figure 16), it is possible to see a comparability of design ethics. At Monza it was a show of art craftsmanship, with the inlaid-wood decorative panel, designed by Frank Brangwyn and made by the Rowley Gallery, wax-polished walnut furniture by Gordon Russell, and hand-crafted textiles and pottery. The living-dining room of the worker's cottage was furnished with the rustic craftsmanship of the carpenter or home craftsman, the gateleg table, Windsor chair, simple framed sideboard, framed prints, set around the cast-iron fire grate; it was a home resolutely utilitarian in materials and construction. Separated by economics, the alternative interpretations shared a similar sense of purpose.

Dorothy Todd and Raymond Mortimer in *The New Interior Decoration* (1929) endorsed these concepts of simplicity. The house was the last refuge for expression, as well as a place of utility, of beauty connected with a sense of convenience and health, informed by an exact understanding of the needs of everyday life. It was the place where the efficiency and precision of the machine combined with the beauty of art. The plan was for spaciousness without unnecessary space, allowing for the collective and individual needs of family life. It had a desire for economy, but not austerity.

> As life grows more uniform and is increasingly dominated by machines, we may wish in our homes to escape from this impersonality. We need fantasy, imagination, wit in our houses. We want to relax, to enjoy intimacy, to feel, as well as actually to be, comfortable ... We require our homes to be quieter, more informal, more personal.[72]

It was a reminder of how restraint and common sense were perceived to be distinctly English characteristics. The concept of the perfect home was one where these expressions of beauty and home comforts were accompanied by the benefits of the latest technology. It was this mood that was captured by the 1930 Ideal Home Exhibition. Electricity took on a new presence with the General Electric Company (GEC) 'Pavilion of Light', in which six rooms showed the latest designs and ideas on interior lighting, including an electric nursery, and a dining room and bedroom designed by Raymond McGrath. There was also the Hall of Ideals by Ediswan, as well as domestic and radio sections.[73]

Poverty

The dilemma was how some part of the benefits of the advances made in the provision of new homes and services could be extended to the good

15 'Breakfast for three, at 8 pm', Monza, 1930

of the nation as a whole, and to those who were trapped in poverty and sub-standard housing. Celebrating sixty-five years of Public Health Administration in the city, in January 1928 Edinburgh held its first Health and Hygiene Exhibition, demonstrating its responsibilities for medical and welfare schemes. It also underlined the importance of its public parks, and the scale of its housing problems with a reconstruction of a recently demolished slum property contrasted with a modern house currently being erected by the city. Two years later the exhibition was repeated and, although there was much to attract the interest of those of moderate means, including a three-bedroom cottage, the Corporation was anxious to give wider publicity to the scale of its housing problems, again contrasting the slum with the replacement house. The message was that there were

> still about 7,340 one-roomed houses in Edinburgh, some of which house whole families, and the size of many of these houses is as small as one quarter of the minimum size prescribed for in the latest Housing Acts. The arrangement of having water closets and sinks which are common to several families is still prevalent.[74]

It was possible to take any British city and town and find a similar kind of story. As this account has shown, throughout the 1920s there was never a time when slums and suburban developments did not attract the attention of the politicians and the professional associations. Linked to electioneering

16 Typical non-parlour house living room for miner's cottage, 1927

and the national economy, there were variable bouts of enthusiasm and despair about the ability to provide the required housing and local amenities. Ideals were undermined by economic depression, but even so it was becoming apparent that the limited progress was less to do with ineffective planning than a growing realisation that the scale of the problem had been far greater than originally envisaged. Consequently by late 1929, the social responsibilities of architecture and design were being given renewed attention. As E. D. Simon put it in *How to Abolish the Slums* (1929), a satisfactory resolution could only be achieved through national subsidies that would support the building of the smallest and cheapest houses to standards consistent with bringing up children in full health in mind and body. With the 1930 Housing Act giving the municipal authorities new powers to instigate slum clearance programmes and tackle the plight of the badly housed working classes, there was much greater optimism that on this occasion the question would be effectively answered.

Notes

1 *Journal of the RIBA*, June 1918, p. 169–77.

2 *Ibid.*, p. 170.

3 *Ibid.*, p. 175.

4 *The Welsh Housing & Development Year Book*, Cardiff, 1919, p. 45.

5 *Welsh Housing & Development Association*, 1918, p. 106. In February 1918, two members of Miss E. P. Hughes' sub-committee were invited to join the Women's Housing Sub-Committee of the Ministry of Reconstruction.

6 Mrs S, Furness, 'Working Women's Views on Housing and Fitments', *The Architects' & Builders' Journal*, 12 June 1918, pp. 268–9.

7 *Ibid.*, p. 269.

8 Raymond Unwin, 'Housing: The Architects' Contribution', *Journal of the RIBA*, January 1919, p. 57.

9 *Tudor Walters Report*, p. 8.

10 *Ibid.*, p. 82.

11 *Journal of the RIBA*, October 1918, p. 261.

12 'Government Housing Schemes and the Gas Industry', *British Commercial Gas Association Bulletin*, October 1918, p. 180.

13 Report also gave a lead on the conversion of large houses into multiple occupancy.

14 *Daily Mail Designs for Ideal (Workers') Homes*, London, 1919, p. 2.

15 *Ibid.*, p. 3.

16 *Illustrated London News*, 18 October 1919, p. 596.

17 Cubley Garden Village, Penistone, for Cammell Laird, used the 'Winget' system: *Municipal Journal*, 2 September 1921, p. 650.

18 The Birmingham Housing Exhibition, July 1919, had had comparable aspirations,

showing a range of model houses being erected by the Housing and Planning Department. Bristol and Liverpool had similar exhibitions in 1920.

19 *Builder*, 2 November 1923, p. 694.

20 Major Harry Barnes, 'National Housing and a National Municipal House-building Service' *Journal of the RIBA*, 22 March 1924, pp. 289–97.

21 The Telford All-Steel house by Braithwaite & Co. was shown at the 1925 Ideal Home Exhibition and the company also had the 'Atholl' house, a bungalow, erected as an experiment by Dundee Corporation; the Reith Steel House, made by the Govan shipbuilders, Stephen and Son Ltd., was exhibited at the 1926 Building Trades Exhibition, London.

22 Included houses at Cardiff, Newport, and Swansea.

23 L. Weaver, 'Subsidy Cottages at Wembley', *Country Life*, 18 July 1925, p. 112. Also see L. Weaver, *Cottages*, London, 1926.

24 The Nissen type steel houses at Yeovil: see *Engineer*, 13 March 1925, p. 287.

25 *Autocar*, 24 February, 1928, p. 324.

26 See *Architects' Journal*, 7 September 1921, and W. Haywood, *Birmingham Civic Society 1918–1946*, Birmingham, *c.* 1946.

27 The 'model' garden village at Woodlands, that had been built for Markham Collieries, was referenced for the qualities of its initial development, and used as a cautionary note over the dangers of lowering of the housing standards.

28 Mr and Mrs F. H. Crittall, *Fifty Years of Work and Play*, London, 1934. p. 124.

29 *Ibid.*, p. 123.

30 Sir J. Tudor Walters, *The Building of Twelve Thousand Houses*, London, 1927, p. 24. It was an important period in designing new mining villages. Noteworthy was the new village at Methilhill, Fife, commenced in 1923 for the Wemyss Coal Company, its houses decked out with classical details, pediments and columns, in a monumental scale ill-suited to a small domestic house. Similarly significant was the work by Messrs Mauchlen and Weightman in Northumberland and Durham.

31 P. Abercrombie, with J. Archibald, *East Kent Regional Planning Scheme, Preliminary Survey*, Liverpool, 1925, p. 80.

32 *Ibid.*, p. 84.

33 *Journal of the RIBA*, 7 May 1927, p. 439.

34 Starting in London with estates at Hayes and Acton, the policy was to provide comfortable homes in pleasant, open surroundings. Other estates were built at Plymouth, Truro, Penzance, Severn Tunnel, Caerphilly, Barry and Swansea, all under the direction of the architect T. Alwyn Lloyd of the Welsh Town-Planning Trust, Parlour and non-parlour houses were built, with the bathroom on the ground floor of the non-parlour house, and on the first floor of the parlour house. See Major Harry Barnes, 'Railway Housing', *Architects' Journal*, 22 December 1926, pp. 775–90.

35 By the time the Act was revised in 1926, 16,295 smallholdings had been established. The scheme for Scotland was run separately.

36 *Journal of the RIBA*, 9 April 1921, p. 314. The scheme had a large team of architects, with H. P. G. Maule as chief architect and John Lee, superintending architect. Maxwell Ayrton, Oswald Milne, and Clough Williams-Ellis had also been involved at the outset.

37 *Ibid.*, p. 320.

38 The Land Settlement (Facilities) Act, 1919, and the Small Holdings Act, 1926: see unpublished report, G. Herbert, *Land Settlement Report*, York, August 1934.

39 Morris Advert, *Autocar*, 22 February 1929.

40 C. Hussey, 'The Architecture Club at Grosvenor House', *Country Life*, 15 March 1924, p. 403.

41 H. Belloc, 'The Importance of Exact Boundaries to Towns', *Architectural Review*, July 1929. It was, as Corbusier argued in *The City of Tomorrow*, a case of pulling down the city centres, starting again, and abolishing the suburbs, to give space for new cities built for traffic, and the businessmen suffering from the increasing speed of working life.

42 C. Williams-Ellis, 'Wales and the Octopus', *Welsh Housing and Development Year Book*, 1930, p. 71. Also see Williams-Ellis, *England and the Octopus*, London, 1928.

43 C. and E. Williams-Ellis, *The Pleasures of Architecture*, London, 1924, 3rd imp. 1929, p. 209.

44 *Ibid.*, p. 210.

45 *Ibid.*, p. 233.

46 Its long-term value was as an open-air museum of architectural heritage, an enjoyable tourist attraction.

47 In January 1912 the Post Office had taken over the control of Britain's telephone service.

48 Redesigned by Scott for the 1936 Jubilee, the box had gone modern in scale and fittings, including a black bakelite shelf, stainless steel frames for the instruction cards and small mirror.

49 J. Wilson, 'Notes on the Planning of Sanitoria, Infectious Diseases Hospitals, and other Public Health Institutions', *Journal of the RIBA*, 8 April 1922, p. 343.

50 *Our Homes and Gardens*, June 1919, p. 1.

51 R. Randal Phillips, *The Servantless House and How to Equip it*, London, 1920.

52 *Good Housekeeping*, October 1924, p. 30.

53 *Our Homes and Gardens*, January 1920, p. 223.

54 'The Physiology of the Working Class House', *Builder*, 3 January 1919, p. 27.

55 J. Gloag and L. Mansfield, *The House We Ought to Live In*, Edinburgh, 1923, p. 15.

56 *Builder*, 23 September 1921, p. 384.

57 H. H. Creasy, 'Government Housing Schemes and the Gas Industry', *A Thousand and One Uses for Gas*, October 1919, p. 173.

58 'The Wonder House', *Municipal Journal*, 27 February 1920, p. 217.

59 Welwyn Garden City Co., formed May 1920. The prizewinner was a five-bedroom detached house: see *Architects' Journal*, 8 February 1922.

60 *Catalogue*, p. 9.

61 From 1926 Manchester had held an annual Brighter Homes Exhibition, in association with the *Daily Dispatch*; Edinburgh had held its own Ideal Home Exhibition from the same year.

62 *The Electrical Age*, January 1928, p. 249.

63 D. Vaughan, 'Electric Washing Day', *The Electric Age*, January 1927, p. 88.

64 Mrs C. Frederick, 'How the American Housewife Achieves Leisure Through Electricity', *The Electric Age*, January 1927, p. 99.

65 See *Journal of the RSA*, 22 August 1924, pp. 689–96.

66 *Country Life*, 20 October 1923, p. 531.

67 The assessors Guy Dawber, President of RIBA, and Louis de Soissons, paid much attention to the kitchen layout and, while all the designs included a garage, felt that none of those that integrated the garage within the house had done so successfully.

68 The Little Gallery and The New Handworkers Gallery in London were significant developments of the 1920s.

69 The highlight of these years was the 1929 exhibition of modern rooms designed by Grace Lovat Fraser, that included the 'Cubist Lounge'.

70 See M. H. Baillie Scott, *Houses and Gardens*, London, 1906.

71 *Architecture and Home Organisation*, Association of Teachers of Domestic Subjects, London, 1926, p. 5.

72 D. Todd and R. Mortimer, *The New Interior Decoration*, London, 1929, p. 28.

73 The formation of the British Broadcasting Corporation (BBC) in 1927 was significant in its presentation of taste and culture, setting out a way of life with which the listeners could share even if there was little opportunity of them ever becoming part of it.

74 *Health and Hygiene*, exhibition catalogue, Edinburgh, 1930, p. 92.

3 ✧ Rationalisation and new dreams, 1931–39

Schemes, settlements and speculation

New order

WHAT started to unfold and then gain momentum over the 1930s was an obsessive preoccupation with order, and having a society under central control. Images invariably portrayed new neighbourhoods where it never rained, nothing broke down or stopped moving, and even stationary objects were made to look as though they could move. Work could be completed at speed to allow more activities to be squeezed into the extended leisure made available by the efficient life. They were places where the sun always shone, the grass never turned to mud and noise was always civilised. Architectural forms reflected this philosophy, planning sought to impose it on the landscape, and new materials and appliances provided the tools to enjoy it.

There was a division of opinion over how the ideal world should be shaped. The traditionalists sought a pre-industrial world, a pastoral Britain, while the modernists dreamt of a post-industrial world, a technological Britain. An amusing yet eminently serious contribution to this debate can be found in the essay 'A Hundred Years Ahead' by Serge Chermayeff and J. M. Richards.[1] Revealing the kind of world the modernists were anticipating, it would be a time when the false ideas that had given society 'smoke and dirty stone houses'[2] and the 'diseased growth of little red villas' would have long since gone, where slums would have been eradicated, and fascism replaced by a European Union of Socialist Republics planning on a grand scale for the masses. It was to be a world of planned obsolescence, that had no interest in buildings of the past, living in the controlled environment of the tower blocks, and on airship stations that were 'complete towns with living-places and offices for 10,000 persons'.[3] Futuristic in concept, but without doubt they were to have a strong influence on the contemporary housing schemes and urban planning.

As part of the BBC series on 'The Changing World', broadcast through

1931 and 1932, J. E. Barton, Headmaster of Bristol Grammar School, presented six talks on 'Modern Art'. Talking of a new spirit of order that would be born of a unity of art and communal life, Barton vigorously denounced Victorian muddle, and the masses of dead rubbish which had been left behind. Joining other reforming campaigners to get 'rid of lumber' Barton spoke of a Modern Art personified as bright, clean and hard, responding to the needs of the time. Represented by the perfectly equipped kitchen, rather than the artistic interior, its purpose was simplicity and freedom. Following on from the economic crisis of 1931, Modern Art was aligned with the government legislation to improve the health and housing of the nation. It was the utilisation of a product style for social and political goals, and in turn was the acquisition of a social and political philosophy to justify the product style. Socialism and fascism were becoming intertwined. Noel Carrington in *Design and a Changing Civilisation*, contemplated an enlightened dictatorship, such as that of Mussolini in Italy, believing that just as economic planning on a national scale was necessary, 'so designing must also be on a national scale if it is to be orderly and efficient'.[4]

New homes for old

The closest any developments came to becoming a national plan were the housing schemes generated by municipal authorities in response to the 1930 Housing Act, beginning what was termed the 'exodus from slums'. This included the families who had nothing.

> We have also had in mind the difficulties of those people who are so poor as not to be able to afford the rent of any of the houses already described, and who are not possessed of furniture or even the means of buying any, and an experimental scheme has been undertaken which provides small maisonettes, each consisting of a living room, 14ft by 12ft and a single bedroom, together with a bathroom and kitchenette, lavatory, coal store and larder, the intention being that a couple could comfortably live in such quarters and remain there until their family got either too large or too old for the accommodation when it is hoped that such families will be in a position to be moved to a larger house. The question of the provision of furniture was solved by providing everything absolutely necessary to enable a couple to commence residence immediately.[5]

The scheme being described was that of Birmingham, which was acknowledged as having one of the most committed and enlightened policies, and it gives a clear view of the scale of the national housing problem. Two years later slum clearance was being talked of as a battle, and photographs of large families living in one-room squalor, neighbourhood decay and unemployment raised public concern, adding to the continuing national anxiety over the precarious state of rural life and industry.[6]

Picking up similar issues to those presented by the Housing Exhibition, December 1931, a themed exhibition 'New Homes for Old' took place at Olympia in September 1932. It dealt with slums, town planning, new building, and local amenities, drawing on American and continental examples as models of good practice. The final feature was a full-size model of a three-bedroom non-parlour flat, using the 750 sq. ft recommended by the Ministry of Health as suitable for one family, and furnished for £40.[7] Formed into a travelling exhibition, two years later the Housing Centre reorganised it for the Building Trades Exhibition at Olympia in September 1934. The implications of slum clearance for housing and planning policies was the dominant theme for which a slum alley had been recreated 'to form a monument to the type of living conditions that we hope will never be tolerated again', and from which the visitor stepped 'into a spaciously planned area which by its very whiteness created a contrast with the sordidness of Susannah Row'.[8] Other sections dealt with town planning, flats and their equipment, outdoor amenities and nursery schools, and a visual analysis of the slums of Bethnal Green by the MARS group.[9] The issues and solutions were far from black and white, but the onset of contributions from the modern movement were to play a significant part in scale and styles of inner city rehousing schemes. Again 'New Homes for Old' travelled the country, and then in January 1935 was included in a Ministry of Health exhibition on the 'Working-Class Flat'. It was eventually reworked under the same title for an exhibition arranged by the Housing Centre in collaboration with the MARS group, which after an initial showing at the Housing Centre in April 1936, was later in the year taken to the 1936 Building Exhibition. Arguing the case for 'for better, healthier, more conveniently situated houses and lower rents for the working-class',[10] the photographs and captions restated the problems facing working-class communities and the ways in which architecture and planning could provide solutions. The importance of social and community provision was as much a concern as homes, and there were sections dealing with infancy, childhood, manhood and old age.[11]

The scale of the slum clearance schemes can be illustrated from examples taken from any British city. In a paper of 1934, for the Scottish National Housing and Town Planning Committee, E. J. Macrae, City Architect for Edinburgh, described one such scheme. Approved in 1931, the plan was to clear an area that had 1,606 dwellings, almost half of which were of one room, housing 5,569 people, served by two baths, neither of which could be used. The commitment was to rehouse as many as possible within the same area, in dwellings that had good light and ventilation, hot and cold water, a scullery, bathroom and effective cooking appliances. Given the existing density of 166 houses to the acre, it was decided to use three-storey tenements that would reduce the density to 39.3 per acre, rather than the garden suburb model of 12 to an acre. The task of acquiring, demolishing and rebuilding on these sites was a slow and expensive process and, despite wanting to retain the rehousing within the cleared areas, building on new land was unavoidable.

While there was little new to be learnt about the poverty, ill-health and disease being confronted by the rehousing programmes, it was the Political and Economic Planning publication *Housing England* (1934), that gave a new dimension to the level of national understanding of the social and economic issues that were integral to the policy issues of working-class housing. Economy was not simply an issue of establishing affordable minimum standards of housing, but to be effective it also had to embrace a system of rent relief that would enable those families living in poverty the opportunity to enjoy the benefits offered by the new housing. In other words, those responsible for rehousing were reminded that while families were leaving infested disease-ridden homes, their poverty went with them. Despite the praiseworthy intentions, there was something rather awesome about the term 'slum clearance', for in concept and execution it obliterated the life and history of communities that had constructed themselves out of a deprived and exploited environment. At the same time the challenge of starting a new life was daunting when faced with the practicalities of running a home for a large family on low income, and coping with the cultural and social implications of relocation.

Many local authorities were aware that families being rehoused were having great difficulties adapting to a move 'in their progress to a more advanced state of civilisation'.[12] There had long been doubts over the ability of the slum dweller to make this transition, and what was now being realised was that there had to be a new approach to the social and financial support if the housing schemes were going to produce the new model citizens. Surveys of tenants in Manchester revealed the scale of these social problems, where having survived the embarrassment of the fumigation of furniture and all personal belongings before the removal from slums was allowed, many families experienced further difficulties adjusting to furnishing and managing their new homes. Despite the popular myths, there was a universal pleasure in having a bathroom, and although faced with increased travel costs and less local amenities, when given a choice, tenants with a family invariably preferred a house with garden, rather than a flat.

Rural housing was just as much of a problem and to stimulate architectural interest, at the beginning of 1933 the Building Centre organised a cottage design competition. For two pairs of cottages that could be built for £900, and let at an economic rent, the emphasis was on the use of local materials and respect for the general amenities of the district.[13]

As a guide to the competitors the Building Centre produced a model scheme which had living room and scullery with bath under a bench, a WC by the front door, and three bedrooms. It was for a rural estate, not more than a mile from a railway station, main drainage and water would be available, but there was no electricity or gas, a reminder that the new appliance age had yet to reach the rural working class. The winning design by N. E. Leeson of Newcastle upon Tyne was to be built for £450 per pair, and let for between 8*s.* 6*d.* and 10*s.* a week each. Essentially the same as the model scheme at the first floor, the design had changed the ground floor to provide a through living room and a bathroom separate from the scullery, in effect reducing the size of the scullery by about a third. Sixty of the competition designs were published as a book of *Three Bedroomed Cottages*, and the winning design was built for demonstration purposes on a site in Aldwych, each house furnished in 'good taste' for £45, from various London shops.[14]

These were basic solutions, but providing all their slum dwellers with a house was a luxury that no British city believed that it could afford, and it was the continental working-class flats of the German cities and Vienna which attracted collective attention. Visiting deputations came away convinced by the benefits of large-scale developments that would provide each dwelling with the essential services and private balconies, and communal facilities that included meeting halls, wash-houses, a garden playground and kindergarten and, where possible, libraries, clinics and shops. Elizabeth Denby wrote enthusiastically about the foresight in the planning, amenities and equipment of housing estates that she had visited in France, and there is clear evidence of its influence on her contribution to the design of Kensal House in Ladbroke Grove, London, and her reference to it as an 'Urban Village'. Scale and cohesion were of vital importance to its success, and the reason why she attacked the failure of many of London's blocks of flats as nothing more than 'cottages above one another, but without the cottage garden or the cottage privacy. In fact, they are the rows of industrial cottages opening directly on to a common balcony street'.[15] She believed that they were schemes that had been born obsolete, but such warnings went unheeded and for a time Quarry Hill in Leeds and Kennett House in Manchester became the monuments to the modern movement's influence on urban renewal. They were very photogenic from the air, but were not without their problems. Quarry Hill in particular suffered from technical difficulties over its construction, its refuse disposal system, and eventually the major disruption that came from the Second World War.

In an attempt to project a more humane, personalised sense of a ready-made community, just as Denby had picked on the village concept as an indicator of the community values embodied in the Kensal House scheme, so many of the immense blocks were referred to as new villages or towns. Few came larger than Nisbet House, Hackney, described as 'an experiment in the construction of a village in modern dress'.[16] In 1935 LCC acquired the 52-acre site of the old White City exhibition and pleasure grounds, and three years later commenced a new housing scheme of five-storey blocks providing 2,166 flats. Anticipating the construction of a range of educational, social and welfare facilities, it was envisaged as the place for the working-class family to enjoy clean living and less housework. The image was of 'a new town' in which well-dressed and cared for children could step out into a bright new future (figure 17).

Coming mid-way between the high rise and the cottage was the 'Hundred New Towns for Britain' movement instigated by the writings of Trystan Edwards in early 1934. Committed to a zoning system of residential, recreational, commercial, shopping and industrial areas, it was promoted as a solution to congested urban development and a safeguard to the countryside. Leading to an exhibition, 'Forbidden Houses', at the Housing Centre in October 1936, it was a reworking of terraced housing, some

17 A town is born, White City, 1939

back-to-back, and without gardens. As this type of housing and layout was a substantial part of the slums that it was trying to replace, it came in for much criticism. However, as the working-class families had made it clear to anyone who asked, they did not want to live in tenement blocks or in the country, and the idea of a new terraced house was not as silly as it first appeared. It was Elizabeth Denby's 'All Europe' working-class house for the 1939 Ideal Home Exhibition that usefully summarised the debate and offered a compromised model solution.[17] Flat-roofed houses with three bedrooms, living room and kitchen, rear garden and open-plan front, linked in an offset terraced arrangement, it was a design that had updated the cottage model for the people. It was a logical outcome of the ideals outlined in the summary and conclusions of Elizabeth Denby's research into continental housing models and published as *Europe Re-housed* (1938). Anticipating the ideals of the Lansbury housing development for the Festival of Britain, it argued the case for city redevelopment that incorporated flats and cottages in the building of new communities, arguing that

> meeting- and games-rooms, swimming pools, restaurants and shops, theatres and cinemas are essential as a focus of common interest, to encourage companionship and direct the varied talents of the neighbourhood into social instead of anti-social channels.[18]

There was a clear concern for the needs of the housewife in the organisation of communal services that effectively recognised the everyday demands of caring for a family and young children, matched by the provision of a comprehensive range of individual facilities for the home, particularly for laundry work. The 'All-Europe' house was a model for social housing that she believed would bring about a revitalised town life, and which would avoid the pattern of the segregation of the poor on 'lonely estates without adequate shops, without enjoyment, without sufficient anticipation of the help which they, as ex-slum dwellers, so urgently need'.[19] Although there was an inclination to over-romanticise certain social aspects of the continental housing schemes that she had visited, it nevertheless showed a determination to rethink the design solutions to the social purpose of national housing. Principles that were partially overtaken by the onset of the Second World War, some of her ideas were picked up in the emergency years' debates on the reconstruction programme. However, at the time it could not have been anticipated that her fears over class segregation would be overshadowed by municiple housing schemes of the 1950s, and that the 'All-Europe' house would became a model more associated with middle-class than working-class housing schemes.

Ideal villages and coastal dreams

In January 1934, the *Builder* launched an 'Ideal Village' competition, to design a self-contained community 'planned on garden city lines, suitable for a population of approximately 5,000 persons, all to be provided with good houses, and gardens ample enough for their needs and to ensure abundance of fresh air and sunshine'.[20] The results were felt to be disappointing, giving too much attention to garden city models, and German and American civic design, rather than the natural beauty of the English village. At the same time the organisers of the Ideal Home Exhibition were preparing 'The Village of To-Morrow', a street of detached modernist houses from the speculative builder that included the 'Sunspan' house by Wells Coates and Pleydell-Bouverie, and the 'Sunway' house by Evelyn Simmons and Cecil Grellier. The same exhibition also had the 'Staybrite City', a monument to the untarnishable and indestructible steel age. Of the nine modernist houses, only three had garages, and in only one, the 'Sunspan' home, was it integral to the house. Set at right angles to the front door, and thereby sharing the entrance canopy, it was also linked to the domestic central heating system, so that the serious problems of engines freezing and cracking were avoided. The following year the Ideal Home Book of Plans had a range of suggestions, for house styles that included Tudor and Georgian, as well as Modern, and by then the double garage was gaining in popularity. Luxury flats were also being designed with underground parking, including a commercial garage, and were incorporated into major redevelopment schemes in central London from 1934 onwards, notably in Berkeley Square, Woburn Place and Park Lane.

It set the cultural climate in which F. R. S. Yorke and Marcel Breuer's fantasy model of a 'Garden City of the Future' for the Cement and Concrete Association's contribution to the 1936 Ideal Home, was not too fantastic.[21] Its blocks of high-rise flats, most with their own terraced gardens, set the pattern of planning that was tailored to the needs of the car-loving professional man. The free traffic systems, parking space and underground car parks, central shopping mall, theatres, cafés and sports facilities, a city of sunlight and clean air, all provided a foretaste of many of the post-war planning concepts. Drawing heavily on ideals from Central Europe, with its images of healthy outdoor life and an architecture to match, the plans looked splendid as models, but in scale ran counter to the resources of the middle-income family. There was a similar spirit to the 'New Architecture' exhibition organised by the MARS group at the New Burlington Gallery, January 1936. A manifesto described the intellectual position of the group towards architecture and planning, its relationship to everyday life, scientific knowledge and aesthetic experience. It made grand statements on the needs of the community, family and individual, and persisted in its denial of style, yet it presented a specific stylistic model of urban life, with its bentwood furniture, fitted furniture, concealed lights and a romantic new world idealism.

It was one thing to entertain the public with the ideals of the modernist dreamland, or incorporate them into municipal schemes, the seaside pleasure parks and holiday camps, but for the middle classes it remained a minority taste. When, at the beginning of 1933, Dartington Hall transferred its allegiance from the cottage-style architecture of de Soissons to the modernist houses of Lescaze, for its speculative development on the coastal site at Churston, part-way between Paignton and Brixham, it little realised how few middle-class families shared its taste.

Dartington made much of the fact that they were developing an unspoilt piece of coastline, and were surprised by the strength of local opposition to their exclusive dreamland. This was primarily because of the desire to protect the landscape, but there was also antipathy towards a proposal that was a mixture of continental and American planning. Beset with economic problems from the outset, there were only a handful of clients with the money and taste to take up the chance of a life of leisure and fun on the South Devon coast. In 1935 Dartington mounted a major publicity campaign to sell the houses at Churston, 'the last word in health-giving and labour-saving planning; superbly and scientifically built; situated on one of the few remaining unspoiled strips of Devon coast; with a value that cannot depreciate by reason of indiscriminate building'.[22] Presented as the place where the sun always shone, and the air was always warm, the new estate was described as a haven for the retired, a playground for the sports-lover, and paradise for children. In the hands of the graphic artist, the blend of rural England and continental modernism was seamlessly achieved (figure 18). But the houses were expensive, of traditional construction, and when set on the headland the architectural limitations of the Lescaze design were exposed for all to see. The coastal dream homes were clumsy in their proportions and details, and the landscape had been spoiled. Yet Lescaze as a convinced disciple of modern architecture believed in its ability to solve contemporary social problems and anticipate the needs of the future. For an age preoccupied with clean healthy living, the white rendered, flat-roofed house had its attractions, but in the layout of living rooms, bedrooms and services it followed conventional patterns, and in construction it employed the traditional building craft techniques. Consequently, no matter how much it was denied that modern architecture was just another style, that was how it was perceived, and the basis on which choice was made. The Churston development collapsed, there were no buyers for modern architecture, or investors for the sea front hotel,

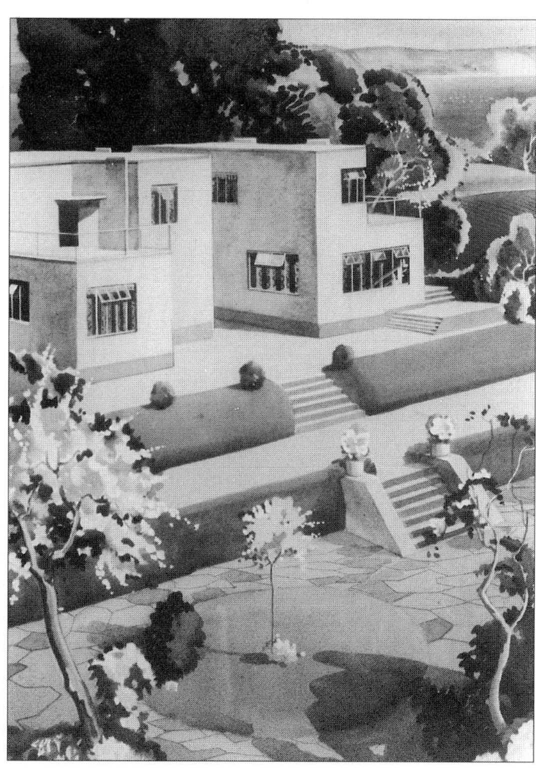

18 Churston, publicity brochure, Dartington Hall, 1935. The Lescaze houses set in an English coastal landscape and garden by the graphic artist

and a partial rescue plan mounted by le Soissons could do little to restore confidence in the scheme.

It was a remarkably similar story to the proposal for a modernist town between Frinton and Walton. The Essex coast at and around Clacton was seen as ideal residential building land for making good money for the speculator, and from 1926 onwards parts of what was known as Frinton Park were being sold for new housing. By early 1933 it was being talked about as a garden town idyll, and later as a new Bournemouth. Compared to neighbouring developments, progress was slow and in February 1934 the central part of the original scheme was taken over by South Coast Property Investment Co. Ltd. Through the early part of 1934 the estate was offering new houses in all kinds of styles, from 'Gothic and Early English to the Ultra Modern', and the idea of a new town began to take shape. Oliver Hill had been appointed as scheme architect, and in the September the Urban District Council had agreed to relocate its offices to a site on the estate. The *Builder*, 7 September 1934, carried the first illustration of the new shopping centre being planned by Oliver Hill, and local advertisements began to appear describing the new modernist township. The sales campaign was kept up throughout November, and the following month *Building* carried an illustrated account of the proposed new town, with its grand esplanade, town hall and sea front hotel: 'The whole of the new buildings are being carried out in the contemporary style. The general appearance of the town will be gleaming white, with parts of some of the buildings colour-washed pink, others treated white and blue, and white and green'.[23]

Work started on six shops and the first fifty houses. By January 1935 talk was of the new town 'likely to become famous throughout Britain, the Empire, and the World'.[24] Nineteen architects and firms were listed as being involved in the proposal, of which six, as well as Oliver Hill, designed some of the houses. Despite the launch, and the offer of labour-saving fixtures, stainless steel 'Savestone' metal sinks, vitrolite bathrooms and automatic garage doors, few houses sold. By August there was a smattering of about 30 houses, which on a plan that had envisaged 1,200 houses made it impossible to grasp any visual idea of how the scheme would appear. The plan for a modernist town was dead, rejected by the middle-class home buying public, which in its retreat to secluded havens around the British coast showed a preference for picturesque chalets and cottage-style bungalows at almost half the price. It was the same public that filled the much abused ribbon development and acres of suburban estates that offered reassuring Tudor details, bay windows and comfortable living space.

The Small House Exhibition, held at the RIBA in October 1938, was an attempt to counter these expressions of popular taste.[25] Arranged in three sections it attacked the unrestricted development and speculative building, specially the bungalow and suburbia, contrasting it to England's proud traditions of town planning, its crescents and squares, and its villages, and putting forward an alternative picture of a planned future that relied heavily on examples of continental modernism. It constructed an image of a nation sinking under an uncontrolled ugliness, which encouraged one of the openers, Ellen Wilkinson MP, to bemoan the lack of control, concluding that 'our only general feeling is that if ever we are going to be bombed, I hope that the enemy will bomb the right things'.[26] J. B. Priestley humanely added that he thought that matters should be changed through education, rather than legislation. He sought to convince his listeners of the merits of the middle ground, for while he had a particular hatred for bungalows, he had little sympathy for the modernist houses generated by excursions to the continent.

> We are now getting away from that, and we realise, like our fine old architects, that a house has to grow out of the soil, as it were; it has to be part of its background, and it has to conform with the temperament of the

> people who are going to live in it. Now, we English like to be cosy. We are cosy people. The Latins are not; they like to spend most of their lives out of doors. The Americans on the whole are very uncosy people. But we do like to be cosy, and you cannot be cosy in one of these functional rooms which are nearly all window. I think that we are getting away from that, and we are effecting a compromise between that rather cosy, narrow, domestic spirit of ours and this new austerity.[27]

Alongside a compromise on style, Priestley wanted to see new communities made up of a cross-section of people, out of which could be developed a 'healthier and happier life'.[28] In a decade committed to building a new way of life, of replacing nineteenth-century disorder with a new order, any ideas of a social mix in any of the new developments were significantly missing as class ghettoes were relocated or recreated. Given the scale of the new housing schemes, this was hardly a surprising outcome, but Priestley was right to identify the importance of social and class balance in the new communities.

A new land settlement scheme

Very little was understood of the social problems attached to resettlement schemes, and the experiences of the new industrial villages and municipal estates were only just beginning to be appreciated. This gives particular significance to a new phase of the Land Settlement Scheme, involving a relocation scheme for families from areas of high unemployment to areas where the prospects for employment were thought to be much higher.

The key concept was for a new Britain to be built on the revival of the yeoman class, with the wife and family also working the land. Announced to Parliament on 17 May 1934, the scheme came from the intervention of Mr Percy Malcolm Stewart, chairman of the London Brick Co. and Forders Ltd, working in conjunction with the Society of Friends, and other associated bodies. Stewart had recently built his own garden village, Stewartby, for the London Brick Co., on a site south of Bedford, but there was no clear indication as to why he should wish to become involved in a move to relocate the unemployed, except for the possibility that he saw it as an experiment in keeping with the spirit of the Halley Stewart Trust, founded by his father to fund research for promoting the Christian ideal in all social life. His adviser and confidant in this venture was the surveyor/land agent Sir H. Trustram Eve, who identified a piece of land at Potton for the experiment to be initiated, believing that if Stewart 'remained absolute boss the thing would be a great success and a lesson to the whole of England'.[29]

In its revised form the Land Settlement Scheme was not without its successes, but it also had its failures. Not surprisingly in the areas in which it was set up there was local opposition. Bad housing and rural poverty was still endemic, aggravated by the fact that agricultural workers were unable to claim unemployment benefit. The 1931 Housing (Rural Authorities) Act, with the prime intention of stimulating the building of new houses at low rents, particularly the provision of three-bedroomed houses had had limited effect.[30] Now rural communities were being confronted with a scheme that offered work and houses, but to which they had no access, it being restricted to the long-term unemployed industrial workers from special areas.[31]

Administered along the lines of a colonial settlement, the scheme was run from London,[32] and from the outset there were problems of selecting what they considered to be suitable families from those who had applied, and then implementing a training programme.[33] Operating in two distinct ways, in the first instance the settlements were organised as a collective of small holdings grouped around a farm which provided seeds and marketed the produce, such as was the case at Potton.[34] Two years later, moves were made to establish cottage homesteads with half an acre, that were meant to meet the needs of the family with adolescent children who could get work in the local area and continue to live at home, as was the case of Caversham, near Reading. The first of the settlements at Potton was divided up into 30 smallholdings, with an average of 5 acres and a semi-detached house. The first men arrived for training in March 1935, and were followed in July by their families. The physical demands of setting up a new smallholding, and the social isolation experienced by the families, meant that at Potton and across the scheme as a whole, there was a persistent high turnover of families, which by the end of the 1930s had averaged at over 40 per cent withdrawal.

The architectural models for the new life, with the neat fields, extensive farm buildings and greenhouse, full orchard, and detached house, were far distant from the reality of working a smallholding. However, in terms of housing, positive efforts had been made to take into account the needs of the families in providing an economic home. The preferred design was a detached house with the eaves coming down to first floor level.[35] This allowed for two bedrooms upstairs, one downstairs, a living room and scullery. The bath was originally placed in the scullery, but later plans incorporated a bathroom. Construction was usually of brick, with weather-boarding, except at Crofton in Cumberland, where the houses were flat roofed, built of hollow blocks and rendered.

Picture Post caught the romance of the movement, when it followed the Turner family from the Durham slums to the trees and green fields of Reading, and the cottage homestead where this long-term unemployed miner could regain his self-respect, and his children would enjoy a healthy

19 The Turner family arrives at their new house on the Land Settlement, Caversham, 1939

20 The Land Settlement, publicity brochure, n.d., *c.* early 1940s

life (figure 19). For them it was new-found luxury: 'Their old home was a bedroom and a kitchen. Now for the first time, they can sit comfortably round the tea-table'.[36] The association's own publicity followed the same line, pointing out the disadvantages of living some distance from community facilities and shops, and the difficulties of working the holding, but emphasising the compensations of 'a healthy life and a fine start for a family to be brought up in the fresh air of the English countryside'.[37] Putting the image of the family arriving at Caversham alongside the one constructed for the Land Settlement's publicity illustrates the credibility gap between the real and the dream (figure 20).

From 1936 Wales ran its own Land Settlement Scheme and by the end of the 1930s had established six settlements. Two used the smallholding arrangement, while the others were arranged as cooperative farms without individual holdings, creating new villages that challenged the principles of the English system. In terms of work, both schemes had their limitations. The English settlements offered the potential of independence, but with the reliance on the central management and payment of commission, a sense of freedom was largely illusory: 'Three acres and a cow are not necessarily as idyllic as is often imagined; family – father, mother and children – having to put in on the land an amount of work out of all proportion to the yield'.[38]

The Welsh scheme was based on a wage earning structure, but with the workers taking a share of the profits at the end of the year. In other words the settlement was modelled on the new industrial villages, with agriculture as the industry, in the belief that the grouping of houses sustained a greater continuity in the social order experienced by those moving from the Special Areas.[39] Efforts were made to provide these settlements with their own village halls, but they were still reliant on the schools, shops and other community resources of the established neighbouring villages, and some form of social integration was essential.

Efficient homes and things

Lessons on taste

The Exhibition of British Industrial Art in Relation to the Home, Dorland Hall, in June–July 1933, was both a response to the Swedish Exhibition in London in 1931 and the Gorrell Report on Art and Industry. It marked the establishment concern for design in everyday life and its desire to raise the standards of British taste and quality of manufacture through exhibitions of industrial art. Commandeered by the modern movement, and arranged by Oliver Hill, it was an expression of functional efficiency, as well as the exotic. Although directed at the householder of moderate means, expensive taste was on show. Displays of textiles, light-fittings, wallpaper, pottery, glass, silver, furniture, floor coverings, ornaments, utensils and tools gave a selective introduction to the products of British industry. But it was the range of furnished rooms that provided the comprehensive picture of the modern home, the Dining Room by Sir Ambrose Heal, Bedroom by Raymond McGrath, Living Room by R. W. Symonds, Study by R. D. Russell, Minimum Flat by Wells Coates, Bathroom by Oliver Hill, Weekend House by Serge Chermayeff, Dining Room by Oliver Hill, Study of a Ruling Prince by Arundell Clarke, Nursery Ensemble by Oliver Hill, Aga Kitchen by Mrs Darcy Braddell and Gas Kitchen by Wells Coates. Contemporary settings for upper middle-class homelife were on display, with the Minimum Flat and Weekend House providing a distinctly innovative interpretation of adaptable space. As important as the exhibition was the recognition that these ideas on design for the home had to reach a wider public, and immediately following on from the 1933 Dorland Hall show, Serge Chermayeff arranged an Exhibition of Modern Living at Whiteley's Department Store, London. Alongside the selection of furniture, lighting, fabrics, rugs, wall coverings, china, glass and metalwork, there was a complete reconstruction of his 'Weekend House'.

These ideals were reinforced by other exhibitions and a series of broadcast talks. The first was on 'Design in Industry' in the autumn of 1932 and then beginning in April 1933, there were ten discussion programmes on 'Design in Modern Life', which were written up and published the following year under the same title. As much concerned with the environment as the home, the approach was based on the premise that the public did not know what it wanted, or more particularly that it had yet to appreciate that 'good modern work' was preferable to 'old-world cult'.[40] This was not just the dismissal of the wasted years of the nineteenth century or the consequence of a cultured aristocracy having been replaced by shopkeepers and merchants, but a condemnation of the continuing obsession with replicating the past.[41] Instead of building a land fit for heroes, England had 'become the slum of Europe'.[42] Coinciding with slum clearance, this was a powerful indictment that heightened the debate on design ethics, and increased the tensions between social and aesthetic responsibilities. With a range of contributions that included essays by Gordon Russell, Elizabeth Denby and Frank Pick, the recurring message was for order and orderliness, but in terms of new principles it was not altogether the radical break that could have been expected. Although demanding a more scientific and rational approach, Frank Pick chose to remind the public that design was also expression, and 'purpose must transcend the merely practical, and serve a moral and spiritual order as well'.[43]

The Exhibition of Contemporary Industrial Design in the Home, October–November 1934, followed a similar thesis, although it attracted criticism for its failure to address the needs of the minimum middle-class householder. Even so it had a number of influential exhibits: the Reinforced Concrete Flat by Lubetkin and Tecton, which was a replica of a flat for the Highgate development, the All-Electric House and All-Electric Office by Walter Goodesmith, and a Living Room by Serge Chermayeff. The Royal Academy Exhibition of British Art in Industry, January–March 1935, similarly faced criticisms, only this time they were directed at the inadequate attention to design for mass-production. In fact the rooms devoted to ceramics and glass were notable exceptions, but the furnished rooms were exclusively for the affluent, and distinctly at odds with the mood of social change and responsibility. A more pragmatic approach was taken by the RIBA, in its 'Everyday Things' exhibition which started its tour in Bristol in May 1936, followed by showings at the Walker Art Gallery, Liverpool, and the City Art Gallery, Manchester.

Closely involved in these events and following on from its efforts of the early 1920s, the Design and Industries Association (DIA) also embarked on a number of collaborative ventures furnishing showhouses, and arranging displays for retailers, selecting articles that it believed conformed to 'principles of fitness for purpose and pleasantness in use', that were 'reasonable in cost' and 'easily procurable'.[44] What was still being overlooked in these models of good taste was the scale of the poverty of many of those being relocated, and while it was perhaps acceptable that a house furnished for £200 at Welwyn Garden City in September 1933 was within the reach of a 'man of moderate means', to arrive at an almost identical costing for a family house on the new municipal housing development at Wythenshawe was unrealistic.[45] Recognising the impracticalities of the approach, in the working-class house the DIA put the emphasis on the cost of individual items rather than the total. Even so, considering that £50 of expenditure would have been normal, and £100 exceptional, good taste was certainly not low cost. In 1935 the Manchester branch of the DIA took a more practical approach when invited to furnish two show flats at Smedley Point, the Kennett House development. Opened on 30 July it showed that for under £60 for a two-bedroom flat, and approx £80 for the three-bedroom flat it was possible to follow the principles of good design, using simple and serviceable furniture, and clean, light colours. The same year the DIA decided to take the lessons of the recent Art-in-Industry exhibitions into the high street, through a display scheme for retailers, beginning with Bowman's in Camden High Street, where it arranged five room settings and displays of fabrics, pottery, glass, carpets and household equipment. In 1937 the Birmingham branch of the DIA published a booklet, *Your New House – The Furnishing Problem*, setting out the costings and ideas for simplicity in style, furnishing and decoration for a young couple of moderate means, recommending light-coloured walls, simple curtains and wallpaper patterns, and well-made furniture in modern materials (figure 21).

Presenting the public with images of a domestic wonderland was a role ably filled by the retail trade, some being more serious than others. In 1932, Lewis's, Liverpool, created a 'Design for Living Department', to cater for contemporary taste, with complete rooms, furnishing, pottery, glass and textiles, and then proceeded to extend the idea to its stores in Manchester and Birmingham. Catching the spirit of the time in 1933 Heals opened some new rooms to display 'Economy Furniture' for 'Wise Spenders', while its Mansard Gallery exploited similar themes as exhibitions.[46] 'Beautiful Homes' was the ideal of many of these in-store exhibitions, and the language and scope of those organised by Heelas, Reading, provide a good introduction to the broader culture and purpose of these events. Held over a two-week period in mid-February, they often had as many as twenty-eight

THE COST OF FURNISHING

To make sure that the suggestions made in this booklet were reasonable and practicable, an attempt was made to find out how much is spent on furnishing a small house when the weekly wage is £2 10s. to £4. Only a few such figures were obtainable, so that these results are by no means comprehensive, but they are actually what did happen and so have some practical value.

Weekly Income	A. £3 0 0	B. £3 3 0	C. £3 10 0	D1. £2 15 0	D2. £3 5 0
	£ s. d.	£ s. d.	£ s. d.	£ s. d.	£ s. d.
Dining Room	41 0 0	19 1 0	26 4 6	11 2 0	34 0 0
Sitting Room	30 10 0	20 15 0	4 5 0		
Kitchen ..	5 10 0	—	14 12 0	—	12 10 0
Bedroom 1 ..	34 0 0	28 8 0	34 6 0	14 10 0	31 12 0
„ 2 ..	6 10 0	—	—	—	—
Bathroom ..	1 10 0	—	1 12 0		
Total ..	119 0 0	68 4 0	80 19 6	25 12 0	78 2 0 25 12 0
					£103 14 0

B and C. These couples only furnished one bedroom on marrying.

D1 and D2 represent furnishing in stages. The couple lived in 2 rooms for 3 years and only bought some furniture (D1). Then they moved into a house and bought more furniture (D2). They also had other furniture for the sitting room and used the furniture originally bought for their own room in the second bedroom.

In order to find what could be done in the way of buying good furniture of simple but pleasant style, the following goods were picked out from local shops. They represent what can actually be bought for cash.

		£ s. d.	£ s. d.
Dining Room 15 x 10ft. or 14 x 12ft.	Table, 4 Chairs and Sideboard	15 15 0	
	Lino (16 yards)	3 0 0	
	Rugs	1 6 0	
	Curb	1 0 0	
	Curtain Materials	15 0	21 16 0
Sitting Room 10 x 10ft. or 13 x 11ft.	3-Piece Suite	19 19 0	
	Axminster Carpet	7 0 0	
	Paper Felt	5 0	
	Curb and Fire Irons ..	2 0 0	
	Curtain Material	1 0 0	
	Small Tables	2 10 0	32 14 0
Bedroom 1 ..	Beds and Mattresses.. ..	6 0 0	
	4ft. Bedroom Suite ..	13 15 6	
	Chairs	15 6	
	Lino (13 yards)	2 10 0	
	Rugs	2 0 0	
	Curtain Materials	15 0	25 16 0
Bedroom 2 ..	Bed and Mattress	3 15 0	
	2ft. Bedroom Suite ..	6 5 0	
	Lino (13 yards)	2 10 0	
	Rug	10 0	
	Curtain Materials	10 0	13 10 0
Bathroom ..	Lino (4 yards)	15 0	
	Mat	5 0	
	Cabinet	15 0	
	Stool	15 0	2 10 0
Kitchen ..	Table	1 10 0	
	Wringer	1 5 0	
	Bread Bin, Pots and Pans, Kettle	2 10 0	
	Brooms and Bucket ..	7 0	
	Chairs	7 6	
	Curtain Materials	9 0	6 8 6
Hall	Mirror	10 0	
	Stair Carpet and Fittings ..	2 12 0	3 2 0
		Total ..	£105 16 6

N.B.—Considerable economy can be made by spending less on such things as curbs and bathroom fittings, and a good sitting-room carpet can be bought for as little as £3.

21 DIA, Furnishing a small house, 1937

furnished rooms in modern and period styles, alongside cooking and product demonstrations, garden designs and ideas on how to furnish a flat. Catering for all interests, in 1938 the exhibition had a stainless steel kitchen and a birch dining room by Alvar Aalto; the following year it was an all-electric labour-saving kitchen, the chintz room, and 'The Pig and Whistle', 'no less suitable for the lounge bar of a private house than for a public one'. They were occasions that offered 'real practical value and interest to the housewife whose main happiness lies in the well-being and smooth running of her home'.[47] Model living was the recurring theme and in March 1938 Lewis's Birmingham store exhibited ideas for two homes, a four-room house, furnished for £65, for a family with an income of £3 per week, and a five-room house, furnished for £165, for a family on an income of £5 a week. Catching the national mood, in 1937 the CWS organised a 'Happy Homes Exhibition' at the City Hall, Manchester. Similar in its approach to displays found in any large department store, the idea was repeated later in the year by the Bristol Society, when the general display was complemented by an all-electric bungalow, and a home furnished for £50 in collaboration with the Council of Art & Industry. The popular ideal was happy homes for happy people, at moderate prices for the model family that had taste in its discreet ornaments, was modern in its furnishing, traditional in its pursuits and considerate in its relationships.[48]

In 1937 Anthony Bertram broadcast twelve talks on 'Design in Everyday Things', supported by twenty identical travelling exhibitions of goods and photographs, that had been organised by the DIA. In the following year the lecture series was published as a Penguin paperback. It included an important section on 'Housing the Workers' and coincided with the publication of the Council for Art and Industry report on *The Working-Class Home, Its Furnishing and Equipment*. It was these and similar kinds of publications that formed the framework and character of the immediate post-Second World War efforts. Bertram outlined the agenda, 'Every one of us should consider the problem of working-class housing ... (as) design is everybody's business ... we must not be satisfied until we are sure that the great service of housing our workers is being as well done as it reasonably can be, down to the smallest details of taps and light'.[49]

In his broader discourse, Bertram chose objects, buildings and interiors that illustrated the concepts of order, cleanliness, light and efficiency. He advocated the environment of the built-in/unit furniture, central heating, electricity, large metal-framed windows, and the fitted wash-basin in all bedrooms, although this sometimes had to be sacrificed for space and economy and might necessitate fitting a basin in the bathroom. His ideal house would have been one that was made to measure to fit the social needs of the family like a suit round a body, but he had to accept that the family would have to fit itself to the type provided for its social-economic group. The solution was 'a big family room for meals, games and conversation, for the communal family life, and a bed-sitting-room for each member of the family'.[50] He avoided any detailed consideration of the kitchen, and the needs of families with young children. His was a blueprint for a modernist society, where towns were more efficient, healthy and beautiful, and the natural beauty of the countryside had been preserved, he argued against the suburbs in favour of a new world constructed for the motorist, with the town dweller escaping on the new roads into the country, and the countryman enjoying the social and commercial facilities of the town.

When the Council for Art and Industry turned its attention to the understanding of the possibilities of furnishing and equipping the working-class home, the investigation and recommendations were directed to the manufacturers. The commentary and data was to explain the economics of working-class consumption with the intention of helping to raise the standard of design among the cheapest domestic wares. Set the task of reporting on the furnishing and equipping of the working-class home, the committee decided that it would demonstrate that it could achieve its objectives with British-made furnishing from firms observing the fair-wages clause. The target group was the two-children family, living on £3 a week, accommodated in a two-bedroom house with living room, kitchen-scullery, bathroom and WC.

Initially it was thought possible to provide a minimum standard for £40, but after investigation the committee realised that £50 was the realistic minimum figure. The maximum was to be £100. In the end the report identified three categories, a minimum standard, a desirable standard, and a desirable additions standard. None of the houses were expected to have labour-saving devices, the primary objective being to provide a good standard of design at the lowest possible cost. The economics of the filtering of taste were considered, and in particular the continuing popularity of decoration. In the end a compromise was reached as they considered it unreasonable to force the severity of some modern taste on to the public. The emphasis again was on an education in what was 'convenient and useful' and 'qualities of simplicity and beauty'.[51] At the same time they felt it necessary to take into account the realities of the market.

> What was fashionable in furniture with the well-to-do becomes, in time, fashionable with poorer folk ... due to the fact that second-hand furniture is a main source of supply for homes where expenditure upon furniture must be severely curtailed. There will, therefore, come a time when the furniture which is now fashionable in more prosperous quarters will find its way down to less prosperous quarters. What we should like to see once more is a living tradition of furniture design which would cover all classes and resist the decayed furniture of gentility dwindling slowly through the second-hand shops from owner to owner.[52]

In the search of classless furniture, the illustrated examples drew from the vernacular tradition of the Windsor Chair, and turned to the simple cabinet-maker furniture that became the forerunner of the designs selected for the Utility range. Progress was overtaken by the Second World War, but the exercise prominently influenced both the utility and post-war debate on furnishing the nation, and identified the need for both the state and municipal authorities to become directly involved in providing furniture at a price that the working class could afford.

Electric or gas

While redefining the products of the everyday, renewed efforts were being made to distinguish the 1930s as the Electric Age. The building of all-electric showhouses as permanent homes that could be purchased at the close of the exhibition period were an important part of the campaign. There was nothing original about using the showhouse in this way, but the British Electrical Development Association's 'All-Electric House' on Vicarage Road, Edgbaston, of 1932, designed by W. N. Twist, was the first house of this nature built to demonstrate the benefits of a modern electrically equipped home. Anticipating the completion of the National Grid System, and the availability of cheaper electricity, the house was on a grand scale and exotic in style. Incorporating the latest technology and planning, 'an ultra-modern Continental elevation' was rejected in favour of the 'dignity and charm of some of the smaller Spanish houses'.[53] Planned as a U-shape, with a range of outbuildings that included a double garage, the rooms were grouped around a central open courtyard facing the garden, with the maid's room, kitchen, servery and dining room, occupying the ground floor on one wing, and the lounge leading into a loggia in the other. It had five bedrooms, all with cupboards and washbasins, but surprisingly only one bathroom.

Much was made of designing a garden appropriate to the character of the house. Restraint was emphasised. Only the front and immediate terraced area was laid out in time for the exhibition. The advice to the future owners was to work with the existing levels of the garden, eventually leading into 'a semi-wild garden as an approach to a rock and water garden'.[54] Overall, in its style and materials, the intention was to integrate the modern with the traditional. Externally the cement walls were finished in snowcrete, and the metal window frames surrounded by faience, as were the doors; there was a wrought-iron entrance gate by the Birmingham Guild, handmade green glazed roofing tiles, and a terrace of buff-coloured concrete slabs. The floors of the lounge, hall and dining room were laid with oak, the service areas with tiles. Electric clocks were provided for all the main rooms, modern light-fittings by Best & Lloyd, and in the lounge and dining room there was thermostatic heating that operated from ceiling panels. The emphasis was on the dustless house, rooms automatically maintained at the correct temperature, constant hot water, refrigeration, perfectly cooked food, and clothes washed with ease. Presented as a model of luxury living, it was also an opportunity to demonstrate how electricity could save British cities from the smoke and grime that excluded air and sunlight. It was to inspire action, to install electricity, and give the 'Old Country' a much-needed spring clean.

Three years later the Bristol branch of the Electrical Association For Women instigated a similar scheme, but on this occasion it was directed at those in search of an ordinary middle-class suburban house. By the standards of The Ideal Home it was small, possibly too small for many of its readers, but it was a model that could be adapted to the larger house. A detached modernist house, with three bedrooms, workroom/nursery, bathroom, through living-dining room, cloakroom, kitchen and garage, it had been designed by A. E. Powell as a labour-saving home to be run by the housewife with no domestic help. It was built on an estate being developed at Stoke Bishop on the western edge of Bristol, to sell for £1,000. From the end of October 1935 and through November, it was opened as an exhibition house attracting some 20,000 visitors and considerable national publicity.

With the exterior walls finished in a pale green distemper, metal windows, modernist front garden, and the modern furnishing by P. E. Gane, a founder member of the DIA, the visitor was introduced to the modern age of electricity. The sense of functional efficiency was reinforced by concealed lighting, flushed doors, fitted cupboards, Columbian pine flooring, and a whole array of appliances from the utilitarian to luxury items. Being marketed as a house for healthy living, much was made of its large windows, sun-bathing roof, and ventilation holes in the ceiling along the dividing line between the living/dining room. Great emphasis was placed on the space saved by not having to include the conventional fireplace and chimneys, and the provision of instant heating throughout the house with inset and directional fires, tubular heaters, and with the fires in the bedrooms being able to be switched on from the bed. The kitchen, with its full range of appliances, built-in cupboards, serving hatch, foldaway table and ironing board attracted great interest, as did the kitchen door which could be used either to close off the opening into the dining area or the hall. An experiment in modern living, it was considered to be a pointer to the future when all houses would 'be air conditioned, have windows which disappear from sight by electricity, and collapsible doors operating in the same way'.[55]

Gas was losing out to electricity in the fight for the lighting market, but in all other appliances for the home, particularly in those houses being built by municipal authorities, it retained its popularity. It was rightly argued that it was just as much automatic and instant as electric, and even more so in the case of cookers and water heaters. In a brilliant piece of publicity, the Gas Light & Coke Co. took the front page of *The Times National Health Number*, to advertise its 'Healthier happier living at a new low level of cost' as provided by its Kensal House.[56] Designed by E. Maxwell Fry and Elizabeth Denby, it was immediately adopted as an icon of modern architecture, but just as important was its representation of 'middle-class amenities' at a cost that the working class could afford (figure 22).[57] J. M. Richards' in *An Introduction to Modern Architecture*, an exposition on taste for and understanding of the stylistic integrity of modern architecture, valued it for its representation of the aesthetics of 'proper civic planning',[58] rather than for the significance of its contribution to the broader debate on working-class housing.

By its sponsorship of *Flats, Municipal and Private Enterprise*, published 1938, the Ascot Gas Water Heaters aligned itself with the social purpose of architecture and its equipment. The gas industry had already identified itself with the slum clearance programmes, drawing attention to the thousands of appliances supplied for municipal estates and housing schemes now it was declaring a closer interest in modernist ideologies. A number of key design points were being made on the basis of the Kensal House scheme. There was no surprise that these all-gas flats were put forward as providing much improved services for the working-class housewife, being fitted with 'a cooker with thermostatic oven control, an instantaneous water heater serving kitchen and bath, a movable wash copper and gas iron in the kitchen, a gas-ignited coke grate in the living room, a gas fire in the main bedroom and gas points in the others, and switch-controlled gas lighting'.[59]

The development had 54 three-bedroom flats and fourteen two-bedroom flats, and although much thought had gone into the layout and general services, living space was kept to a minimum. For example, the three-bedroom flat had just 576 sq. ft. of living space and a 40 sq. ft. balcony. Stores for prams and cycles were on the ground floor.

22 Modernism goes all gas, Kensal House. E. Maxwell Fry and Elizabeth Denby

Despite the limitations on living space there were three design decisions that ensured success for the scheme. Being designed for a derelict industrial site there was the imaginative exploitation of the shapes left by the abandoned gas holders and preservation of some fine plane trees, then there was what Elizabeth Denby described as the 'urban village' concept which included clubrooms, nursery school, playground, quiet space and allotments, managed by a tenants' committee, and finally the arrangement of the flats around internal staircases, thereby allowing for the bedrooms to be grouped on one side, with the living room and balcony on the side that had the afternoon and evening sunshine. It was much more than the outcome of a woman designing for women, it was the design of a woman who believed that homes should be designed to offer a quality life to poor people, who after paying their rent would have 3*s.* 6*d.* to 6*s.* a head left for food and clothing. Her aim was to provide more than the basics, offering 'a reasonable degree of comfort, convenience and leisure'.[60]

Similar design concepts were present in the two model working-class flats shown at the Empire Exhibition, Glasgow 1938.[61] A two- and three-bedroom flat were on show, with a balcony and approached from an interior staircase. Equipped with Belling 'streamline' electric cookers, Ascot heaters, and solid fuel back-to-back grates, the emphasis was on simple craft furniture, built-in cupboards, distempered walls in pale colours throughout,

23 Model working-class flat, Empire Exhibition, Glasgow, 1938

and geometric patterned rugs and linoleum floor coverings. The craft flower vase, Roland Hilder print over the fireplace and simple functionalism of the wireless denoted simple taste and new life enhanced with sunshine and clean air (figure 23).

Housework

The 'Age of Electricity' brought into question not only the questions of efficiency, but the value of housework and role of the housewife. The Fifth International Scientific Management Congress, Amsterdam, July 1932, devoted one of its sessions to papers on 'The determination of standards which make it possible to establish a budget of the expense of money, time and energy in the administration of the household'. The British delegation based its submission around an account of households living on a weekly income from £2 to £3. It pointed to the failure of architects and builders to deliver the standards outlined by the Tudor Walters Report, and compounded by the inadequate design of the kitchen in relation to the living room. The argument was for a greater standardisation of equipment, with a lowering of costs and raising of standards, but recognising the pressures on family budgets, it also accepted that the possibilities of family allowances that would enable families to live above the 'poverty line' should be explored.

The report considered that it was impossible to find any meaningful way of quantifying the amount of time needed to care for children, although recognised it as demanding. Nevertheless, determined to establish a clearer idea of the demands placed on the housewife for managing and running a house, the report set out to estimate the hours devoted to cleaning, cooking, washing up, washing, mending and sewing. It was a workload averaged at 56 hours over a seven-day week. Converted into employment terms it was argued that

> All these women ... have to perform skilled as well as unskilled work for not only do they wash, cook, iron, make and mend clothes, but their job is definitely a managerial one, since they have to plan and expend the available income, train the children, and direct the whole life of the little community dependent on them for everything except the actual monetary supply, and they should therefore, be able to command at least the higher price paid to the daily help with a knowledge of cooking.[62]

Quantified as labour costs, the estimate was over £3 a week, in effect doubling the family income. Realising that this strategy and analysis would be met with scepticism, the paper emphasised that it was an effective way of bringing attention to the importance of design standards that would eliminate unnecessary wastage of time and effort used in running a household. What was being accounted for in these debates on the working week did not match the widely accepted social conventions. Despite having a house full of gadgets, and hints on efficiency, the work of the good housewife was still being illustrated as a 14-hour day, seven-day week, with or without a daily help (figures 24a and 24b). Twenty-five years after the demand for women to be more directly involved in planning and general design matters, the same arguments were being made and the same prejudices being expressed. The general expectation was for the modern mother to be clever and efficient, promoting the well-being and happiness of her family.[63]

In the design debate Noel Carrington's comments were typical.

> Social observers have laid much emphasis on the emancipation of women in England, and possibly in some classes and groups of society women now have all the freedom they themselves desire. What is important to civilisation is the fact that they are in the main the great spenders of national income, not only for food, but for all manner of things, from houses to motor-cars, and that on their education and taste the future must largely depend. It is thought by some that they will prove themselves more realist than men, but there is nothing in the past from which any such deduction can be made, having regard to the absurdities of feminine fashions.[64]

He thought it possible that in time women would exercise more responsibility in terms of birth control, and that with their knowledge of home management they could influence political policy, particularly in the areas of slum clearance. But outside of the home few thought that women could play an influential role. This meant that as the appliance home became the model of a new utopia, campaigns were focused on women, and their responsibility for delivering home comforts. The fact that going all-electric remained outside of the reach of most families was irrelevant: it was the imagined dream world for all women.[65] For example, Manchester's Electricity Department leaflet on 'Electricity in the Home', was illustrated with the housewife cooking, ironing, reading in bed, and having a bath.

The obsessive interest in reducing housework led some commentators to look towards the feasibility of schemes that removed most of the household chores from the responsibility of the individual housewife altogether. L. B. Atkinson, Chairman of the Royal Society of Arts, put forward the idea of blocks of apartments in which all the chores of cooking, washing and caring for children would be done on a communal system, reducing the workload to a fifth. He had a picture in his mind of a kind of holiday camp service centre where occupations would be 'carried on in clean, beautifully lighted, and well-warmed, properly ventilated and spacious apartments, and if a costume approaching the modern American

PLAN OF WORK FOR MISTRESS AND ONE HELPER

Kitchen, Scullery, Dining-room, Sitting-room, and 4 Bedrooms

HOUSEWIFE'S DAILY DUTIES

7.0.	Get up and open bed.
10. 20. 30. 40. 50.	If there are children, help them to dress ; bath and dress baby, as this is likely to ensure a peaceful breakfast. Cook breakfast, if helper is not resident.
8.0.	Have breakfast.
10. 20. 30.	
40. 50.	Take children to school if necessary.
9.0. 10.	
20. 30.	Make beds and tidy bedrooms. Mop floor and dust.
40. 50.	
10.0. 10. 20. 30. 40. 50. 11.0. 10. 20. 30. 40. 50.	Special weekly work, such as preparing sitting-rooms or bedrooms for the helper to turn out. Washing smalls, ironing, using vacuum cleaner, household sewing, special silver cleaning, etc.
12.0. 10. 20. 30.	Shopping when required or taking the baby out.
40. 50.	Cooking or supervising the lunch.
1.0. 10. 20. 30. 40. 50.	Have lunch.

2.0. 10. 20. 30. 40. 50.	Help with clearing away and tidying when there are several in family. Look after children when necessary.
3.0. 10. 20. 30. 40. 50. 4.0. 10. 20.	Free for visiting, receiving friends, social work, sewing, gardening, preserve making, amusements, or supervising the children.
30. 40. 50.	Tea.
5.0. 10. 20. 30. 40. 50.	Looking after baby or supervising children's studies.
6.0. 10. 20. 30. 40. 50.	Supervising or cooking of dinner or supper when necessary.
7.0. 10. 20. 30. 40. 50.	Have supper or dinner.
8.0.	Clear away supper if daily helper only is kept.
	Reading, recreation, letter writing, accounts from 8.40 onwards.

HOUSEWIFE'S WEEKLY DUTIES

From 11.30 to 12.30.

MONDAY.	Brush all clothes used over the week-end and put away. Collect large articles and send to laundry or do laundrywork at home. If all family laundry is done at home, help may be necessary. Wash silk and woollens, followed by white things. These can be done alternate weeks if preferred.
TUESDAY.	Help turn out dining-room. Clean silver.
WEDNESDAY.	Special turning out of one or two bedrooms each week.
THURSDAY.	Special turning out of sitting-room.
FRIDAY.	Thorough weekly clean of bathroom, W.C., landing and stairs. Baking for the week-end.
SATURDAY	Special cleaning of hall, kitchen and scullery. Extra cooking for week-end.

PLAN OF WORK FOR A SMALL SERVANTLESS HOUSE

(3 or 4 in family)

Time	Duty	Time	Duty
7.0.	Get up; dress.	2.0.	Wash up, tidy kitchen and scullery.
10.	Strip the bed and air the rooms.	10.	
20.	Unlock the house.	20.	
30.	Stoke the boiler.	30.	
40.	Light living-room fire if necessary.	40.	
50.	Prepare breakfast.	50.	Change.
8.0.	Have breakfast.	3.0.	
10.		10.	
20.	Clear away, wash up breakfast things. (Accompany child to school when required.)	20.	
30.		30.	Recreation, resting, visiting or special duties such as ironing, gardening, needlework according to weather and season. Minding young children if necessary.
40.		40.	
50.		50.	
9.0.	Sweep porch and steps.	4.0.	
10.	Lay sitting-room fire if needed.	10.	
20.	Do dining-room and sitting-room carpets with vacuum cleaner. Mop the surrounds and dust.	20.	
30.		30.	
40.		40.	Prepare and serve tea.
50.		50.	
10.0.	Make beds.	5.0.	
10.	Mop and dust upstair rooms and W.C.	10.	Wash up tea things.
20.	Attend to bathroom. Wash out bath and lavatory basin. Sweep and mop bathroom floor and landing. Sweep stairs.	20.	
30.		30.	
40.		40.	
50.		50.	
11.0.	Look over larder.	6.0.	Prepare food for supper or dinner, and cook the meal.
10.	Prepare vegetables or pastry for midday or evening meal.	10.	
20.		20.	
30.		30.	
40.		40.	
50.		50.	
12.0.	Shopping when required and special weekly duties.	7.0.	Put children to bed.
10.		10.	
20.		20.	
30.		30.	
40.	Finish off cooking, and prepare lunch.	40.	Serve and have dinner.
50.		50.	
1.0.	Serve lunch or dinner.	8.0.	Clear away meal. Wash up if liked, but this can be deferred until the morning.
10.		10.	
20.	Have lunch, and clear away.	20.	
30.		30.	
40.		40.	Reading, recreation, letter writing, accounts.
50.		50.	

As meal-times vary considerably in different families and in different parts of the country, according to the nature of the husband's work the principal meal is sometimes taken in the middle and sometimes at the end of the day. As a general rule, when the husband's work is near at hand and he can take all meals at home, the principal meal is taken at midday, and the housewife's morning will be necessarily busier, but she should have more leisure between tea and supper.

HOUSEWIFE'S WEEKLY DUTIES

From 11.30 to 12.30.

MONDAY.	Brush all clothes used over the week-end and put away. Collect large articles and send to laundry or do laundrywork at home. If all family laundry is done at home, help may be necessary. Wash silk and woollens first, followed by white things. These can be done in alternate weeks if preferred.
TUESDAY.	Turn out dining-room. Clean silver.
WEDNESDAY.	Special turning out of two bedrooms each week.
THURSDAY.	Special turning out of sitting-room.
FRIDAY.	Thorough weekly clean of bathroom, W.C., landing and stairs. Baking.
SATURDAY.	Special cleaning of hall, kitchen and scullery. Extra cooking for week-end.

above and facing 24 The housewife's book, *Daily Express*, late 1930s sun-bathing costume were adopted, ultra-violet lamps in winter would do much to maintain the resistance against pathological germs'.[66]

The issue of household services and equipment was neither a new one, nor a problem exclusive to the introduction of electricity. What was happening, and what continued to happen, was an outcome of the major differences over what constituted minimum standards and the reality of the communal facility. Washing, and all its associated tasks, was the one major activity that continued to expose class differences. There can be no better illustration of its consequences than shown in the communal laundry of the Quarry Hill Housing Scheme, opened three days a week for the residents, and the image of the home laundry as part of the efficient home.

While exaggerated claims of 'half-time housework' could be ignored, there were improvements in the demands and time required of the housewife, partly due to the availability of new equipment and attention to kitchen design. The manner in which the kitchen equalled efficiency owed something to the fascination with the concept of the house as a machine, and to the transfer of management 'time and motion' ideas to the home. It was a case of the kitchen as the 'workshop and office'.[67] The all-electric kitchen was widely used as the ideal model, and much publicised by the British Electrical Development Association, through competitions, such as one held at the end of 1933, out of which the winners were exhibited at the Building Centre, and popular exhibitions, as that of May 1936, when three ideal kitchens were put on show at Charing Cross District Station. With competitions in journals and newspapers, planning the dream kitchen almost became a national pastime.

Glass and adaptability

Glass made a bid to be the material of the decade, and could not have got off to a more flamboyant start than in 'Glassholm – the Sunlit House' at the 1931 Scottish Ideal Home Exhibition. It was not an ideal house, but a series of rooms configured into a modern house type to demonstrate the colour possibilities of a range of new glass materials. Starting from the ground there was a 10 in. deep vitreous black marble band, a two-feet dado of sea-green, a narrow band of black, and the rest of the exterior wall surfaced with a crushed jade green marbling dashed on to a cement coat. Inside the exotic persisted, with glass panels of pink and grey in the bedroom, and black and green for the bathroom in a riot of hygienic expression.[68]

Pilkington's sought to introduce a similar exuberance to the trade. Its reputation had been established for quality and technical advances, such as in its production of plate glass.[69] Yet, by the early 1930s, as they brought a range of new materials on to the market, they realised the need for generating a greater public awareness of their uses in the domestic and commercial environment. Beginning with the opening of its London showroom in Albemarle Street in 1932, the company was going modern. John Gloag was appointed as consultant, and Oliver Hill's 'Glass Ensemble', of a dressing table, stool, small table and couch, at the 1933 Dorland Hall Exhibition of British Industrial Art in Relation to the Home, underlined the design possibilities of the new glass age. By 1934 the range of glass included coloured vitrolite for interior and external use, vitroflex, vita-glass that allowed sunrays into rooms, armourplate, and triplex toughened glass.

Vitrolite gave the 1930s modernism a distinctive characteristic; used in bathrooms and kitchens, chip shops, milkbars, cinemas, garages and shops, the Savoy Hotel and lining the walls of the recently constructed Mersey Tunnel, Britain was coated in the wonder material. Publicity brochures made great play of its before and after qualities. It was easy to keep clean, bright and colourful, and in 1934 Pilkington's built a hotel at Kirk Sandall, opposite its factory, to demonstrate to its potential customers its decorative and exterior uses. Modernist in style, designed by the local architects, T. H. Johnson & Son, and with a later extension by Kenneth Cheesman, the hotel attracted national publicity. The exterior was faced in shell-pink, with black base, and a turquoise blue canopy supported by a silver plated column. Every room was different in colour and material: the larger of the two smoking rooms was finished in an engraved grey silver double-rolled glass, designed by A. S. Pollitzer. Nothing could have been more different in design from the cottage garden village of Kirk Sandall, or the public buildings of neighbouring Doncaster and, not surprisingly, local interest was roused, although the attention was not always of the desired kind.[70]

1937 was a significant year. It saw the publication of *Glass in Architecture and Decoration* by R. McGrath and A. C. Frost, that had been funded by Pilkington's, and the conversion of two London and North Eastern Railway (LNER) coaches as a touring exhibition centre.[71] Designed by Kenneth Cheesman the company had acquired a 'Glass Train', that was practical, in that it used the full range of glass, and visionary in its imaginative creation of glass rooms. Starting out from Doncaster in the first week in November, technicians, architects and builders were still the primary audience, but the train constituted the first occasion on which a large-scale appeal was made to the general public, showing householders and potential householders what could be done with glass.

The exterior, apart from the roof, was covered in strips of 'Vitroflex', a flexible mirrored glass, with 'The Glass Age Exhibition Train' in glass letters. Going through the entrance hall of black 'Vitroflex', to a pink and ivory bathroom, a vestibule of silvered plate glass, tango walls of 'Vitrolite' and 'Vitroflex', and a cocktail bar of ivory and cadmium yellow (figure 25), the highpoint of the tour was 'The Rotunda', achieved by the semi-circular hall reflected by a wall of mirror glass. It was furnished with a plate glass table, decorative lighting of radiating fins of 'Armourplate' glass, a floor of silvered glass tiles, and an illuminated screen of glass rolling pins set in front of clear prismatic glass. There were other displays illustrating the technical and decorative uses, but it was the rooms that captured the magic of glass and captivated the public imagination in the railway sidings of provincial railway stations.[72]

New materials and services had contributed much to the redesigning of living space, but as significant had been the growing attention to the demands for adaptability. The 1937 Ideal Home Exhibition had been a curious affair. Anticipating the Coronation celebrations it had a Golden Hall of Homage, with the statue of the King and decorations representing the people of the Empire, installations on historic Scotland in honour of the Queen, and reproductions of rooms of historic monarchs. It also gave a glimpse of the future with an extensive display of televisions, and the

25 Kenneth Cheesman, 'The Glass Age Train', 1937. Cocktail bar, in cadmium yellow and pure bright blue, with a clear and silvered prismatic glass ceiling.

'All-in' home by R. A. Duncan, which, while being a conventional model of the upper middle-class detached house, had internal steel supports that allowed the interior walls to be rearranged and adapted to meet new family requirements. It was this move to large living spaces that could be sub-divided by the rearrangement of the furniture and the greater use of lightweight and multi-purpose furniture that was comprehensively recorded in *The Flat Book* of 1939 by J. L. Martin and S Speight, husband and wife architects. Although describing the equipment, furnishing and layout of the flat, in its observations and arguments it was just as relevant to house design.

> The object of the designer is to provide more space and greater freedom. One urgent demand, particularly in the case of the low rental family flat, is for a form of planning which will meet the needs of large families or even make possible an enlargement or decrease in the size of flat to satisfy changing family conditions.[73]

That summarised the basis of both the current and future design objectives.

New services and people's pleasures

Family welfare

At its outset the 1930s had anticipated change, even expected change to characterise the new world. Architects, designers and planners had hoped for a new unity of expression and order of purpose out of which would come a modern society freed from the anachronisms of the past. It had been anticipated that just as mass-production would put the products of industry within the reach of all sections of society relieving social inequalities, so art would play its part, 'essential, in one form or another, to the life of every intelligent and civilized human being'.[74] This influence did not produce the social progress that had been expected, but in promoting the ideals there had been a growing recognition of the importance of the new means of communication in shaping a cultural democracy. For example, it was not just that there were more exhibitions on homes, artifacts and neighbourhoods, but their ideological purpose was increased by booklets and broadcast discussions. In a radio talk on 29 January 1932, Dr C. Delisle Burns identified how 'The new machines for entertainment make for similarity of outlook and attitude among people of very different occupations, incomes or social class ... The gramophone, cinema and radio are bridging the traditional gaps between distinct groups of people.'[75] These changes were part of the inheritance from the 1920s, but what distinguished this new phase of development was the authority now attached to the radio broadcast. *The Listener*, first issued in January 1929, had established itself, and with the new Broadcasting House coming into use in the spring of 1932, the BBC had a capital presence which enhanced its national identity.[76] In terms of the assimilation of ideas and outlook, it was perceived as a revolution, 'the invasion of the narrow world of home by a wider world outside',[77] an essential part of the pleasures of the home, in which the ideal family was imaged as following serious pursuits, the father reading the newspaper, mother knitting, and children reading a book or doing their homework (figure 26).

It was already well understood that if this model of a stable family life was to be achieved then more progress would have to be made on the quality of the nation's health and the provision of more adequate neighbourhood centres. Through the 1920s health centres and child welfare clinics had become an established part of community provision, usually housed in practical undistinguished buildings. The change of approach came as a consequence of distinguishing between health and healthy living. The first and most radical expression of this thinking was the private Pioneer Health Centre, Peckham, 1934–35, by Sir E. Owen Williams, with its swimming pool, gymnasium and theatre, as well as children's playground and nursery, which had for the first time designed facilities with the family

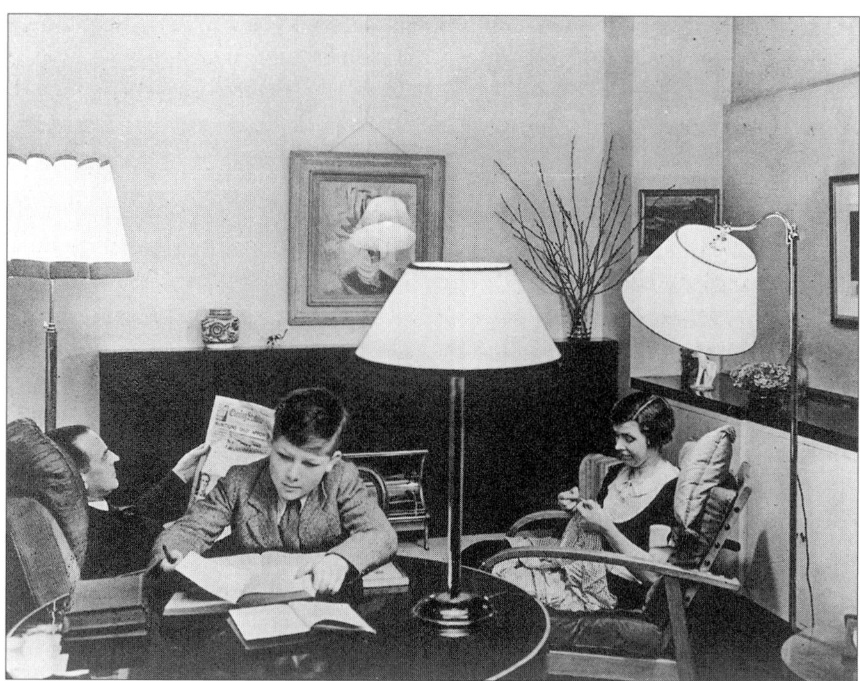

26 The electric home. The dining room as sitting room. Each person with their own lamp, late 1930s.

in mind. The only comparable initiative was to be the local authority Finsbury Health Centre, 1935–38, by Tecton. While these were both city area developments, there was a growing awareness of the lack of community amenities on the new out of town housing estates. By 1935 these views were being articulated in a number of official pamphlets that underlined the problems of living on estates that had had no natural organic growth, were limited to a social-economic group of one class and, unlike a village or town, had no local government status to enable them to take action on their own future, or resources to establish their community identity.[78] The proposition was to construct community centres for general civic needs, catering for young and old, providing libraries, meeting halls, sports facilities and performance space. A broader strategy was outlined in a published memorandum of 1936 by the Department of Health for Scotland, when recreation grounds were added to the community centre. This developed into a national movement and, at a conference in April 1937, Sir Kingsley Wood summarised its ambitions.

> The ultimate aim of good housing, as of all other social services, was the establishment of a full and happy life. The provision of good healthy houses, though of fundamental importance, was not enough. There was a real need for the development of communal and social interests. This meant the provision on large estates not only of shopping centres and schools but also of open spaces for outdoor games and recreations and community centres with assembly halls, clubrooms, and work-rooms, which should provide for a wide range of activities.[79]

New building programmes were overtaken by the war years, but it was an important step towards ensuring that greater provision for physical education and fitness became a recognised part of the health programme and social framework of the family.

The running of clubs, associations and recreational facilities had been dependent on voluntary and charitable commitments, but with the passing of the Physical Training and Recreation Act in July 1937, a new national responsibility emerged. By October 1937 it had been constructed and launched as a campaign for national health. Following on from a general introduction, it concentrated on the health of the mother and child in the November and December, the schools' medical services in the January, topical problems of such diseases as tuberculosis in February, and culminated with fitness in March 1938. Nothing and nobody was left out of the campaign, 'It behoves the good citizen, then, not only so far as he can to keep himself and his family fit and try to make them fitter, but to take a practical interest in the health of the community'.[80]

The importance of the outdoor life was only exceeded by the emphasis placed on the quality of homelife, with the woman, as mother and housewife, playing a pivotal role caring for and encouraging child development.

> The desiderata for women as wife and mother are charm and gentleness; a balanced personality, which is the outward sign of inward harmony between body, mind, and spirit; a physique that has never suffered undue strain and so will enable her to companion her husband in all his various outdoor pursuits; a law of health, if there be one, to make motherhood an event fraught with the minimum of risk, both to herself and to her progeny; finally, a knowledge of the body's functionings, which will equip her to lead her children expertly, out of ignorance, to faulty figures and unsound health. Woman is the creator, or the potential creator, of generations to come, the architect of the future.[81]

Not for the woman, strength and muscles, but grace, poise and self-expression, as promoted by the Women's League of Health and Beauty.

During 1938, the 'National Fitness Campaign' held non-partisan public meetings across the country, promoting the case of decent conditions and health to enjoy them.[82] A major exhibition on 'Health, Sport and Fitness' was organised by the Royal Institute of British Architects and, after showing in London, it travelled the country. Its theme was constructed around the uses of open spaces, walking and cycling, and the provision of organised facilities. It gave a hint of things to come with a model of a Sports Centre and recreation ground for a town of 250,000. Against this background it was little wonder that health and fitness was a significant feature of the Empire Exhibition, Glasgow. Opened to the public on 3 May 1938, there was a Physical Fitness pavilion on the edge of the exhibition, and the Fitter Britain Hall formed a prominent part of the United Kingdom pavilion. Overall, in architectural style and themes, there was a continuous referencing of a clean and healthy future.

It was a time when the greatest number of schoolchildren were still attending schools that had no gymnasiums, sports fields, and no specialist sports/PE staff. Any direct involvement in sport was dependent on local clubs, and unless this was organised by young people's groups, such as scouts and girl guides, most children would not become involved in sports until they left school at 14 years of age and accessed the works or local club facilities. The one exception to this pattern was access to the public swimming baths. Other amenities were slow to be provided, but, nevertheless, considerable progress was made in securing new playing fields for public and school use. Local authorities were obliged by the new legislation to make the necessary provision in schools, and such was the level of poverty amongst the pupils that the schools had to be equipped with

27 The mobile shop, 1936

boxes of assorted sizes of pumps for children to use during the lesson. No other sports clothing was expected.

Improvements in bus travel were slowly increasing the opportunities for those living in outlying districts to take advantage of city facilities, and the city dweller was able to escape into the country. But, for the municipal bus companies serving the new housing estates built as part of slum clearance programmes, maintaining a reasonable service throughout the day was creating great problems. In a paper delivered by the Leeds Transport Department Manager to the 1934 annual conference of the Municipal Tramways and Transport Association, these were identified as inadequate roads between the city and the new estates, the demands of operating adequate morning and evening peak services, and the financial difficulties of meeting the off-peak needs of the casual passengers. The result was a serious underprovision for shopping and social needs. In this context the travelling shop gathered increasing importance (figure 27). Available in a diverse range of bodies, including streamlined and highly colourful livery, the vehicles served outlining villages and estates, and catered for passing trade, sports events and other recreational outlets. In 1934 Vauxhall launched a major campaign to promote 'The Bedford Shop on Wheels', the 'Big Income from Shops That Move'.

> Already there are Shops that Move in use as boot repairing vans, optical sight-testing rooms, hot lunch conveyances, ice cream vans, fried fish shops, ironmongery stores, electrical equipment demonstrator-sales shops, and so on and on – but there is plenty of rooms for cafés, country produce shops, arterial road shops, farmer-butcher dairy produce shops, hairdressing establishments, grocers and greengrocers, and fishmongers.[83]

Service to urban and suburban homes was also extended from 1933 onwards with the growing popularity of the light electric van, particularly popular for milk delivery. It was not just commercial interests that took advantage of these developments, municipal authorities also began to employ them for a range of public services. The mobile library was introduced of which Manchester claimed to have been the pioneer, while Northumberland took delivery of a trailer fully equipped as a dental surgery.

Family outings

Steadily the motor industry had moved from the specialised to the mass-produced, and the second-hand car market extended ownership further down the social line. In 1920 there were some 90 car manufacturers, which by the end of the 1930s was reduced to 20 organisations, with Austin, Ford, Nuffield, Rootes, Standard and Vauxhall accounting for 90 per cent of the market. Output had increased from 71,000 in 1923 to 390,000 in 1937. Luxury cars, coachbuilt and streamlined, caught the public imagination and inspired a new aesthetic for British cars that sought to express speed through elegant lines. But the age of the small family car was in place, and it was the economic utilitarian models that changed the culture of motoring and extended the potential of car ownership. By the early 1930s there were three small standard cars that offered middle-income motoring, the Austin Seven, Morris Eight and Ford Popular. The time had come when the motor car was 'regarded as much an essential part of the household equipment as the wireless or gramophone'.[84]

Accepted by many as an indispensable part of modern life, the new car owners found themselves accused of unsocial behaviour, being blamed for spoiling Britain's beauty spots, and guilty for 'the enormous growth of the great suburban rings of shoddy villas surrounding London and the big provincial towns and their derivative satellite bungalow communal groupings'.[85] The fact was that the professionals and upper middle classes disliked even more having to share the freedoms that came with motoring with those families that would have put the car away for the winter, and spent Easter getting the car ready for summer months of picnics in the country and runs down to the coast (figure 28).

The grandeur of Victoria Coach Station, the new coach stations for the Green Line services for the home counties and at seaside resorts, such as

GETTING READY FOR EASTER!
Exide
EASTER OFFER of
battery inspection and tuning up

28 Bringing the car out of winter store. Family motoring, 1932

the one at Bournemouth, confirmed that luxury coach travel had arrived. The established seaside resorts were enjoying record trade as the coach trippers swelled the rail excursions. Blackpool claimed to have the largest number of visitors of any British resort, with some 6,000,000 to 7,000,000 coming during the season. There were over 1,000 coach operators licensed to run tours into Blackpool, while the town had forty coach companies running day trips to other Lancashire seaside resorts and Lakeland towns. Astutely they had extended the season with the illuminations running on into late October.[86]

The scale of this industry is well illustrated by the account of the last weekend of the 1934 illuminations.

> The number of trains additional to the ordinary time-table today totals 129. The first reached the town from Newcastle before six o'clock. A second followed it half-an-hour later from Cardiff. Not until 3.30 to-morrow morning will the last train depart, its destination Swansea. The total number of special trains during this grand finale week-end reaches 215.[87]

Although not yet complete, Blackpool was in the process of going modern. Conscious of the symbolic significance of the Midland Hotel at Morecambe and the plans for the De La Warr pavilion at Bexhill on Sea, the architect Joseph Emberton was in the middle of a total redesign of the Pleasure Beach: the Fun House recently completed, the Grand National under construction, and a new Casino projected for future development.[88] Blackpool was well established as the pleasure centre of working-class culture,[89] and yet there was a sense in which modernism was being used to attract a new audience, the middle classes. They were not alone in making this connection between style and class. Equally good examples can be found in the designs by W. A. Johnson for new retail stores for the Cooperative Society, which in a deliberate move to attract the middle-class customer were going modern, first at Southport in July 1934, followed by Bradford in 1936 and Huddersfield in 1937. Of course in the process of this change the working classes were also enjoying the pleasures of the modern store.

Time and again the evidence is of social exclusivity being breached for mass enjoyment. Trippers traditionally satisfied with the established resorts, through the construction of new roads and improvement of existing roads were travelling greater distances and discovering new landscapes. For example, with the construction of the road from Perth to Inverness, and from Glasgow through Glencoe to Inverness, and road improvements between Glasgow and Carlisle, and Edinburgh and Berwick, a new era of tourism was opening up for Scotland, and not just for the private motorist: 'To-day men and women in the humblest walks of life may travel with their families by luxuriously-furnished motor coaches in the most perfect comfort, and enjoy the delights of the countryside or seaside at comparatively little cost.'[90] This idea of freedom, whether it was collective or individual, became a major part of British culture, and the escape from the drudgery of urban life into the countryside or the coast was one of the pleasures of the new age of motoring. The family picnic in a pastoral corner of Britain became a popular image, as did the weekend trip to the new roadhouses, but it was the growth of caravanning that brought a new dimension to middle-class family holidays, fulfilling the role of a weekend cottage on wheels.

The concept of the moving house had been integral to motoring since the legalisation of motor transport on British roads. Initially the development was through the construction of a motor home on a commercial vehicle chassis, complete with dining rooms, bedrooms and servants' quarters. Being heavy, and with limited manoeuvrability, their freedom to travel was extremely limited. However, by 1920 the value of a lightweight trailer, with an ash frame, covered in plywood, canvas or aluminium had been accepted as the future model, even to the extent of being offered as an alternative home on a permanent basis. The trailer tent was also being developed, and smaller versions of the motor homes. The cosy, comfortable trailer caravan, with bay windows and chintz curtains was a popular choice, and at first it is easy to underestimate the important design developments taking place as stoves and storage, and foldaway beds were fitted into the minimum space. Eccles, which had rapidly established itself as one of major manufacturers, put considerable emphasis on its bed design, that could convert into a settee and also provide luxurious sleeping. The trailer caravan was expensive to purchase, ranging from £200 to £400, but from the mid-1920s it was possible to hire one for holidays, while the trailer tent at a cost of £45 to £50, catered for the small car owner.

In 1932 an event of national importance took place, when on Saturday, 27 August, the first caravan rally was held at Minehead. Organised by the *Autocar*, there was a competition for the best-presented caravan in a variety of categories, a parade of caravans on the Esplanade, and concluding in the evening with a ball at the Hotel Metropole. The meeting had assembled the night before.

> Caravan enthusiasts are happy, carefree folk and friendships were soon formed, so that cocktail parties were being held to the music of gramophone or wireless, or visits were being exchanged and happy half-hours spent in examining the various caravans and the many cunning devices for increasing comfort or saving space which they one and all contained.[91]

During the 1920s caravans had been shown at the annual motor show at Olympia as part of the coachbuilding section, but in 1933 they were given their own much enlarged section and as with the rest of the industry enthusiastically embraced streamlining. In April 1933, The Camping Club of Great Britain and Ireland held its first National Exhibition of Camping at the Imperial Institute, and while as a family pursuit it was still essentially a leisure activity for the middle classes, camping was broadening its appeal. Short-term holiday camps had operated since the 1890s, run by religious and political groups, organised by companies for their workers, and by local authorities for poor children. Steadily through the 1920s permanent sites of caravans, prefabricated huts and converted railway coaches began to fill coastal sites around Britain. Along with speculative housing development it became the focus of intense campaigning by the Council for the Preservation of Rural England (CPRE). By 1934, the weekend bungalow popularised by the Edwardian families, in its mass-produced form and vernacular forms was seen as the creeping menace strangling Britain's natural beauty.[92]

Although they did not prevent this type of erosion, the development of the designed holiday camp marked an important stage in the recognition of the leisure needs of working-class families.

> The passion for camping spread because it was cheap, a complete change from everyday life, romantic, and took place in the country. But of the very large number who embarked on camping holidays the very great majority had no appreciation of its less obvious pleasures. This majority did not want to be by themselves, did not like being three miles from the shops, did not understand how to look after camping gear; and the wives especially did not like cooking on unfamiliar contrivances with the children on top of them.[93]

With the opening of Skegness in 1936, Gorleston-on-Sea and Clacton in 1937, Rogerson Hall, Corton, in 1938, and the impressive Prestatyn Holiday Camp, by W. H. Hamlyn for LMS railway company (London Midland Scottish), in 1939, the mass holiday that blended freedom with care was in place.[94] Squires Gate, Blackpool, publicised itself as the 'Californian Holiday Camp', offering every imaginable facility, and providing a healthy time for all the family.

From April through to May 1939, a Holiday Camp exhibition was held at the Housing Centre, London, but at the first meeting of the Board of the National Camps Corporation, Ltd, on 4 April, a different type of camp had to be planned. Preparing for the evacuation of children was the priority. Thirty sites were selected, and by August 1939, fourteen camps were under construction. Architectural responsibility for the scheme was given to Sir John Burnet, Tait and Lorne, with a designated local architect responsible for any adaptation to the site. Prefabricated western red cedar buildings were chosen as the standard model, both for ease of assembly and cost.

Circumstance had brought the architectural debate back to the prefabrication of temporary structures as solutions to the housing problem, and to fundamental questions regarding the practical and expressive purposes of design. There was now a better understanding of the benefits of new technology and the requirements of small living spaces, but opinions on the relative merits of flats and houses remained deeply divided. Unresolved, this problem shaped an agenda that was to preoccupy architects, planners and politicians throughout the emergency years.

Notes

1 *Architects' Journal*, 10 January 1935, pp. 75–86.

2 *Ibid.*, p. 80.

3 *Ibid.*, p. 82.

4 N. Carrington, *Design and a Changing Civilisation*, London, 1935, p. 128.

5 H. H. Humphries, 'Municipal Housing', *The Listener*, 30 September 1931, p. 541.

6 See BBC series, 'Other People's Houses', *The Listener*, 18 January 1933, p. 73.

7 Designs were by Miss Janet Fletcher and Mrs Alison Shepherd.

8 J. G. Ledeboer, 'New Homes for Old', *Design for Today*, November 1934, p. 408.

9 Modern Architectural Research group (MARS) was established in 1931.

10 *Architects' Journal*, 23 April 1936. p. 609.

11 The exhibition was available for touring.

12 *Architect & Building News*, 22 July 1932, p. 86.

13 The overall dimensions gave 735 sq. ft., but in real living space this was probably nearer to 650 sq. ft.

14 These included Bowmans, Camden Town, John Lewis & Co. Ltd, The Rowley Gallery and Michael Dawn, Bedford.

15 E. Denby, 'Planning Future Cities', *Design for Today*, April 1934, p. 126.

16 D. Brooke, 'Brighter London', *Electrical Age*, 1938, p. 425.

17 See *Ideal Home*, April 1939; *Architect & Building News*, 17 March, 1939.

18 E. Denby, *Europe Re-housed*, London, 1938, p. 269.

19 *Ibid.*, p. 272.

20 *Builder*, 19 January 1934, p. 121.

21 Less well known, yet just as interesting, was the exhibition pavilion designed by Marcel Breuer and F. R. S. Yorke for the Royal Agricultural Show, Bristol, in 1936, which combined traditional squared-rubble walls with a flat timber roof and large plate glass windows, to create four distinct living spaces to display furniture.

22 *Churston South Devon*, Dartington Hall Ltd, 1935.

23 'Britain's First Modernist Town', *Building*, December 1934, p. 486.

24 *Clacton Times & East Essex Gazette*, 5 January 1935, p. 14.

25 The exhibition was to tour the country, starting in Stoke, moving on to Cheltenham and Luton, and other venues arranged by the RIBA.

26 *Journal of the RIBA*, 7 November 1938, p. 25.

27 *Ibid.*, p. 25.

28 *Ibid.*, p. 26.

29 Letter from Eve to Stewart, 7 December 1933.

30 See *Architects Journal*, 5 August 1931, p. 167, on discussion of its impact on the countryside. The Housing (Rural Workers) Act, 1937 put the focus on grants to modernise rural workers' cottages, and was much publicised by leaflets, posters and in the December through an exhibition at the Housing Centre, London.

31 By 1939 it was being suggested that these restrictions should be relaxed.

32 The chief executive officer was L. D. Gammans, recently retired from the Malayan Civil Service.

33 A variety of training programmes was in operation, particularly in support of allotments for the unemployed. For example, Sheffield had one at Derwentwater, there was a school of Reconstruction & Land settlement at Hillend, Edinburgh, and a training centre at Chisledon, near Swindon.

34 Twenty-four sites were identified for development, of which twenty-one were

established. The Forestry Commission, that came into being with the 1919 Forestry Act, favoured the continuing use of smallholdings, whereby seasonal work could be supplemented by the holding.

35 Designs for the early developments were by Pakington and Enthoven, and the cottage homesteads by A. G. S. Fidler.

36 *Picture Post,* 11 February 1939, p. 48.

37 *The Healthy Future for you and your Family,* Land Settlement Association, London, n.d., p. 23.

38 T. Alwyn Lloyd, 'Land Settlement Schemes in Wales', *Journal of the RIBA,* 22 May 1939. p. 719.

39 These settlements were at Boverton and Fferm-Goch in Glamorgan, Sealand Major in Flint and Llanfair-Discoed in Monmouth.

40 J. Gloag (ed.), *Design in Modern Life,* London, 1934, p. 24.

41 E. Maxwell Fry, 'The design of dwellings', in *ibid.,* p. 33.

42 J. Gloag, 'Who knows what the public wants?', in *ibid.,* p. 26.

43 F. Pick, 'The meaning and purpose of design', in *ibid.,* p. 133.

44 *Design for To-day,* September 1933, p. 186.

45 From 1937 local authorities were instigating hire purchase schemes to help provide furniture for the families being rehoused in slum clearance programmes or from temporary dwellings. St Helens were prepared to allow up to £11 credit, Chesterfield £12. It could be used for purchasing new and second-hand furniture. Blackburn had a scheme which allowed an expenditure of up to £18, but the furniture remained the property of the authority, while Worcester arranged for repayment of loans by including it in the rent.

46 An exhibition of contemporary furniture, April 1936, by seven architects, Marcel Breuer, F. R. S. Yorke, E. Maxwell Fry, Brian O'Rorke, Jack Howe, Raymond McGrath and Christopher Nicholson was probably its outstanding event of the 1930s.

47 Heelas, *Beautiful Homes Magazine,* February 1939, p. 1.

48 The extent to which these values were being adopted by mainstream popular taste is well illustrated by the Times Furnishing Company's publication in 1939 of six free booklets on how to furnish the modern home in style and with modest outlay, by reputable writers such as Derek Patmore, Grace Lovat Fraser and Elizabeth White.

49 A. Bertram, *Design,* London, 1938, p. 39.

50 *Ibid.,* p. 74.

51 Council for Art and Industry, *The Working Class Home Its Furnishing and Equipment,* London, 1937, p. 46.

52 *Ibid.,* p. 42–3.

53 British Electrical Development Association, *All-Electric House,* Vicarage Road, Edgbaston, 1932, p. 2.

54 *Ibid.,* p. 6.

55 'The E.A.W. House at Bristol', *The Electrical Age,* January 1936, p. 21.

56 The R. E. Sassoon House, Peckham, 1934, by Maxwell Fry in association with Elizabeth Denby, was also an all-gas block of twenty working-class flats.

57 The Times, *National Health Number,* 1937, p. 1.

58 J. M. Richards *An Introduction to Modern Architecture*, London, 1940, p. 111.

59 B. Friedman (ed.), *Flats, Municipal and Private Enterprise*, London, 1938, p. 282.

60 *Ibid.*, p. 279.

61 The Exhibition also hosted the Electrical Association for Women conference, 'The New Way of Living: Women's Work in the Modern World'.

62 'Scientific Household Management', *The Electrical Age*, October 1932, p. 407.

63 See M. G. Reading, 'Tuesday I Clean', *The Electrical Age*, Spring 1939, p. 534.

64 N. Carrington, *Design and a Changing Civilisation*, 1935. p. 55.

65 Although costs of using electricity were coming down, the £30 per annum suggested for the all-electric Bristol house were still high for a working-class family budget,

66 L. B. Atkinson, 'Women and Electricity', *The Electrical Age*, July 1930, p. 8.

67 C. Creedy, 'Kitchen Affairs', *Electrical Housekeeping*, October 1933, p. 3.

68 See *Design and Construction*, December 1931, p. 94.

69 Pilkington's had shown the largest sheet of plate glass in the world at the 1924 Wembley Exhibition.

70 In time there were problems with the adhesive, and in 1957 wholesale alterations removed all of the external surfaces and details.

71 In 1934 HMV had a three-coach national show train, decorated in chromium, rose and cream, and displayed more than thirty different radios and gramophones. In the mid-1930s Fry's had its chocolate train.

72 The 'Glass House' competition run by the Building Centre for the 1938 *Daily Mail* Ideal Home Exhibition had little of this design flair, although the winning design by N. H. Cuthbertson and D. W. Notley using a pre-cast reinforced concrete frame, was partly rescued by being set on a terrace in the exhibition hall, that gave an added expression to the cantilevered first floor.

73 J. L. Martin and S. Speight, *The Flat Book*, London, 1939, p. 9.

74 J. E. Barton, *The Changing World. Vol. 6 Modern Art*, London, 1932, p. 3.

75 Dr C. Delisle Burns, 'Modern Entertainment the Leveller', *The Listener*, 3 February 1932, p. 183.

76 BBC royal charter on 1 January 1927.

77 *Ibid.*, p. 183.

78 *New Housing Estates and their Social Problems*, National Council of Social Service, London, 1935. *Report on the Need for Youth Community Centres on New Housing Estates*, Board of Education, London, 1935. *Community Life in New Housing Schemes*, Department of Health for Scotland, No. 88, London, 1936.

79 *Builder*, 16 April 1937, p. 843.

80 Sir Kingsley Wood, 'The March to Health', *Times Supplement*, 30 September 1937, p. iv.

81 P. Stack, 'Physical Culture for Women', *Ibid.* p. xvi.

82 Coincided with the 'National Mark' campaign, 1938, organised by the Ministry of Agriculture & Fisheries, for quality foodstuffs to get housewives to buy home produce.

83 *Big Income from Shops that Move*, Vauxhall advertising campaign, *c.* 1934, p. 11.

84 *The Scotsman*, 8 January 1935, p. 13.

85 'Current Architecture', *Building*, September 1935, p. 350.

86 See *Commercial Motor*, 5 October 1934, p. 244.

87 *Blackpool Gazette & Herald*, 20 October 1934, p. 24.

88 The original Pleasure Beach had been opened in 1894, on what were undeveloped sand dunes, but the real beginning was in 1910 with the ejection of a gypsy encampment and the formation of a limited company. Three years later a baroque-style casino was opened, and a pleasureland that was not dissimilar to those created for major national and international exhibitions was in place.

89 The largest Woolworth's department store in Britain, 1936–38, was built on an island site next to the Tower. Commercial American in style and concept, the basement and ground floor was given over to merchandising, and the first and second floors to self-service cafeterias.

90 *S.M.T. Magazine*, May 1935, p. 123.

91 *Autocar*, 2 September 1932, p. 435.

92 This did not reduce its popularity for the middle classes. The main attraction of the 1938 Woman's Fair, was the Week-End Cottage designed by Clive Entwhistle, in association with Le Corbusier. A rectangle, 44½ ft. × 32 ft., the living accommodation was effectively an 'L' shape, with a patio/carport, and enclosed lawn taking up about a third of the space. In an effort to emphasise how modern architecture could blend into the countryside, the external walls were finished in a pale-green colour wash, the steel beams a grey-tinted lilac and the flat roof covered in turf.

93 'The Army Under Canvas', *Architects' Journal*, 1 September 1938, p. 47.

94 Holidays with Pay Act, 1938, boosted the number of holidays being taken.

4 ✧ Emergency, economy and modernisation, 1940–53

Planning for the future

The emergency years

On 31 August 1939 the Ministry of Health ordered the evacuation programme of large towns. The following day London began the evacuation of children, expectant and nursing mothers, invalids and the blind. Food rationing commenced on 8 January 1940. These were totally new experiences for British society, and together were to give a new edge to the debate on national standards and the failure of architecture and design to meet the basic social needs.

Throughout the 1930s municipal authorities had struggled with the demands of slum clearance and the social problems that accompanied the unremitting poverty endured by as much as 15 per cent of the urban population. Research reports and newspaper campaigns had well publicised the scale of the problem, but it was the evacuation which brought middle-class families and country towns face to face with the reality of poverty. The scale of the differences of expectations and opportunities, health and hygiene, education, social behaviour and morality, diet and lifestyle were exposed. It was as though the country had discovered a primitive tribe living in its midst.[1]

A time when much emphasis was placed on self-help, the growing of vegetables and making new outfits by restructuring pre-war fashion are well-known examples. The significance of making more of home town resources for leisure and holidays has perhaps been less appreciated. Every local authority arranged 'holidays at home' programmes, with organised events and entertainments in the public parks, and some even continued this provision after the war.[2] Increasingly there was a belief in the social benefits to be gained from national initiatives and central control. In some instances this was only for the short term, such as the opening of the civic restaurants for the blitzed and emergency workers. By October 1940 there were about 60 civic eating centres in London and, at their peak in 1943, there were over 2,000 restaurants across Britain serving more than 500,000 meals a day.[3]

The emergency was tangible: rationing, rising costs and dispersed families all tested national resolve. Little could be done about the present, and attention concentrated on discussing, dreaming and planning for the future, considering the residue of unfulfilled plans, while at the same time projecting hope for the future life of the family in peacetime.

Dream homes

In 1940, Ralph Tubbs arranged the travelling exhibition 'Living Cities', which was subsequently published in book form by Penguin. The theme was that decay could be stopped if planning was implemented on a sufficiently large scale. Dismissive of nineteenth-century exploitation, and alarmed by traffic congestion and suburban sprawl, Tubbs restated 1930s ideals, urging that positive advantage should be taken of the destruction by bombing. In effect this meant pulling down the Victorian 'follies' and clearing the revivalist and ribbon development crimes of the twentieth century, whilst keeping the medieval cathedrals and eighteenth-century squares in new plans. Family life was at the core of his thesis: 'The father will want to be near his workplace, his wife near a market for household shopping and near smart shops for special things. The whole family will want to be near a park and to have opportunities for social life.'[4] There was considerable concern that the needs of children should be catered for, and families would be living in a healthy sun-drenched environment, enjoying the open-air life, theatres and concerts. The vision was for trouble-free areas by mixing blocks with terraces to create squares, zoning services and amenities, all interlinked by roads, yet it showed a limited understanding of the mechanics of family life, the social problems of poverty and unemployment, and community as an integration of localised resources. Nevertheless it was a popular vision, enthusiastically endorsed by the *Picture Post* 'Plan for Britain', 4 January 1941, with its proposals for a 'juster, healthier, happier Britain'.[5] Great importance was attached to the selection of photographs to reinforce the ideas, and none was more powerful than the front cover with the laughing, shouting nursery children sitting on a slide, enjoying the sunshine in nothing other than their shoes. It was for this generation that the country was fighting and planning. Maxwell Fry, writing about town planning, argued the modernist theme, anticipating a cheerful, civilised, coherent plan replacing the current hap-hazard development. Image after image reinforced an argument for the wholesale demolition of existing urban settlements, setting the evils of the unplanned against the planned grid system that would separate commercial, industrial and domestic facilities. Considering the limitations of the inter-war reconstruction it was astonishing that the blueprint for the future was seen in such simple terms, but there was no doubt of the popularity of a thesis that argued for a greater level of public ownership and standardisation to overcome social inequalities. Elizabeth Denby developed the same ideals for the working-class home, although in offering a picture of the planned kitchen as the housewife's dream, the image was of the spacious, fully equipped middle-class kitchen. Attempting to resolve the tensions between the home as a 'machine' that would enable the housewife to operate with maximum efficiency and economy, and to which 'the family returns with relief and satisfaction',[6] was the core of the proposals on the layout and services. The recommendation was for living rooms to be west or south facing with maximum privacy, while 'the kitchen, the workshop, should look on to the street, so that the woman can join, however indirectly in the life of the neighbourhood'.[7] Explaining the benefits of a dining-room-kitchen and study bedrooms, her ideas acutely anticipated the demands of minimum living space. On the problems of the family laundry, Denby reiterated her objections to the communal laundries in favour of a cheap efficient laundry service, leaving small items for the housewife to wash. As a special issue it was powerful and influential material that, in dealing with work, welfare, education, health, land and leisure, prompted an avalanche of letters which in the main were enthusiastic at the prospect of a new democratic civilisation in which culture would become accessible to the general public.

The following month *Ideal Home* began a series of articles on houses, 'Planning for the Future', which ran intermittently through to 1945. Serving as a reminder that the rich families would also need homes, the emphasis was on design of the large luxury detached house, outlining ideas on thatched, neo-Georgian, modernist or just modern. Space and services were much discussed, offering advice on the easy-to-run, and the quiet and compact houses. After the introductory article the series became a platform for invited architects to expound their vision of the post-war house, starting with the 'House that Grows' by Mrs Doris Howard Robertson. A house with a sun terrace and air-conditioning, it was designed with bathrooms on both floors, so that it could be used as one house or two flats. There were references to Frank Lloyd Wright's 'Falling Water', detailed discussion by F. R. S. Yorke of the house he had designed with Marcel Breuer, and an 'inexpensive house' by Elizabeth Denby. R. Myerscough-Walker attacked the 'horrid man-made rectangles' that were imposed on the landscape and, considering the standardised housing as emergency shelter, he looked forward to the time when 'The house of the future will grow out of the earth; it will be moulded to the site'.[8] It was left to Erno Goldfinger to put the case for the public housing of the multi-storey block.[9] Goldfinger was concerned that each member of the family had his or her own individual space, that the dwelling should have good storage, central heating and maximum amount of sunshine. Visualised as a home for a family with two teenage children, significantly it made no reference to the problems of the family laundry, a problem of many pre-war housing schemes, and the basis of many of the problems of post-war housing.

The most articulate introduction to the way in which the ideals were taking shape was provided by the lecture series at the Royal Society of Arts, from November 1941 to May 1942, and published as *The Post-War Home: Its Interior and Equipment*. It championed the rights of the wage-earner, the happiness of the children and the home as symbol of national values. Decent living conditions, with new standards of finish and space was the basis of Howard Robertson's introductory lecture. Elizabeth Denby focused on the need for 'the illusion of additional space',[10] by astute interior design of arrangement and colour, and effective grouping of services, and vigorously argued in favour of the dining-kitchen, objecting to the way in which refined middle-class taste had conspired against its use. F. R. Yerbury outlined the needs for standardisation and prefabrication. Mrs Darcy Braddell yearned for the lost traditions of English furniture design, hoping that by returning to the values of the arts and crafts movement and the more recent example set by Sweden, matters would improve. Having dealt with the aesthetics, she explained how the practicalities of the contemporary home should be met by concentrating on built-in furniture.

The underlying theme of the series was one of social responsibility, and it was George Hicks, Parliamentary Secretary, Ministry of Works and Buildings, and Helen Masters, Head of the Battersea Domestic Science Training College, who forcefully made the case for the family. Hicks was concerned that proper attention should be given to the tenants' viewpoint on housing needs and general preferences of the working-class family. As in the aftermath of the First World War, he saw the home and needs of the mother and child as the priority issue: 'the home is rooted in the imagination and environment and the life of the occupier ... If we want to help in lifting mankind to the position in society and in life of the world which he should occupy, we must create a home where a man and his wife can live in health and happiness'.[11] Masters gave a timely warning of the dangers of an overemphasis on the efficiency demanded of the housewife, with routines that imposed on the comfort of the family and made no provision for emergencies or necessary modifications. In taking this line her real purpose was to attack the social and intellectual snobbery shown towards domestic work, asking, 'Would it be too much to hope that we might after the war see the opening of a new era in home life, based on the realisation that the running of the house and the home should be a co-operative family affair in which all must have a share, and to which all must make a contribution?'[12] Her dream was for a Swiss Family Robinson home life of shared responsibility, but few were listening to this ideal.

There were others who kept the home and the housewife at the centre of debates on the post-war reconstruction. From June 1942 through to 1944, the Cooperative Building Society issued thirty-five booklets in two series on 'Design for Britain', underlining the social imperatives of housing and planning for post-war Britain. Deserving more attention than can be offered in this study, good housing was the dominant theme meeting the needs of the family and strengthening 'British life that, in the days of peace ahead, this country will have the means wherefrom in the greater ennoblement of her own people she may add to the dignity, culture and happiness of the world itself. Good houses, the need of all, must contribute to the good of all'.[13]

Ethel Mannin argued the case for women architects, for women of all classes on town planning councils, and an increased cooperation between architects and housewives. Other papers had accepted that if housing targets were to be met then it would be necessary for some flats to be included in the building programme. Mannin was adamant that this should not happen, and neither should there be distinctions in provision because of differences of class. She believed that by cooperative effort

> the humblest may realise their dream of a house worth living in, that dream inherent in every home-loving person's heart, of a little place that is really one's own, that really represents security, the little place that 'lies high', like the best people's places, and stands alone in its garden. It is probably the most common of all English dreams, for the English dearly love a little house and garden.[14]

Such desires were also the substance of Mrs M. Pleydell-Bouverie's *Daily Mail Book of Post-War Homes*, based on the ideas and opinions of the women of Britain. Claimed to be the result of 3½ years of research, the popular demand was for a house or bungalow with a garden of its own, in pleasant surroundings, 'within easy reach of Shops, Churches, Health Centre, Maternity and Child Welfare Clinic, Day Nursery or Nursery School, Residential Nursery and Community Centre'.[15] The ideal was a house of not less than 1,000 sq. ft., with three bedrooms, kitchen, living room and sitting room, bathroom and utility room. There was no support for the communal laundry, and while there was a demand for electric or gas fires in all rooms, few favoured central heating. The opportunity was taken to introduce chapters on planning, prefabrication, the Ideal Homes since 1908, and to describe the 'Dream Kitchen'. It was published in the hope 'that the war will have taught men that a woman's views are often sound and should be considered, and that although still a female she need no longer be considered dangerous, stupid, interfering or incapable'.[16] Similar to the expectations voiced at the end of the First World War, they were destined to meet with the same limited success.

Of course the dream of a house and garden was not exclusive to women, and the eventual confused response owed much to the limitations of the building industry, the lack of financial resources, and a fundamental inability to resolve how such expectations could be satisfied within the modernist conceptual framework of the city. A stark illustration of this dilemma was provided by *Changing Britain*, with its contrasting images of the industrial town, smoke belching from a forest of factory chimneys, set against the regularity of the clean blocks and tree-lined boulevard of the modern city of tomorrow (figure 29). No one, professionals, politicians or the public, appeared to give any adequate thought to the timescale and resources for bringing about such a change, and the landscape implications of replicating such plans across the country. Nor did they give sufficient attention to the potential social tensions from an idealised urban development imposed on a nation committed to cottage architecture, which was believed to be 'the universal plan': the three-bedroom house, with scullery, living room, parlour, inside lavatory, and bathroom; 'the living room opening on to the garden; convenient scullery overlooking it; and the pleasant "close" with fine trees' (figure 30).[17] Herein was the friction of rebuilding Britain, with city planners embracing towers and the public dreaming of a house and garden.

Any of the new city plans illustrate the complexity of this point. The Erno Goldfinger and E. J. Carter introductory guide to the County of London Plan provides a good example of the attempts to harmonise public and private needs. The integrity of their ideas on social architecture, the importance they attached to neighbourhood units and adequate living space was not in doubt, but their commitment to the concept of a 'new London clean, humane and beautiful'[18] was problematic. It was an aesthetic of social order that looked not only to rebuild the war damage, but those areas that stood in the way of sweeping traffic routes, esplanades and imposing blocks of buildings set in parkland. As illustrated by Thomas Sharp's plan for Exeter, it was seen as an opportunity to create 'a much improved city',[19] not only replacing the 'out of date' houses, the 'ugly and outworn'[20] areas, but also bad taste, which in Exeter's case included a proposal to pull down the museum, now recognised as an outstanding piece of Victorian architecture,

CHANGING BRITAIN

ILLUSTRATING THE INDUSTRIAL REVOLUTION : 1750–19..?

29 Front cover, *Changing Britain*, Bourneville, 1943

30 'The Universal Plan' house and garden in *Changing Britain*, 1943

but then regarded as 'an architectural horror'.[21] The plan was not without merit in its attempts to respond to the underlying layout of the city, but the proposed changes of scale marked a change of character and, in common with other city plans, its renderings raised unrealistic expectations of what urban life would be like after the war. However, it was an appealing picture of a new society, and one for which the electorate voted in 1945, returning a Labour government with an overwhelming majority.

Reports

Many of the social difficulties were compounded by the way in which reports and policy decisions overlapped making it impossible to take full account of how decisions and recommendations could be implemented. Through the 1944 reports, *Design of Dwellings*, by the Ministry of Health, and the *Planning our New Homes*, by the Scottish Housing Advisory Committee, attention was focused on the economic pressures that would limit the provision of living space, and the economic impracticalities of over-reliance on domestic appliances. Primary attention was devoted to families with children, although the needs of single people and those of old age were also included in the reviews and recommendations. Both reports showed concern about the creation of social class ghettoes, the nature of community life and importance of neighbourhood centres. They also felt that there would be a need for the new tenants to be helped in making the most effective use of their new housing, and given positive assistance with the task of furnishing their new homes.

Intended to inform government policy, the reports were directed at local authorities, but it was also hoped that this would help to raise standards in speculative developments. The experiences of the inter-war years, when an increasing number of local authorities began to operate hire purchase arrangements for their new tenants, was a major part of the Scottish inquiry. Either because some of the relocated families owned no furnishings to start with, or those they had had been destroyed because of vermin, some of the families being rehoused had neither possessions nor the financial means to acquire them. In the opinion of the Scottish Committee, in addition to the essential built-in facilities of the new houses, it was considered critical that all homes should have, in order of priority, beds and bedding, tables, chairs, chest of drawers and floor coverings, and that local authorities should be prepared to set up schemes to help families in need.

Both reports gave a clear recognition of and support for the widespread preference for the cottage type of house, but had to accept that despite considerable public opposition, flats would have to be provided for inner city redevelopment. Good design was called for in the architecture, and a sensitivity to the landscape in the new schemes. The core of the proposal for England and Wales was the three-bedroom house, with bathroom and separate WC, two main rooms comprising either a kitchen-diner with living room and small utility room, or a kitchen with living room/dining recess. Set at a minimum of 900 sq. ft., space was limited, but in the expectations for general standards of services and fitments there were dramatic improvements on the Tudor Walters standards set just over twenty-five years earlier. There was a distinct levelling out of the differences between working-class and middle-class housing. Significantly garages and space for car parking were now on the list of requirements for neighbourhood planning.

The *Design for Dwellings* report recommended that local authorities should take notice of the views of housewives, and where possible co-opt women on to their Housing Committees. It was not clear how seriously such advice would be taken, particularly after reading the dissenting notes and reservations of Jean Mann in the Scottish Advisory Group report, where she objected to the recommendations on cooking, heating and washing, arguing that such decisions should be left to women. Whether it was the size of the kitchen, provision of a utility room, choice between gas and electricity (of which gas got her vote), she argued strongly that the choice should remain with the housewife. She outlined the same case against the developments being based on high-rise flats rather than the preferred 'cottage' concept, believing that any such moves would contribute further to the undermining of a sense of community.

The 1946 *Housing Digest*, compiled by the Electrical Association for Women from official and association reports that had been published between 1941 and 1945, provided a comprehensive view of popular opinions on the layout, setting and equipment of homes. It confirmed the collective position that had been reached on standards of housing, the qualities and facilities of neighbourhood, the essential features of family living space and equipment. The demand was for bigger rooms, bigger windows, space for healthy living and relaxation. Based on a minimum of 950 sq. ft., there was a need to balance personal and shared space, establish an efficient layout of the kitchen, and use the kitchen-dining room as a core facility.

It was an unassuming agenda: 'Our people desire to live in surroundings, external and internal, that conform to their modest conception of beauty in design, of comfort and convenience of modern equipment, and of the pleasurable contact in environmental proximities.'[22] Part of the popular ideal for a future of better homes, healthier cities, and improved standards of living, where people 'would live a full life without class barriers',[23] it was not an excessive list, but it was to prove an elusive set of objectives.

Attitudes towards and legislation for town planning went through a more radical and permanent change. The speed with which this took place owed something to the Royal Commission on the Distribution of the Industrial Population (Barlow) Report of 1940, and its recommendations on dispersal and diversification from large towns, the destruction from the blitz, and the growing fear of the atomic bomb. The immediate result was the New Towns Bill introduced in April 1946, which by the November had received royal assent. The Final Report of the New Towns Committee had opted for the development of entirely new towns: and by May 1947 approval had been given for building four new towns, Stevenage, Hemel Hempstead, Harlow and Crawley. The expansion of a number of existing towns, including Newbury, Aylesbury and Bletchley was also approved. What was to emerge in these developments was the complexity of constructing new communities and the difficulties of providing what Ralph Tubbs had referred to as the passion and personality of architecture, 'the relation it bears to life'.[24]

Prefabrication and conversions

What came to be known as 'the house out of factory' became the centre of attention. In 1943 R. C. Tarran Ltd, put on a demonstration at Conway Hall to show that its prefabricated bungalow could be erected by twelve men in nine hours.[25] The firm held a similar promotion event on 2 May 1944, showing that its house could be erected in eight hours, and completed, decorated and furnished within four days. Understandably there was great interest in the Tennessee Valley Authority project that had been launched in 1933,[26] as one of the earliest New Deal projects. It covered an area of 42,000 square miles, and in scale and population it was unlike anything in Great Britain. However, its concepts of coherent planning that took care of the community, in its housing, education, work and recreation, had some interesting principles for a time of emergency. This was particularly so with its experimentation in the provision of demountable houses, consisting of four or five sections, that could be transported by lorry and re-erected on new sites as required. In fact as events emerged the demountable issue was less important than the provision of prefabricated temporary structures capable of meeting emergency housing needs. A government delegation had visited America in 1943 to study its housing developments, and national awareness was enhanced by the exhibition 'American Housing in War and Peace' organised by the Museum of Modern Art, shown at the RIBA in 1944, and backed up by a full issue of the *Architectural Review* devoted to American housing. The message was clear, the mass-production of houses, when well designed and controlled, could improve popular standards and taste, and make beautiful homes.

31 Prefabricated kitchen unit

The 'Portal' prefabricated bungalow was first publicised in the spring of 1944, but when shown alongside the 'Arcon' at the Tate Gallery, summer 1944, it had incorporated some important revisions. Designed for young families, with just 616 sq. ft., it provided comparatively small living space, but with the hall enlarged to take a pram, the ceiling height raised from 7 ft. to 7 ft. 6 inches, the bathroom extended and the introduction of a back-door to the kitchen, it was an efficient and well-equipped family dwelling that far exceeded the conventional pre-war housing. Bedrooms had built-in storage units and the living room had bookshelves, but it was the kitchen with the built-in cooker, refrigerator, washing copper, and cupboards that embraced all the labour-saving principles associated with the modern home, that attracted attention (figure 31).

Of the various construction systems to be used, the aluminium bungalow, manufactured by five former aircraft factories, was the most prefabricated.[27] Made in four units, with the plumbing in one unit, and incorporating the Ministry of Works designed kitchen-bathroom, it was an effective assembly line production, that had reduced site work to a minimum. It was emergency housing, predicted to last for ten years, but it was a dream that had become a reality. There were difficulties in finding suitable sites for the emergency housing, the limited living space was a problem for families with children, and the basic functional appearance had little appeal, but it was an outstanding solution that had surprisingly little long-term influence on an architectural profession attracted to the idea of the house as machine.

Following on from the publication of the 1944 *Housing Manual* and *Design of Dwellings* the Ministry of Works built thirteen blocks of housing at Northolt, Middlesex, as a demonstration of the layout of houses and flats to assess the building costs and practical problems of using traditional brick-built structures in comparison to new prefabricated building methods.[28] Steel frame and concrete-clad structures showed positive savings in time and costs, but it was still felt that new developments would be best carried out using a mix of new and traditional methods of construction. What was clear was the expectation that the estimated post-war demand for four million new houses would be based on the three-bedroomed house with either kitchen-living room or dining-kitchen arrangement. By September 1946, Aneurin Bevan, Minister of Health, was able to announce ten types of prefabricated houses available for local authority building programmes. Only the 'Easiform' system which used concrete walls cast on site was available for anywhere in the country, the others were restricted to designated areas. All used a standard plan of three bedrooms, living room, kitchen, bathroom and outbuildings.

The Cornish Unit House, a prefabricated concrete structure, with mansard roof, was introduced in 1946 by the china clay industry, and added to the approved list. These were not temporary buildings, even though they tended to be perceived as such. Consequently, while they were coming on line, the government still felt obliged to hold a competition for permanent post-war housing, and with the results announced at the end of August 1945, from the 27 selected plans, 30 demonstration houses were constructed in different parts of the country to encourage public debate on their design. The first sets of pairs were opened on 31 January 1946, at Hayes and Eastcote, with one house in each pair furnished by the recently formed Council of Industrial Design (CoID). The Hayes model designed by T. P. Bennett, and built by Taylor Woodrow, had a through living-dining room with separate kitchen; the Eastcote house, by E. Collins, built by George Wimpey & Co., had a kitchen-diner with separate drawing room.[29] Although I have separated the discussion of architecture from design, in this instance it is important to recognise the close relationship in these demonstration houses of national reconstruction. Altogether eighteen of the houses were furnished in a mix of utility, inherited and second-hand pieces for families of moderate means, by the Council of Industrial Design. It was recognised that few families would be able to furnish the whole house at one time, or spend the £300 that some of the schemes had cost, but along with the house they were offered as models of real value for money, which would 'help to familiarise new housewives with good design in a form which is well within their means and in a style which will give them more pleasure for a longer time than the old; and the more they are able to follow this lead the more they will do, unknowingly, for the future well-being of British Industry'.[30] The 'simple style' was on show and the visitors were invited to complete a questionnaire on some sample objects and the Utility furniture. Further confirmation of these developments as a national movement came in the contemporary publication of *Homes for the People,* endorsed by the Minister of Health.[31]

The *Conversion of Existing Houses,* the 1945 report of the Sub-Committee of the Central Housing Advisory Committee, introduced the importance of conversion as part of the solution to the housing problem, estimating that not only was there a need to make well-planned conversions of new properties, but also to remedy the inadequacies of the existing 75,000 multi-occupied dwellings. It was thought that these would be particularly suitable for single tenancy, small families and old people, ideas that were further developed in the Scottish Housing Advisory Committee Report, *Modernising our Homes,* 1947.

The Scottish report was working from the deficiency of its existing houses: that nearly a third of its households were sharing WCs, and a large number were without baths or separate kitchens. In other words the immediate post-war need was not just for 500,000 new houses, but a programme of modernisation. Included in its recommendations was the important recognition that modernisation could preserve communities by enabling 'groups of people to continue to live in the locality with which they are familiar, near to the shops and places of recreation they are accustomed to visit, near to school and church, and probably, near to their place of work'.[32] It was also an argument for a respect for the unpretentious architecture, that with its local materials brought a harmony of scale and colour to neighbourhoods.

Despite the desperation at the scale of the task facing the nation, there was a recurring theme that post-war housing should provide more than shelter, enabling all family members to lead happy, comfortable and useful lives.[33] In the excellent *Houses into Flats,* published by the Ascot Gas Water Heaters Ltd, in 1947, outstanding among a series of informative essays on the practicalities of conversions was 'The City Family' by Mrs Muriel Gee. Working on the model of a three-storey house with basement, the suggestion was for families to occupy the ground and first floor, single person tenancies on the second floor, and communal facilities such as storage and shared laundry in the basement. Her proposition was that design should work from the psychological needs of the family, of which having its own front door was the first priority.

> Thereby it becomes an entity, a complete little circle with its own interests and privacies. Next, families need space in which to organise their several activities, with sufficient suitable rooms in which to indulge in noise without repressions. There must also be a well-planned domestic circulation, which will allow the parents a certain degree of peace and charm of living.[34]

It now seems such an obvious list of requirements that the only surprise is that it was felt necessary for it to be outlined with such clarity. In fact it was a clear indication of the way in which conversion work frequently fell outside the conventional safeguards attached to the purpose built, and fears that during the emergency standards of workmanship and facilities would be allowed to fall further behind. 1947–48 was a difficult time; although the New Look in fashion had arrived, and the nation had enjoyed the Olympic Games, the bleak winter mirrored the economic climate, prompting a growing pessimism in the sense of social purpose.

Hoping to reassure the general public, the Ministry of Health took space at the 1948 Ideal Home Exhibition to bring attention to the new standards and progress in house building. Four houses were selected to demonstrate 'Housing Progress': two concrete houses, the Airey Rural House and the Cornish Unit House, the Aluminium House, and the reconstruction of a traditional municipal terraced house designed for Worthing. The intention was to convince the public that quality was not being sacrificed to quantity: homes were better-looking and better planned, grouped to enhance neighbourliness, adapted to meet the different needs of the town and country, based on a revival of traditional social and aesthetic values. Statistics were provided on the repair, conversion and the number of new houses built since April 1945. '100 New Houses an Hour' was the proud claim, but the output was still far short of the need.[35]

At the same time the Ministry of Health also published advice on 'Gardens', and 'The Appearance of Estates'. In the case of gardens it was a reminder to both the public and the professionals how they gave a sense of comfort, were cheerful and welcoming: 'English cottage gardens are world famous. Let us carry on this charming tradition in our towns and suburbs to ensure that our housing estates shall be worthy of our landscape heritage'.[36] There was a similar tone to the recommendations on the appearance of estates, but with a far wider set of objectives, including the planting of trees, shrubs, fruit trees and creepers, care of open-plan areas, provision of garden sheds, colour washing of houses to introduce variety, and an area of rough ground with all its natural features where children could play free of restrictions. It was a garden city approach, understanding space as multi-functional, active and managed from the outset by a sharing of responsibility between tenants and authorities.

Alternative housing

The ideal of new homes and a new society was now under severe threat with the failure to build sufficient houses quickly enough. A warning of difficulties to come had already surfaced in September 1946, when the London Trades Council deputation to Ministry of Health raised the lack of progress on housing, and the problem of families forced into squatting. A whole range of alternatives was being used, from vacated camps to converted buses and holiday caravans. Hard pressed, there was no doubt that the Government and local authorities had willingly accepted this development as a short-term emergency solution, but by 1947 concern over the lack of control was growing, particularly over the use of the caravan as a permanent home. There was little that could be done as the economic crisis of the August undermined the reconstruction, and increased the prospect of a longer period of emergency.[37]

In October 1947, the Movable Dwelling Conference was convened and, meeting over the next two years, in 1950 published its report on *Movable Dwellings*. Most of the report was concerned with the popularity of tourist camping and its dangers to the landscape if new sites were not properly controlled both in location and design. But the longer-term ad hoc settlements were just as problematic, and part of an escalating situation. The report bemoaned the fact that the shacks put up by the poorer classes in the 1930s had been joined by townspeople's demand for holiday and weekend retreats. These were now multiplied by the emergency homeless being forced by circumstance to use 'dilapidated and unsuitable second-hand structures and material, including worn-out public service and goods vehicles, ex-Service bodies, and even aeroplane fuselages and chicken-houses'.[38]

Making a clear distinction between movable homes, such as tents and towing caravans, and the movable homes that were in effect being used as permanent residences, the demand was for all the latter type to be removed, even though eviction would add to the number of homeless families. This was an unrealistic recommendation, for even though new caravans were not cheap, costing between £400 and £1,800, it was estimated that as many as 80 per cent were being bought for use as family homes. Caravan manufacturers recognised the growing demand and began to advertise them as the answer to the housing problem, designed as 'a mobile flat, containing a large kitchen and separate toilet room including a shower bath. Although some of the furniture is built in, some items are based on the design of normal domestic furniture, and can be moved at will'.[39] Able to be arranged into two bedrooms, the idea was to convey an interior and furnishing that was as close as possible to a normal home, to the point where some were being marketed as fully furnished four-roomed homes.

During the 1930s the interior design and fitments of the caravan had been effectively resolved. Foldaway beds and tables, chemical WC, cylinder gas for heating, cooking and lighting, cupboards and, in some luxury models, even a refrigerator and bath were included. Space was minimal, but the designs were well thought out. Even so, on sites that were nothing more than fields or derelict urban plots, lacking basic amenities, they were not a realistic answer to the longer-term need for permanent family homes. But for many there were no alternatives, and by the mid-1950s this had created a major planning problem, ultimately resulting in new legislation for the regularising of 'mobile' home parks.

At the end of September 1950 the *Builder* decided to make its contribution to resolving the housing problem, with a competition for 'Low Cost Housing'. The proposal was for a three-bedroom family house, in a terrace of four, for under £1,000. It was accepted that in order to bring costs down, some space reduction would probably have to be made. In their report the assessors showed a distinct preference for traditional building methods, good access between kitchen and dining space, and open-plan living. The winning design,[40] by J. L. Womersley and G. Hopkinson, had put the kitchen on the front of the house, with the L-shaped living-dining room giving access to the rear garden, and its ideal fire heating water for the kitchen, bathroom, and radiators on the landing and one of the bedrooms.

At the same time other experimental schemes were being carried out, notably by the Department of Health for Scotland which built demonstration houses at Toryglen, Glasgow and Sighthill, Edinburgh. They used traditional building techniques, but cut costs by the reduction of living space. In contrast the Ulster Cottage for rural areas was a prefabricated concrete shed with asbestos roof.[41]

The Festival of Britain and new town landscape

Such was the level of anxiety over housing and rebuilding Britain, that questions of community needs in the new development plans were in danger of being overlooked. Many cities, equipped with new civic plans that presented them with grand boulevards and new zoned urban landscapes, had the problem of acquiring the quality architecture to go with the plans, and the resources to make a meaningful start. Yet stimulated by the grandeur of the new city plans, municipal authorities began to demolish urban centres on a scale unmatched by the blitz, and the advantages of taking a more restrained humanitarian approach was largely overlooked. This is probably why the lessons set out by the 'Live

Architecture' exhibition of the Festival of Britain were substantially unappreciated. Designed for the Lansbury neighbourhood, a 110-acre redevelopment plan for Poplar, in concept and ambition it was a serious attempt to construct a real community in a bombed working-class district of London. Introducing housing in two-, three- and four-storey blocks, it offered a range of accommodation appropriate to different sizes and types of households. With public buildings that included a shopping precinct by Frederick Gibberd and a school by Yorke, Rosenberg and Mardall, it was an expression of restraint and appreciation of the ordinary. Nothing demonstrated this better than the show flat, furnished and decorated to the schemes drawn up by Mrs Lovall Fraser on behalf of the CoID, and supplied and carried out by the CWS. Its message was that the working-class family could have an attractive, cosy home, with hard-wearing, practical and reasonably priced furnishings.

In December 1951, as a supplement to the 1949 *Housing Manual,* new national guidelines on local authority housing, illustrated with twenty specimen plans, set out to reduce the recommended living space as the only way of cutting house building costs and hopefully making it possible to recover the growing shortfall on new housing. To give the sense of authenticity and approval, one of the two-bedroom plans, promoted as the 'People's House', was constructed by John Laing & Son Ltd, for the 1952 Ideal Home Exhibition, and in consultation with the Townswomen's Guild, the interior furnishing was planned by Marjorie Holford for the CoID. The first floor distribution of space followed the well-established conventions of the small house, but ground floor living space was radically altered. The hallway and passage were removed, and the staircase incorporated into a living room that was fully open plan and centrally heated. Designs to fit the national economy, for politicians, such as Harold Macmillan, Minister of Housing, were an essential part of a national crusade for more new houses. Architectural opinion was divided on the merits of reducing living space by as much as 50 sq. ft. on the minimum recommended back in 1944, and there was unease over the emphasis placed on two-bedroom houses and lack of storage space.[42] No matter how it was presented it was a retrogressive move, contributing to a climate in which large blocks of flats were beginning to be considered as an attractive solution by politicians both at national and local level.

Flats had never been popular with families, and it was clear that the intention of the government report *Living in Flats*[43] was to try to introduce caution in the scale of any new schemes. The importance of the Lansbury model was referenced as a mixed development that offered a way of avoiding putting families with children in flats. Using words like variety, homeliness, neighbourly and privacy, the preference was for future estates that would be small-scale, have some garden or allotment provision, and playgrounds. While recognising the value of private balconies, costs made the committee accept that the balcony access would have to be retained, despite its disadvantages of noise and loss of privacy. General awareness of social and practical problems was apparent in the report, but in details, for example the provision for washing and drying of clothes, it was unable to make a clear distinction between communal and individual needs, or fully appreciate the everyday difficulties of mothers with young children. As an indicator of progress since Britain had first started to engage in planning for rebuilding, it illustrated the continuing uncertainties over the social responsibilities of architecture, and the limited understanding of changing expectations and the commercial changes surrounding family life. For example, car ownership had not been ignored, but committee doubts over whether families living in subsidised accommodation should own a car, revealed that for public housing schemes provision of car space was not a serious consideration in planning for the future. This raised an important issue of how much policy guidelines, and architectural and planning practices, should anticipate the potential changes of lifestyle extending down through the social classes. In this instance, despite a range of social indicators, there was difficulty gauging the planning implications of the onset of a new consumer age. They could, for example, appreciate that one day domestic washing machines could become cheap enough for every ordinary home to have one, but that day had not yet arrived and therefore it was not a concern for planners.

Somehow the lessons of the prefabricated kitchen units of the emergency years were being overlooked. The working-class housewife would not have expected to get the all-steel 'Kitchen of Tomorrow' as shown at the 1949 Ideal Home Exhibition, but to hope for the mass-produced government issue was not an unreasonable expectation. Instead the flat dweller was offered the communal laundry, perhaps satisfactory for the single occupancy, but difficult for a family with children. There were those who argued that this was sound economics and socially responsible, but equally it showed a lack of attention to the mechanics of family life.

There was no doubt of the collective desire to rebuild Britain, but the delays and economic restrictions were beginning to erode national confidence. An effective building programme for the planned new towns had not begun until 1951, and while no one would have disagreed with D. Rigby Childs' observation, 'that the towns must be efficient as places to live in and work in, to go to school in, to bring up a family in, and to enjoy the years of old age in',[44] the lack of any clear identity was beginning to attract attention.

From the new settlement developments of the inter-war years there were numerous examples of the problems arising from the failure to match amenities with housing, yet the same thing was being repeated in the building of the new towns. As the programmes got under way, it became apparent that there was no clear view of what constituted a twentieth-century town, of the stages in which the plan should be delivered, or how the plans would accommodate the cycle of the age-group changes of the family. Even so there were those who saw it as a bright new beginning: the happy enthusiastic community of Harlow New Town, with its 'houses, so pretty, slim and full of colour',[45] and Crawley New Town where,

> Front doors were painted in delightful colours; primrose yellow, sky blue, soft green and peach pink are among the most charming. The gardens were bright with flowers, and as we saw small faces peering out of windows as we passed, we could not help thinking what a healthy, happy race of children would be brought up in such surroundings.[46]

By 1953 a major difference of opinion had opened up in the architectural profession on the new town landscape, with the *Architectural Review* leading the attack on the new town interpretation of urban planning. Gordon Cullen constructed a picture of its desolation as 'Prairie Planning'.[47] J. M. Richards, dismissing new towns as the building of suburbs dignified by the name of towns, suggested that it 'might have been wiser, when it became apparent that shortage of capital was going to slow down the construction of the new towns to such an extent, to have concentrated all the available resources on one of them, enabling it to grow up fully equipped and within a reasonable time'.[48] Even if Richards could have had his instant new town, the possibilities of engineering the complexity and variations associated with British towns, which over the centuries had given them their distinctive characteristics and personality was unlikely to happen. Frederick Gibberd's explanation of the rationale behind the planning in 'The Design of Residential Areas'[49] identified that priority had been placed on the environment of the home life of the family, and the needs of the immediate neighbourhood in terms of amenities such as schools, shops, playing fields and other communal facilities. It was from this neighbourhood plan of mixed development that the town as a whole would be constructed. Lionel Brett, in 'Are Architects Becoming More Human?', pertinently described the problem as the 'conflict between design and spontaneity',[50] the imposition of scale and monumentality that excluded use and interaction by the people.

In the split over the vision of a rebuilt Britain, there was a very obvious feeling that the spirit of adventure that had produced the South Bank development for the Festival of Britain was being lost. The reclaiming of the derelict South Bank site had raised expectations of a new age, colourful, gay and optimistic for the future. It was the image of a new modernised, pedestrianised landscape, 'an exhilarating example of townscape',[51] rather than the community scheme at Lansbury that had captured public and professional imagination, but together they were received as the beginning of a new spirit in Britain. Hugh Casson, who had coordinated the Festival plans since it was conceived in the autumn of 1948, saw it as the transformation of a derelict central site into 'a New World'.[52] Osbert Lancaster talked about it as marking the 'End of the Modern Movement in Architecture', with its 'frenzied rejection of the past'.[53] The Festival was not the beginning or the end of things in quite the way that these comments suggested, but it was a key stage in a re-evaluation of style, taste and values of architecture and design, and the attitudes towards their history. It was, for example, important in the rehabilitation of Victorian architecture and taste with a miniature Crystal Palace at the Ideal Home Exhibition and the 1851 Centenary Pavilion on the South Bank.[54] Rather grandly described as a 'united act of national reassessment, and one corporate reaffirmation of faith in the nation's future',[55] the Festival gave a boost to interest in popular taste, and nationalism, albeit with a growing emphasis on England and Englishness. It was a contemporary representation of a nation proud of its past, and of its national character, land and the people.

> The land, endowed with scenery, climate and resources more various than any other country of comparable size, has nurtured and challenged and stimulated the people. The people, endowed with not one single characteristic that is peculiar to themselves, nevertheless, when taken together, could not be mistaken for any other nation in the world.[56]

It was an occasion to applaud the nation's agriculture, industries, welfare, discoveries and the people's history. The designers had successfully repackaged Britain, raising expectations that harmony and lightheartedness would replace the years of austerity. It was understandable that the Festival should have been optimistic and reassuring, but having lifted the national spirit, there were still the problems of reconstruction to be addressed and, as has been indicated by the housing debate and changes in national policy, the experiences of a partially rebuilt Britain that surrounded it had already begun to unravel the post-war dream.

Design matters

Minimum and low-cost

The underlying message of the emergency years and post-war reconstruction was how to make the best out of the minimum and low-cost, and adapt to reduced living space. On furnishing the home, advice was offered on how to mix old with new, what could be home-made, and being prepared to accept only the essentials.

Minimalist by necessity, recycling and renovation became a national priority, and in 1943 what the poor had always accepted as an integral part of family life became a national campaign. 'Make Do and Mend' was the reminder for middle-class families to get the last possible ounce of wear out of their clothes and household things. Hints were offered on mending, washing and ironing, on unpicking and re-knitting, and turning out and renovating.

The Utility Furniture scheme had been evolving over 1942, and in the October was shown to the public at an exhibition at the Building Centre. The following January the first Utility Furniture catalogue was published, and through 1943 the exhibition was shown at major regional centres.[57] The furniture was good, simple and well made, heavily influenced by Gordon Russell in his role as chair of the Advisory Committee. Looked at as a social experiment, it was very obvious from the room settings that the style and range was typical of that which had represented the furnishing of the working-class home in the 1930s exhibition room, such as was shown at the 1938 Empire Exhibition. Now it was for the nation, and it was interesting to note that in the publicity photographs of the living-dining room and the kitchen, the table settings and decorative details introduced touches of middle-class taste. For sale at reasonable prices it brought a new dimension to the public understanding and appreciation of minimum standards, standardisation, and the provision of cheap well-made products. It was also an opportunity to give a new perspective on the concepts of comfort and convenience, and notions of good taste. There was no settee or three-piece suite in the range so that the merits of the easy chair were well publicised.[58] The kitchen cabinet, rather overshadowed in the 1930s by the obsessive interest in the fitted kitchen, also received a renewed attention that then survived through to the 1950s.[59]

Prompting questions on the future of consumer goods after the war, and the problems of marketing costs, a series of articles in the *Financial News* at the beginning of March 1944 saw no reason why a continuing pattern of standardisation should not be continued without it leading to drab uniformity. It was a case of using the principles of the Utility scheme to prevent the self-indulgence of the minority penalising the interests of the majority. The anticipation was for a retail expansion along the lines that had been established by Woolworth's and Marks & Spencer's before the war, supplying a guaranteed quality at the lowest possible cost.

Raising professional and public awareness of art, design and environment was recognised as a matter of national importance. Following a deputation to R. A. Butler, President of the Board of Education, a Committee for Education in Appreciation of Physical Environment was formed. Eventually renamed Council for Visual Education, its objectives were to promote 'by the application of higher standards of design to buildings, their lay-out, their furnishing and their surroundings, a more beautiful as well as a more healthy environment for the everyday life of the people'.[60] Concurrently the Council for the Encouragement of Music & the Arts (CEMA) was promoting an 'Art for the People' series, that included a 'Design in Daily Life' exhibition, 'to show objects of daily use produced under conditions, which are well and truly made, and therefore have a claim to be considered works of art'.[61] Held at Heal's in March 1944, it then toured Edinburgh, Glasgow and other Scottish centres. Similar in its aspirations to the work of the Cotton Board's Colour Design and Style Centre[62] that since 1940 had played an important role in raising the profile of cotton within mainstream and modern domestic design developments, it was part of the growing mood to provide a lead on national taste.

In September 1944, the Federation of British Industries (FBI) declared its support for a central design council to help raise standards of British industrial design, and in the following month Sir T. D. Barlow spoke of the agreement to set up such a council, with the possibility of setting up design centres for different industries. In January 1945 the Council of Industrial Design was introduced to the nation. All of this now meant that national taste in architecture, planning and industrial design had been brought under central control. This move increasingly dominated the shape of the post-war reconstruction.

At home

The urgent problem was to convince a sceptical public that the functionalism of the utility range could be happily absorbed into the traditional British family home. For this reason the 'Design at Home' exhibition at the National Gallery, June 1945, took 'Good Furnishing For Little Rooms' as its theme. Designed by Milner Gray for CEMA, as a touring exhibition for the provinces, the room settings introduced Utility furniture into the modern house. Reinforced with a mixing of bright sunny colours, touches of Regency decoration and an inherited eighteenth-century dining table, the rooms also attempted to show the most effective use of small space for the needs of the family.

The study-bedroom, with its bed-divan and storage drawers, the kitchen-diner, the living-room diner, complete with foldaway table and corner settee, the study-lounge lined with built-in shelves, the day and night nursery furnished with bunk beds, had rationalised the multi-purpose use of the small house or flat in post-war Britain. None of this was particularly new thinking; after all working-class families had never lived in anything other than minimum space, but it was a clear indication that in the future these standards would also be applied to the middle-class professional family. They were displays that gave a new level of respectability to the home-made, and initiated a culture that was ultimately to find its expression in the do-it-yourself movement of the mid-1950s.

The Kitchen Planning Exhibition, Dorland Hall, in February–March 1945, was the outcome of Jane Drew's research for the British Commercial Gas Association. With ten package and full-scale kitchens, it was an indication of the importance attached to kitchen design for new and reconditioned houses, and a further reminder that it would be the core of post-war house design. Five full-scale kitchens were also included in the *Daily Herald* Post-War Homes Exhibition of the same year, along with scale models of nine houses built by various methods of prefabrication, a display of wallpapers and furnishing fabrics, and the Housing Centre's neighbourhood planning exhibition, 'Up Your Street', designed by Walter Segal. This showed the good and the bad of taste and planning. It set the sun-filled well-furnished home against the sunless badly-furnished example. It was an argument for more planning control, from which would come the good neighbourhood with its community centre, and facilities for shopping and recreation. The following year, at the *Daily Herald* Modern Homes Exhibition, there was a wider range of utensils and fabrics on show, including the prototypes of the new range of utility furniture, and scale models of houses described for the future. But it was the three kitchens designed by Mrs Darcy Braddell, setting out the electric, gas and coal alternatives, and the one-room flat, furnished from the Utility range and designed by Jacques Groag that attracted public attention. Efficiency remained the ideal, employing the principles developed in the 1930s, except that the concept had moved on from the time and motion model, to the smooth running cafeteria model, one domestic activity linking up with another in the way that one might fill a tray.

In the configuration of the living space, the provision of a scullery essentially for washing clothes was no longer a serious option. The Ministry of Health recommended three types: the 'Working Kitchen' designed for all the household chores of cooking and washing, a 'Dining-Recess Kitchen' that had a small foldaway table, and the 'Living Kitchen' modelled on the traditional country cottage type. Where space allowed the dining-recess model was also developed as a 'dinette', with room divider, leaving more space to be added to the living room, and when designed as the 'kitchen-dining room', incorporating a folding dining table, it provided a play area for young children that could be further enhanced by the use of an 'L'-shape room plan.

Throughout the 1920s and 1930s a better understanding had developed of the relationship between class habits, amenities and income and patterns of consumption. In 1945, with its publication, *The Market for Household Appliances,* PEP brought the methodologies of social science research to the question of the social and commercial benefits of concentrating on the manufacture of cheap well-designed products that would bring them within reach of low-income families.[63] Appliances were discussed as necessities that would reduce the demands of the unpleasant and unpopular household tasks, rather than as luxury items for the upper and middle classes. Displaying a future that was much further away than anyone appreciated at the time, the 'Britain Can Make It' Exhibition of 1946 had similar social ambitions, even though in modelling family types to fit the living spaces it reinforced the perceptions of the taste and needs of the conventional social groups. Hugely popular, it was a deliberately lively and colourful presentation of a new and better standard of life, 'a serious attempt to react against any tendency to war weariness or sense of frustration in Britain itself';[64] it effectively raised the profile of the recently formed Council of Industrial Design, and secured the dominant principles of industrial design in post-war Britain.[65]

Being primarily about products and furnishings for the home, with some fashion, the most influential section in terms of taste and ideas on living space, were the sixteen furnished rooms with their imaginary families. Brilliantly illustrated by Nicolas Bentley, with cryptic personal details, the product to family identity provided a fascinating insight into the establishment view of national taste and standards of living. Determined to exploit these ideas Gordon Russell was given the opportunity the following year to produce a short guidebook on *How to Buy Furniture,* and Miss P. J. Owen represented ten of the rooms with additional text as *Furnishing to Fit the Family.*

The primary message was to convince the public of how the average British family would fit into a small house. There were degrees of smallness, and the working-class family invariably had to be satisfied with less space than the professional middle-class family. Types of services and furnishing followed a similar pattern, with an emphasis on room arrangements that could meet the different demands of the family, and a 'judicious' approach to decoration, using pale colours set off with touches of bright contrasting colours. Variations of types and arrangements were offered within the different social groups. The kitchen of the cottage in a modern mining village for the middle-aged coalminer, wife and three children was tinged with modernism from the metal window frames, gas cooker, boiler and refrigerator to the central heating and other detailed fitments. The artisan on the new estate was provided with a mixture of craft furniture and

'Cotswold' utility furniture, and the railway engineer's family living in an industrial town was provided with walnut and plastic Coop furniture.

Reviewing the furnished rooms' section of the exhibition Gordon Russell expressed disappointment at the way in which the rooms had been interpreted as being for different classes rather than for people doing different jobs, yet the class system of taste was unmistakable. Compare, for example, the Living-Room with Kitchen Recess in a small house (figure 32), to the Kitchen plus Dining Space (figure 33). The former had been designed for 'The storeroom clerk, middle aged; collects stamps, reads thrillers; regular picture-goer. His wife; same age and interests. Their daughter, turned twenty-one; loves excitement. Their son; schoolboy and aircraft spotter'.[66] Designed to convince the working-class housewife that eating in the kitchen was a good idea, and that with fitted cupboards to keep everything tidy, the multiple service unit for family cooking, heating the water and the room, oak furniture from Heals and aluminium sink, it was comfort with economy. The living-dining room with kitchen range of the 1920s had been reworked to give a sense of the modern kitchen entering the working-class house. In contrast the professional family, of young architect-painter, with a wife keen on amateur dramatics and a young son, had a much higher standard of living. Their home in many respects personified the core principles of the Council of Industrial Design good taste guide. The dining space emphasised natural materials, an open-air country atmosphere, which with its French window and loggia allowed for out-of-doors eating. The kitchen was austere, scientific, an efficient workshop, a model of modern middle-class living.

Taste and gender were also issues. For the late middle-aged woman journalist, the feminine character was brought out in whimsical decorative features, and bright striped wallpaper setting off the dark walnut panelling. In contrast, the single man, sports commentator for the BBC, was provided with a study that was more daring and experimental in its approach. Symbolically, his beer and pint mug contrasted with her Regency coffee-pot, the anxious hard-working woman compared to the casual club-loving man. Similar characteristics were displayed by the other families, more often with a cautious traditional woman and an adventurous husband. Russell reinforced the official line in *How to Buy Furniture*, offering advice on materials and construction, as well as taste. There was the usual Victorian versus modern interior, 'the abandoned profusion' with the 'commonsensical and pleasant', and in keeping with the times there were illustrations of how to combine a mahogany dining table of about 1800 with utility chairs, and match the utility table with country-made chairs of about 1840.

Organised by the Scottish Committee of the Council of Industrial Design the 'Enterprise Scotland' exhibition, Edinburgh, August–September

1947, set out to do for Scotland what the 'Britain Can Make It' had done in London. Arranged by Basil Spence, it presented Scotland yesterday, today and tomorrow, through a comprehensive range of domestic products, furnishings and furniture, and eight room settings, eccentrically eclectic, including a country house room, a low-income living room, a Regency-style bedroom, a simple and extravagant bathroom, a modern kitchen, a nursery with a bed covered in tartan, and a board room. The future projected through photographs and text was constructed around the family.

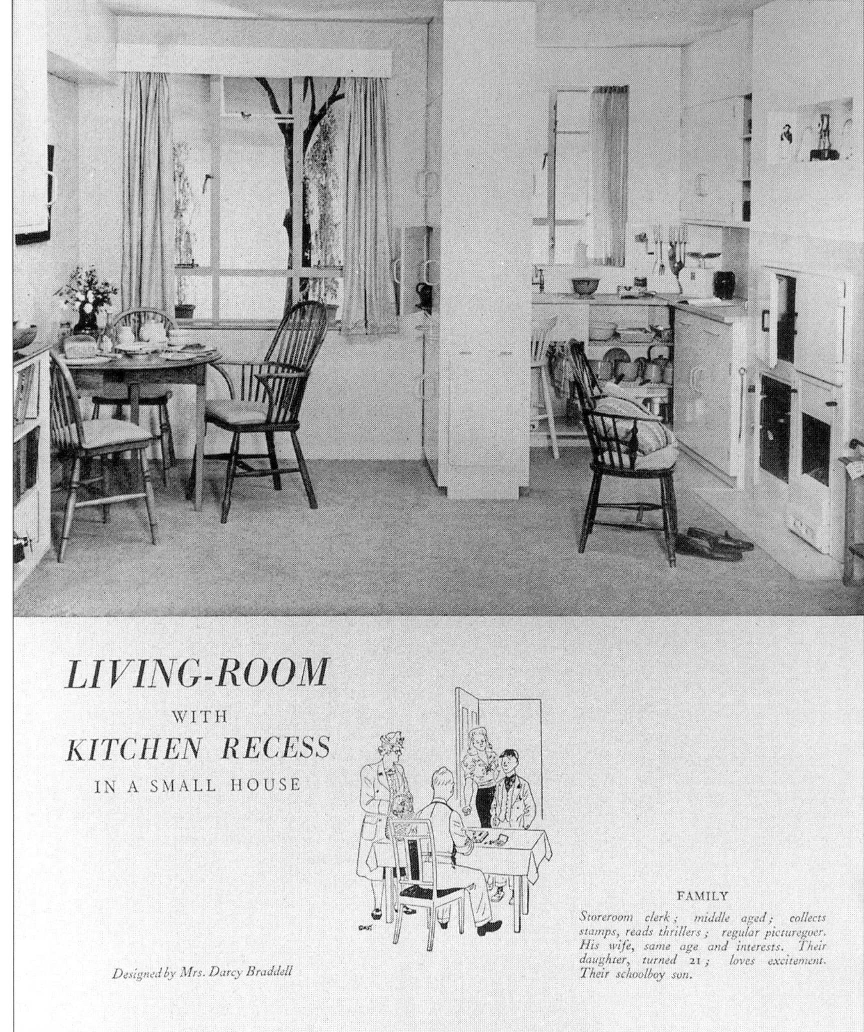
LIVING-ROOM
WITH
KITCHEN RECESS
IN A SMALL HOUSE
Designed by Mrs. Darcy Braddell
FAMILY
Storeroom clerk; middle aged; collects stamps, reads thrillers; regular picturegoer. His wife, same age and interests. Their daughter, turned 21; loves excitement. Their schoolboy son.

Good and popular taste

Brightening and lightening the housework was a common theme of trade advertisements, but the culture surrounding the role of the housewife remained unchanged.

> You will have to face that kitchen every day – spend most of your life in it – and then face your family with a smile in your eye and a song in your heart; at least, as a family man, I sincerely hope you do. That means your

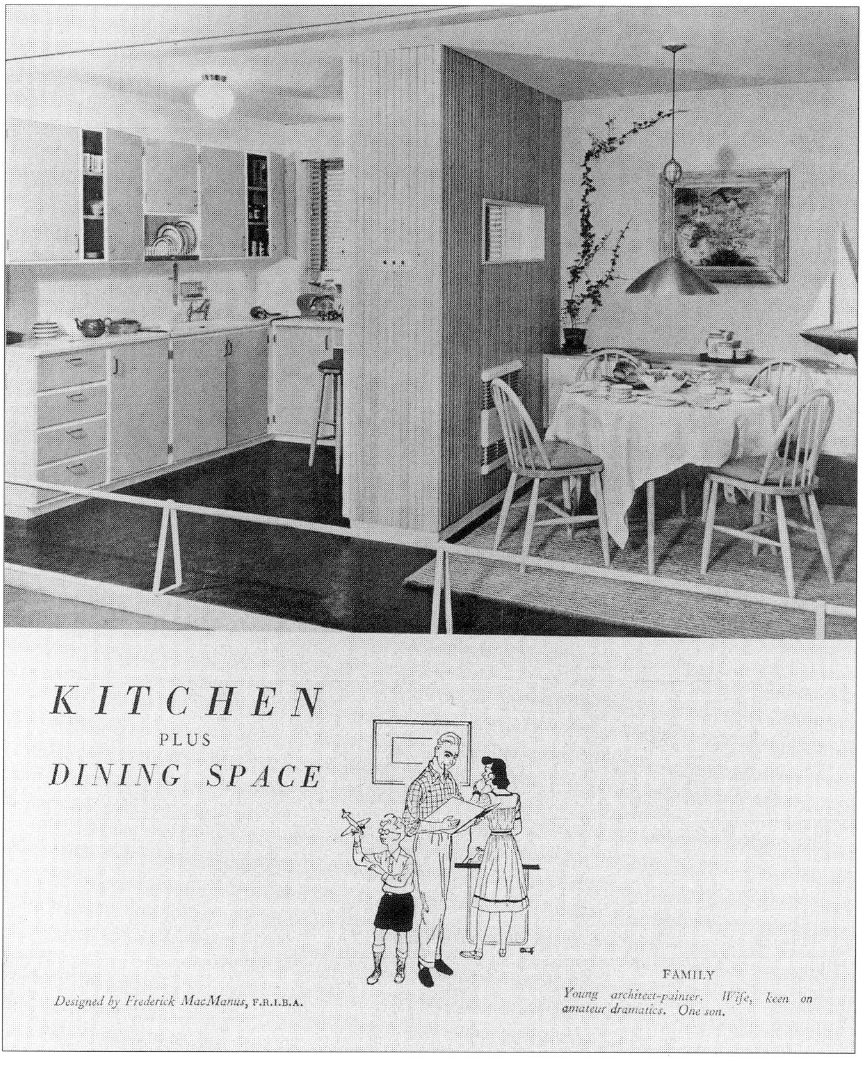

above and facing **32, 33** Room settings first used in 'Britain Can Make It', 1946. Used in *Furnishing to Fit the Family*

> kitchen must be a human (generally womanly) place, light and sympathetic, on the one hand, and thoroughly well arranged on the other.[67]

Principles of good design picked up where matters had been left in 1939. There was a preference for the discreet and the modest, and abhorrence of vulgarity and show. Intent on developing a critical interest and understanding of the general public in things around them and things that they might buy, and prompted by the Council of Industrial Design, in 1947 Penguin Books Ltd began *The Things We See* series. Commencing with *Indoors and Out* by Alan Jarvis, a wide range of subjects were to be embraced including houses, furniture, pottery, public transport and ships. The essays shared a common set of principles, a refined modernism that in its attempts to be both elegant and carefree, gave rise to the style that became known as contemporary. National identity and values were at the core of these works, and consumption and taste were presented as a choice between good and evil. Alan Jarvis set the tone with an extraordinary pairing of images. Intent on explaining the possibilities of achieving diversity through uniformity, he grouped a late nineteenth-century terrace of bay-fronted houses with a line of Nazi soldiers on parade, and then set it against a grand Georgian terrace, and a casual, jolly line of British tommies walking along the roadside. This was not just a case of linking fascism with Victorian design, an extraordinary statement in itself, but was an admiration of the British spirit that had brought victory over adversity, and came from the nation's natural awareness that greatness came from the balance of personal freedom and collective order. The books and the CoID were intent on keeping order.

There were many instances that suggested the CoID rather enjoyed the idea of being the keepers of national taste, and welcomed the possibilities of continuing standards imposed by the Utility regulations, even though style and materials might change. After a time the cultural snobbery of broadsides on good taste became tedious, the only relief was that the extreme prejudices displayed towards the 'man in the bus, the mill girl in the factory, the labourer in the field'[68] by Herbert Read in his introduction to *The Practice of Design* became less pronounced.

Scandinavian influences resurfaced in November 1946, when the Building Centre held an exhibition of flat-pack, self-assembly furniture from Nordiska Kompaniet, Sweden. The Danish Design Exhibition, sponsored by the Arts Council, started at the RIBA at the end of February 1947, running through to 15 March, and then toured Britain throughout the rest of the year. Although still heavily restricted, there were signs that normality was returning to Britain, and this was confirmed by the revival of the Ideal Home Exhibition and Birmingham's Ideal Home Exhibition.

As the official retailers of good taste the CoID issued a series of Design Folios, published between 1948 and 1951 for schools and colleges, and, in association with the Federation of British Industries, Association of Chambers of Commerce and Civic Authorities, organised 'Design Weeks' in regional centres. The first was held in Newcastle from 7–12 July 1947, and was followed by Manchester, June 1948, then Birmingham and Cardiff. The Potteries, Nottingham, Bristol, Southampton and Bradford had their design weeks during 1949. They were extraordinarily successful, and it was reported that an average of over 2,000 attended the public meetings and some 400,000 people visited the exhibitions over a two-year period. Programmes included conferences, meetings, shop window displays, and a 'housewives' forum' to discuss ideas on improvements to household goods and equipment. One interesting outcome of this collaboration was the exhibition 'Background for Living' organised by Grace Lovat Fraser for the David Morgan department store, Cardiff, which ran for six months from early 1949. Working in association with the buyers it was agreed

> that the exhibition, to be really useful, must be a selling exhibition; we would show only goods which were available at the moment to the public, and moreover could be backed-up by a reasonable amount of stock. We all felt that the public was weary of frustration and that it was time to show good design that could be bought as well as admired.[69]

The exhibition consisted of a corridor of five furnished model rooms, two halls with a wide range of furnishing schemes, a model kitchen-dining room, a large kitchen, and bathroom. The emphasis was on furnishing and decoration, offering traditional and contemporary design, but hoping to gain converts to the contemporary styles.

When the CoID launched its monthly journal, *Design*, in January 1949, Gordon Russell led the way with an article on good design. It set out the Council's manifesto for re-establishing Britain as a world leader in design, and upgrading its standards for national prosperity. In July the journal began its stock list as a comprehensive catalogue of excellence, partly for the Festival of Britain, and also as a permanent reference collection for trade and industry. Amongst the first selection was the 3½-litre Jaguar, which gave Morton Shand the opportunity to describe good contemporary design as elegant, 'its significant refinement, its contemporary English accent'.[70] Time and again this was the emphasis that the CoID brought to its furnished rooms, such as those arranged for the Ministry of Health house at the 1949 Ideal Home Exhibition, and which later in the year were shown at Brown's of Chester.

It was a time when other regional shows began to fill the calendar. The Manchester Brighter Homes Exhibition was revived in the spring of 1948, and each year the latest and the modern, the luxury and the modest, the dream and the practical, were on display.[71] The Scottish Industries Exhibition, Kelvin Hall, Glasgow, September 1949, designed by Basil Spence, was one of the first major post-war trade fairs. It was hugely popular, and of particular interest was the unit furniture, much of it self-assembly, in the Utility range designed by R. Y. Godden and R. D. Russell for the Scottish CWS. Being 'cosy' became compatible with the development of a 'contemporary style', a rejection of the austerity of modernism and utility. But products were still in short supply, even second-hand items were expensive and quality difficult to obtain. The general message to the consumer was to obtain furniture at a reasonable price, that could serve more than one purpose, be compact and easy to clean.

Modern living

In retrospect it is possible to see how the coinciding of three new phases of development inspired a sense of optimism of better things to come for the people in the shape of family motoring, television and the self-service supermarket. After a ten-year gap, in October 1948, the London Motor Show was on again. It had been a bad time for private motoring, and still was for many motorists. Petrol was rationed, the industry which had recommenced manufacture in June 1945 was directing its efforts towards export, and new cars could only be acquired with permits for special categories of users. Motoring journals had satisfied some of the enthusiasm and stimulated debate on style and technical issues, amongst which discussion of the concept of the people's car and European minicars raised some interesting questions for austerity Britain. For example, in November 1944, the press release on the prototype 'People's Car' had given a new edge to the debate on the future of the small car. Known as the Kendall, after its promoter W. D. Kendall MP, it was to be a 565cc three-cylinder rear-engined car to sell for £100. A version was driven from Grantham to London in August 1945 as a publicity stunt, but by the November the proposition had been abandoned and Kendall had taken a licence to build a 600cc Gregoire. It was a time when interest in the minicar had been developing on the continent, and at the 1946 Paris motor show the established Fiat 500 was joined by a 2-cylinder Panhard and 4-cylinder Renault. There was no obvious new response to these developments in Britain, although in the same year there was justified excitement over the technical and aesthetic innovation of the Jowett Javelin.

It was the London Motor Show that at last provided some answers, with two new models that were not only of international significance, but helped to define further the economy style of British design. Neither were modifications or adaptations of earlier models; they were both radical in their design and technology, and cars for the future. The Morris Minor and the Land Rover were on show. In their own ways they were to make a major contribution to the redefining of minimum and functional. In the case of the Morris Minor it was a massive step forwards in the thinking through of a car design for an average family. It did not meet the demands catered for by the European minicars, or fulfil the role previously played by the Austin Seven, but it set important new standards for the design of the small family car. By combining the body and chassis in one all-steel structure, it had retained structural strength while saving weight, thereby improving performance, and at the same time increasing the interior space and for the first time providing a small family car that could adequately accommodate four adults (figure 34).

Family motoring was now prominent in all the advertising campaigns, but although new models were being introduced, such as the Standard Vanguard and Hillman Minx, it was post-1950 before the market began to show its anticipation of the lifting of the emergency restrictions. With the new Austin Seven, and then the Anglia and Prefect in 1953, the British family was being provided with a new age of motoring. Unfortunately in planning terms it was an age for which Britain was ill-prepared. In May 1946 Parliament had been introduced to the idea of new motorways from London to the Midlands and then on to Lancashire and Yorkshire, and one running down to South Wales. Other major links to the south-west, north-east and Scotland were to be catered for by improving existing trunk roads. It had been hoped to complete the construction programme over the next ten years, but two years later it was announced that plans had

34 'Reliability all over the world' advertisement, 1952. Copyright BMIHT/Rover Group

35 'Television in the average home', 1947

been deferred until the economy improved. The only obvious sign of any awareness of the seriousness of designing for the motor car was probably prompted by the sight of London traffic almost coming to a standstill at the time of the Coronation, and the beginning of the debate on the merits of parking meters at the end of 1953.

Television was still a national novelty, and it was felt necessary to explain its relationship to homelife: 'a welcome guest and not a dictator of family life'.[72] Services had been closed down in 1939, and had not recommenced until June 1946, when they were still only available to homes within thirty to forty miles of Alexandra Palace. Screens were small, 8 inch or 10 inch, and viewing was very much based on the notion of going to the cinema, with the family grouped for evening entertainment (figure 35). It was not until December 1949, when transmission arrived in the Midlands, that television services extended beyond London and the Home Counties. So the 1950s opened with a determination to make national television a reality.[73] The North received its first programmes on 12 October 1951, and Scotland on 14 March 1952, with the Glasgow Modern Homes Exhibition's 'Television Arcade' introducing the city to the latest models. It was a new experience, advice was given on the costs and lifetime of the television set, its positioning in the room and viewing conditions: 'There is no need to view television in the dark. It is more comfortable and better for the eyes if you have a shaded light beside or slightly behind the set.'[74] For the first time, working class homes acquired reading lamps, to watch television.

Gardening, cookery and programmes about the home were regular features, invariably scheduled for the mid-afternoon, for women in general, or directly for the housewife. Topical subjects, such as town planning and the Festival of Britain were discussed, there was a short series on British craftsmen, and on 3 October 1951, the first children's competition was announced to make a model of a modern house out of a shoebox. The winners were to be invited into the studio to work with students from the Architectural Association and Peter de Francia in making a full-size room, and end up having tea.

The media family was already established. In November 1951, *Radio Times* celebrated the 1,000th edition of the radio serial, *Mrs Dale's Diary*, with a photograph of the Dales taking tea in the lounge, and an 'At Home' photograph and article as a forerunner to the 250th edition of the equally popular farming family, the Archers. The Dales, the upper middle-class doctor's family living at Virginia Lodge in the suburb of Parkwood Hill, secured middle-class values for the nation. Television's first family, *The Connovers*, introduced at the end of 1949, were also an upper middle-class suburban family, complete with a cook.[75]

As home entertainment changed, so did shopping for the family. The retail trade had been slowly changing, more goods were being packaged, frozen food was being introduced, and since the early 1940s there had been recognition that the American systems of self-service superstores would be the future base of British shopping. The Coop had been in the vanguard of this movement, with the London Society experimenting in some of its stores during 1944.[76] Other department stores soon followed, such as Marks and Spencer (M & S) and Littlewoods, while J. Lyons & Co. decided to introduce the self-service cafeteria into its tea-shops. *The Economist*, on 12 November 1949, ran an article on the supermarket as the revolution in shopping habits, and by 1950 it was recognised as the future pattern of retailing, introducing economies in operational costs and the price of goods, and creating a new sense of freedom and choice for the consumer.[77] It confirmed the heightened awareness of the importance of the housewife as consumer and, despite the continuing rationing and financial restrictions, the target of aggressive advertising campaigns, as for example the 'Battle of Detergents' begun in 1950, which reached new proportions in September 1952, when first 'Surf' and then 'Tide' were launched, and in the November 'Daz' was marketed as 'the most efficient washing product in the world'. While confirming that a contemporary civilisation was about to dawn, it contributed to the frustrations and confusions of everyday life, with many families still trying to find a new home and furnish it, while surrounded by images of part baked bread, expansion of quick frozen foods, and packet soup to feast the family.

Going contemporary

Streamlining and the exuberant styling of cars and household products from America had caused much discussion in the post-war period, distressing Gordon Russell's design sensitivity, and stimulating the CoID into great activity to try to minimise its impact on domestic products. Scandinavian influences were at least as great, and as the plans for the Festival of Britain gained momentum so did the interest in the nature of British design and taste. The Council continued to exploit its links with the retail trade and the Ideal Home Exhibition, where in 1950 it furnished rooms for the Unity House which were then used as illustrations for the publication *Ideas for Your Home*, and formed the basis of a touring exhibition to department stores across the country.[78]

At this stage the discussion was of contemporary design, contemporary style and contemporary canons of decent design, as attention was drawn to the characteristics of post-utility developments. Department stores began to arrange displays of the contemporary, while the Wallpaper Manufacturers Ltd travelling train, which had converted two coaches to the designs of

Kenneth Cheesman, suggested the latest wallpaper patterns and 'contemporary' furniture for a reception room, dining room, living room and bedroom that could be defined as a new movement. The stylistic aspirations were for tasteful and elegant design, conceptually locating the new forms generated by new materials and methods of manufacture as part of a continuing tradition rather than as a radical break with the past. Assimilation rather than revolution was the ideological basis of contemporary as the expression of the new.

It was the Festival of Britain that provided the CoID with the opportunity to secure the refined contemporary style that it had adopted as its own as the taste of the nation, and also created a climate that stimulated interest in popular taste, design progress and the British tradition of the well-made craft object. The Ideal Home Exhibition of 1951 reflected these interests, with the British Electrical Development Association's century of electricity display, and the ideal home designed in response to the suggestions from over 400,000 members of the Federation of Women's Institutes, and with furnishings that gave attention to the handmade curtains and bedcovers of the members. A similar theme of setting contemporary design alongside traditional crafts was to be found in the 'Living Traditions' Festival Exhibition at the Royal Scottish Museum, Edinburgh, while the 'Black Eyes and Lemonade' exhibition at the Whitechapel Art Gallery brought the traditions of popular art into the debate on national identity. What was emerging was a similar design critique to that being developed

36 The house of the future – the garden room, Festival of Britain, Travelling Exhibition, 1951

for architecture, so that while in the 1940s home necessity had demanded that utility furniture stood alongside the antique, in the modern home the new could cohabit with the traditional.

In the Festival the CoID took a more vigorous line in its representation of good design and the role of industrial design in modern life. On the South Bank and in Battersea Park the environment was one of gaiety. In the *Homes and Gardens* section featuring six themes of home life, the intention was to display successful ways of dealing with reduced living space for the child in the home, the bed-sitting room, the kitchen, hobbies and the home, home entertainment, and the parlour. It was predominantly a restatement of the ideals set out in the 1946 'Britain Can Make It' exhibition, but with added colour, the pale pastels with splashes of bold colour contrasts, and the decorative patterns ranging from a regency floral to an abstract crystal selection. Glasgow had a special exhibition, while Birmingham, Leeds, Manchester and Nottingham took the travelling exhibition that was primarily devoted to themes on 'The People' at home, work, play and travel. The garden room of the future, with its picture window, natural materials and Ernest Race bent metal chairs, ably captured the contemporary mood that the Festival had worked so hard to portray (figure 36).[79]

To reject the contemporary was regarded as old-fashioned, and despite its links with the CoID, this was the category into which many of the trade and the consumers had put the Cooperative Union Ltd. The growing feeling was that the Coop was reluctant 'to go contemporary', and embrace a design policy. This was not altogether true, although some of the local societies, particularly in northern areas, believed that there was limited interest in contemporary styles. Looking through *Design and our Homes*, a CWS publication of 1951 by Margaret Llewellyn, reveals an acceptance of the CoID principles of good design and models of good taste, and a willingness to encourage their implementation in the stores and the education of staff. The following year a weekend conference was organised at Harrogate for senior managers, on 'Design and the Cooperative Movement'.[80] There were no real surprises: Gordon Russell led the team of speakers, and it confirmed the importance attached to getting the CWS support for the CoID's efforts to improve public taste.

Throughout 1952 the CoID toured an exhibition to retail stores in eleven regional centres, based around seven room corners of contemporary furniture for the sitting room, dining room, bedroom, garden and study. At the beginning of year it also furnished a show house at Manchester,[81] and then in September through to November, working with the *Manchester Evening Chronicle*, it furnished municipal show houses in districts of Manchester and Stockport.[82] In between the Council had furnished three houses shown by the Ministry of Housing at the Ideal Home

Exhibition, as being representative of the preferences of the members of the Townswomen's Guild, the Women's Institute, and an old people's welfare committee.

Other comparable events that reinforced the manner in which contemporary as a style was being popularised and endorsed as the taste of the young and new consumers included the 'Setting Up Home for Bill and Betty' exhibition at the Whitechapel Art Gallery,[83] with its room settings by Anthony Lewis and Mrs Psyche Pirie. Suggested as the home of the returning honeymooners, while introducing what was believed to be a 'common-sense approach' to contemporary taste, supported by catalogue notes on the uses of new colours, patterns and materials for decoration and furnishing, it remained traditional in its reassuring response to social conventions, providing Bill with a good big easy chair to relax in after work, and Betty with an easy chair without arms so that she could sew in comfort. Similar in its intentions, was the Peter Jones' furnishing of the Davis House at the 1952 Ideal Home Exhibition, for the WVS 'Mr & Mrs Thrift'. An imaginary family with two children, girl of 17, boy of five, mother active for WVS, and her house a focal point for the village, they were provided with a contemporary setting, not too 'daring' or 'different'. The bedroom for the girl, who had just started working, provided a good indication of the flavour of the whole scheme, 'white walls with a papered ceiling in red and white with a scalloped valance of the same paper edging the top of the walls. The divan cover and the covers of the small chairs are blue and white striped chintz. The whole room is gay and youthful'.[84] It was considered to be tasteful with economy, a blend of imagination and ingenuity. Furnishing the house had not come cheaply, although it had been kept within its budget of £1,000. The DIA exhibition of two suburban living rooms at Charing Cross Station, February to March 1953, was much more forthright in its intentions.[85] The rooms were furnished in contrasting styles, and the public were invited to vote for their preference. Of the 30,300 votes, 53 per cent of people over 35, and 63 per cent of those under 35 preferred the contemporary room, as did two out of three young women. Replicating the CoID's policy on good and bad design, Paul Reilly in his review revelled in being able to compare the conventional chair, 'opulent, flatulent, corpulent' with the contemporary 'light in line and weight'.[86] As for the rooms as a whole, one was reviewed as being 'overcrowded, restless in detail, sombre in tone; dark colours to conceal dirt, high glosses for glamour, electric candle lights and shades for nostalgia'; the other had 'fresh colours, reds and oatmeal and blues for upholstery, olive-green wallpaper with small pink and lime pattern on chimney wall; ... modest sideboard ... all furniture ... for easy moving and cleaning'.[87] It was assumed that the young and those accustomed to making careful decisions would have had no difficulty in selecting the contemporary model room.

Having moved the design debate into one of consumption, actual choice was still severely limited, and questions of economy, low-cost and minimum were dominant concerns. One of the most realistic introductions to the social climate was the booklet *Furnishing Your Home ... A Guide to Wise Spending*', 1952, sponsored by ICI and produced by the industrial designers, Taylor and Associates of Macclesfield. It addressed the questions of the 'minimum furniture required in a council house for a man and his wife and two children, and then to obtain that minimum at the lowest possible cost'.[88] Accepting that in some instances solutions would be short term and would eventually be replaced, the guiding principle had been to obtain good value for money. So the accompanying show house in Northwich was furnished with Ercol chairs and CWS sideboards and cupboards. Matting and linoleum, or stained wood were the suggested floor finishes. Curtains and linen were made up from remnants bought on Birkenhead or Northwich market, as were many of the kitchen utensils, supplemented by equipment purchased from Woolworths. Repainted

THIS FAMILY 'ROBINSON' cheerfully do the chores gaily arrayed in our new and colourful aprons. Teenager Jane is happy in the Hostess apron she has chosen in gingham with its deep frilled hem and ric-rac trimming. Available in green, blue and red check, with contrasting ric-rac and applique of tulips. 15/11d.
On the Cover
"The New Yorker" Apron in varied guise to show how it will take you thro' the day. Gaily printed cotton on blue, green or pink ground.
In Minor and Major Sizes. 7/11d.
Mother knows that her attractive "Jonell" smock is essentially practical for any household job, as the elasticated cuffs will turn back easily when required. In cotton finished rayon printed on grey, green, yellow, rose or smoke blue. 21/9d.
Father, too, can easily be persuaded to lend a hand when he is offered this smart but workmanlike apron in chalk striped navy butchers' ticking. Inexpensively priced at 7/11d.
The youngest member lends colour to the scheme with a well-styled apron-over-frock effect in gingham and plain cotton. In blue and pink. Length Sizes, 24"–33". 6/11d. to 8/6d. according to size.
Grandmother presides in a Paisley print overall of fine spun rayon with comfortable button-through front. In six colour combinations. Sizes W. 19/11d., W.X. 27/9d. and O.S. 23/9d.

37 Knight & Lee, John Lewis Partnership, advertisement, 1953

second-hand furniture was included as was the home-made, such as a hardboard wardrobe with a curtain, an orange box shelf unit or bookcase, and a work-box stool or toy chest from a soap box, with legs made out of a broomstick. The outcome was a fully furnished house for £177 6*s.* 0*d.*, and if only the absolute essentials had been purchased costs would have been reduced to £135 19*s.* 10*d.*[89]

Few families were in a position to enjoy the new lifestyles, but a culture of modernisation was being created that embraced existing homes just as well as new homes. Furnishing and decoration were the dominant expressions of this movement, but there was also a more pragmatic strand which recognised that the plans for a modern Britain were becoming increasingly dependent on financial support for the modernisation of nineteenth-century terraced houses, 'to modernise the kitchen-living room, to provide an efficient modern cooker and piped hot water service, to contrive the installation of a bath, to warm the parlour, to insulate the roof'.[90] These were the basic needs and as the festival excitement subsided the popular desire of modern Britain was for a tasteful and modernised home. There also remained a strong belief in the possibilities of a new social and cultural democracy that would deliver the same Family Robinson spirit that had been referenced as the ideal by Helen Masters in her paper to the Royal Society of Arts in 1942. Delightfully imaged in the advertisement for new aprons, it was the modern British family of the new Elizabethan age, all sharing the household chores, the ideal picture of the happy, caring family of contemporary Britain (figure 37).

Notes

1 See M. Bondfield, *Our Towns a Close-Up*, London, 1943.

2 In post-war Britain it was being suggested that government hostels and service camps should be brought into use as holiday centres, and that efforts should be made to encourage canvas and country-based holidays, and convert country houses into hostels.

3 In December 1946 over 1,000 restaurants were still being operated by 361 out of 419 authorities, but the scheme was steadily being phased out. Although seen as a threat to commercial trading, these civic restaurants had been allowed to continue if municipal authorities so wished. By 1 January 1949 numbers were down to 678.

4 R. Tubbs, *Living in Cities*, London, 1942, p. 36.

5 Readers' work on the Plan for Britain, *Picture Post*, 8 March 1941, p. 14.

6 E. Denby, 'Plan the Home', *Picture Post*, 4 January 1941, p. 21.

7 *Ibid.*, p. 23.

8 *Ideal Home*, September 1941, p. 131.

9 *Ideal Home*, September 1942, p. 128.

10 Royal Society of Arts, *The Post-War Home: Its Interior and Equipment*, London 1942 p. 13.
11 *Ibid.*, p. 84.
12 *Ibid.*, p. 108.
13 A. Mansbridge, *Wise for thy Houses*, London, 1942, p. 5.
14 E. Mannin, *Castles in the Street*, London, 1942, p. 13.
15 M. Pleydell-Bouverie, *Daily Mail Book of Post-War Homes*, London, 1944, p. 23.
16 *Ibid.*, p. 132.
17 W. E. Brown, *Changing Britain*, Bourneville, 1943, p. 26.
18 E. Goldfinger and E. J. Carter, *County of London Plan*, London, 1945, p. 31.
19 Thomas Sharp, *Exeter Phoenix a Plan for Rebuilding*, London, 1946, p. 58.
20 *Ibid.*, p. 45.
21 *Ibid.*, p. 98.
22 Electrical Association for Women, *Housing Digest*, London, 1946, p. 35.
23 *Coop News*, 1 April 1944, p. 13.
24 R. Tubbs, *The Englishman Builds*, London, 1945, p. 73.
25 It had a living room, two bedrooms, kitchen and bathroom sharing the same plumbing unit, entrance hall and coal store.
26 See J. Huxley, *TVA Adventure in Planning*, London, 1943.
27 Orders were placed for 54,500 bungalows to be delivered by August 1947.
28 Ministry of Works, *Demonstration Houses*, London, 1944.
29 House-Building Industries' Standing Committee, *Your New Home*, London, 1946.
30 *Ibid.*, p. 95.
31 A. Boyd and C. Penn, *Homes for the People*, London, 1946.
32 Scottish Housing Advisory Committee Report, *Modernising our Homes*, London, 1947, p. 30.
33 See Electrical Installations, No. 11, Post-War Building Studies, 1942; also M. Gilbert, 'Open Sesame to Simpler Living', *Electrical Age*, January 1945.
34 Ascot Gas Water Heaters Ltd, *Houses into Flats*, London, 1947, p. 51.
35 Ministry of Health, *Housing Progress*, London, 1948.
36 Ministry of Health, *Our Gardens*, London, 1948, p. 4.
37 October 1948. Britain introduced its Four-Year Recovery Plan to meet its balance of payments.
38 Movable Dwelling Conference, *Movable Dwellings*, London, 1950, p. 11.
39 *The Berkeley 'Ambassador'. Catalogue*, 33rd International Motor Exhibition, London, 1948, p. 267.
40 Examples were built at Delapre, Northamptonshire.
41 Prefabricated houses and buildings were being exported to Australia, and in June 1952 a prototype 'Commonwealth' aluminium house was put on display in London.
42 See C. Barr, 'The People's Houses', *The Listener*, 7 February 1952, pp. 214–16; A. G. Sheppard-Fidler, 'Homes for the People', *The Listener*, 24 April 1952, pp. 666–8.

43 *Report of the Flats Sub-Committee of the Central Housing Advisory Committee*, London, 1952.

44 D. Rigby Childs, 'Housing Layout in London's New Towns, Progress Report', *Architects' Journal*, 10 April 1952, p. 449.

45 *Good Housekeeping*, October 1953, p. 75.

46 *Electrical Age*, January 1952, p. 581.

47 G. Cullen, 'Prairie Planning', *Architectural Review*, July 1953.

48 J. M. Richards, 'Failure of the New Towns', *Architectural Review*, July 1953, p. 30.

49 Ministry of Housing and Local Government, *Design in Town and Village*, London, 1953.

50 L. Brett, 'Are Architects Becoming More Human?', *The Listener*, 11 October 1951, p. 594.

51 'Festival of Britain 1951' *Journal of the Town Planning Institute*, May 1951, p. 156.

52 H. Casson, 'South Bank Adventure', *The Listener*, 17 May 1951, p. 792.

53 O. Lancaster, 'End of the Modern Movement in Architecture', *The Listener*, 18 October 1951, p. 640.

54 Nicholas Pevsner gave four talks on 'How to Judge Victorian Architecture', the first one published in *The Listener*, 19 July 1951.

55 I. Cox, *Guide South Bank Exhibition London Festival of Britain*, London, 1951, p. 6.

56 *Ibid.*, p. 9.

57 The emphasis was on the arrangements for the kitchen, living-dining room and bedroom. An all-steel bed was introduced in 1945, and in March 1946 the range was being extended, and expanded still further in 1947. The scheme finally ended on 21 January 1953.

58 There was a bed-settee, but only available to those living in a bed-sitter.

59 December 1946. Colours allowed in Utility kitchen cabinets were green, blue, cream and primrose.

60 W. F. Morris, *The Future Citizen and His Surroundings*, London, 1945, p. 5.

61 *Architects' Journal*, 9 March 1944, p. 181.

62 Intent on heightening the public appreciation of cotton, and developing stronger links with art schools and young designers, in the post-war period it held important international shows, with the Swedish Textiles and Furniture, spring 1947, and the July 1949 exhibition of textile samples from twelve countries.

63 PEP, *The Market for Household Appliances*, London, 1945. It claimed that 85 per cent of the British net national income was in the hands of families with an income below £500.

64 ColD, *Design 46*, London, 1946, p. 12.

65 Despite this emphasis it had not proved possible to include any work from the motor industry. For discussion of these developments see P. Sparke (ed.), *Did Britain Make It? British Design in Context 1946–86*, London, 1986; J. M. Woodham, 'Managing British Design, Reform 1', *Journal of Design History*, vol. 9, no. 1, 1996, pp. 55–65, and 'Reform 2', *Journal of Design History*, vol. 9, no. 2, 1996, pp. 101–15.

66 *Britain Can Make It*, exhibition catalogue, London, 1946, p. 141.

67 A. L. Osborne, 'A Man in the Kitchen', *Daily Mail Ideal Home Book 1947–48*, London, p. 88.

68 H. Read (ed.), *The Practice of Design*, London, 1946, pp. 9–21.

69 'Enterprise in a Cardiff store', *Design*, May 1949, p. 16.

70 *Design*, July 1949, p. 2.

71 October 1949 Manchester also had the *Evening Chronicle* Better Housekeeping Exhibition.

72 *The Festival Exhibition 1951, The Land Travelling Exhibition*, London, 1951, p. 23. Television service had first commenced on 2 November 1936.

73 The 14,560 licences of 1947 had increased to 343,882 in 1950.

74 *Television & You*, n.d. 772/s xii, JLP Archive.

75 The Grove Family, April 1954–56, and the Appleyards, October 1952–57, followed the same pattern.

76 It was claimed that the Kingskerswell branch of the Newton Abbot CWS was the first purpose-built store, opened in September 1949. In 1948, Portsea Island Coop converted its mobile shop into self-service, and the following year the Walsall Society constructed one on a low-loading trailer, which allowed for rear entrance and off-side exit.

77 Even while these changes were being absorbed, note was already being taken of more profound changes in America, with one-stop shopping and the out of town shopping centres for motorists (see E. Topham, 'Cash and Carry by Car', *Cooperative Review*, December 1952).

78 The booklet *Ideas for the Home*, had space for the name of the host store on the front cover; in the first year it was shown at Bainbridges, Newcastle; Hemingway's, Leeds; Plymouth Coop; Ebbutts, Croydon; O'Brien & Burroughs, St Leonards on Sea; W. H. Gibbs, Ashford.

79 'The old striped wallpaper regime, rooms with their ancient lamps and aspidistras, stand alongside the new – the ultra-smart dining room, living room and kitchen of the twentieth century': *Manchester Evening Chronicle*, 17 April 1951.

80 The lesson was well received, but the independence of the societies made it difficult to develop what might have been understood as a corporate design strategy.

81 See *Coop Review*, April 1952.

82 *Design*, September 1952: Newall Green, 3–17 September; Blackley, 25 September–8 October; Urmston, 16–29 October; Stockport, 6–19 November.

83 *Setting Up Home for Bill and Betty*, Whitechapel Art Gallery, London, 1952.

84 *The Gazette of the John Lewis Partnership*, 8 March 1952, p. 74.

85 Exhibition was shown at Manchester in May 1953.

86 *Design*, April 1953, p. 9.

87 *Ibid.*, p. 9.

88 *Furnishing Your Home*, ICI, Northwich, 1952, p. 2.

89 Wise spending was also the theme of three television programmes, 'A home for the Smiths', broadcast in November and December 1952, in which the designer Hulme Chadwick set about advising a young couple on home furnishing.

90 E. Bellingham, 'Britain's Forgotten Homes', *The Listener*, 4 December 1952, p. 926.

5 ✧ Convenience to confrontation, 1954–69

The post-rationed age

Ideas for modern life

RATIONING was finally coming to an end, and when it was removed from bacon and meat in July 1954, this only left coal on the list. With the lifting of Board of Trade restrictions on hire purchase arrangements in the same month, Britain was to enter a phase of consumer boom that cut across all sections of society. It was a time of 'Credits for Everyman', as the middle classes were joining the working classes on the easy instalment plan to home comforts and the family car.[1] A regrouping that was recognised as a new class of mass-consumers, self-service was endorsed as the future for the large multiple store.[2] The excitement of the Coronation Year lingered on, and the steady appearance of the Italian 'Espresso' machine brought the arrival of the new small coffee house, and the coffee bar culture. After the years of restriction, it was a buoyant start, but even as attention focused on new-found luxuries of homelife, other broader social problems remained unresolved. Not enough homes were being built, traffic congestion was getting worse, and most of the new housing estates were surviving without essential services.

Throughout the year the CoID travelling exhibition 'Round the Table' toured department stores in major regional centres, displaying modern tableware in six furnished bays for different meals, and a central arrangement of eight different place settings.[3] Good manners and good taste were on show. At the end of the year the Council was to celebrate its tenth anniversary, as it entered a new phase in which it set out to consolidate its position as a national institution. The RIBA was doing the same for architecture, arranging touring exhibitions to promote the work of the architect, and having successfully put together 'Home and Surroundings' in 1953, followed it up in 1954 with 'Your House'. Modernisation as well as new development was being given attention, and in August 1954 the government grants for modernising old houses were revised to include the conversion of large old houses into flats. To launch the new legislation the Ministry of Housing built four late Georgian terrace houses, on part of the bombed Holles Street site of the John Lewis department store. One was made up to look like a Victorian home, the second and third were converted into three self-contained flats, one being furnished in contemporary style by John Lewis for £500, and another furnished by the WVS in second-hand furniture painted in 'attractive' colours. The fourth house was arranged to show the latest labour-saving appliances contrasted with the old kitchen ranges, coppers and sinks. Open from 16 June to 14 August they were seen by 169,206 visitors.[4]

It was a climate in which the concept of 'do-it-yourself' as a generic title under which it would be possible to market the various activities undertaken by the home handyman and decorator was gaining wider recognition. This was an important move away from the ideas associated with 'handicrafts' and trade links. The Board of Trade was drawing the attention of exporters to the importance of the already established market in the United States, and the message was being picked up for the home market. In February 1954, Bon Marché, Liverpool, opened its 'Household Boutique', where 'From a wide selection of modern labour-saving equipment and gadgets you are sure to find something to solve your particular household problem, and give you more precious hours of leisure'.[5] Directed at do-it-yourself beginners and enthusiasts, it was a marketing strategy that had drawn women into its audience. John Lewis Partnership stores, Heelas in Reading and G. H. Lee, Liverpool, also opened departments in February 1955. The trend had been set. In September 1956, the first of the annual Do-It-Yourself Exhibitions was held at Olympia, and from November 1957 Manchester also had an annual DIY exhibition.[6]

Home entertainment and taste was being reshaped by television, and with the launch of the Independent Television Authority programmes in 1955 so was consumerism. The 'Design Review' feature on the BBC's 'Mainly for Women' was started in the autumn of 1955 and in 1956 continued as a monthly series. Both the CoID and the BBC recognised the significance of the role television could play in stressing the importance of good design, not only in this type of specialised programme, but in the sets and background furniture used in other programmes.[7] Part of a general mission to develop a discriminating public, lessons on design were now appearing everywhere, introducing ideas on restrained colour and elegant form, alongside schemes for luxury bathrooms and dream kitchens. It was, as the CoID explained about its relationship to the Ideal Home Exhibition, a 'marriage of convenience between advanced design and established taste'.[8] The smaller-scale ideal home exhibitions in Manchester and Birmingham during the 1950s and 1960s followed a similar pattern, as did those for regional centres which supplemented a touring exhibition of national organisations, with work from local companies.[9]

'The Happy Home', was how the Good Housekeeping Institute guide for all housewives and home lovers described the modern family home.[10] It provided a detailed account of how to manage a home, from choosing goods and appliances, planning work, nursing the family, entertaining and modernising, so that with ease and charm the housewife would create a happy and cheerful home life. Days were fully timetabled, with times for leisure and special work (figure 38). There was advice on 'Looking Your Best', changing into a frock and renewing make-up before the family came home, and guidance on 'Living Together', 'Happy Parenthood' and 'Brighter Homes'. With its middle-class images and values it was representing established family lifestyle values, and at a point where these were under question, reminding its readers of the dignity of running a family home.[11]

It was a similar picture of moderate good taste that the CoID constructed for the British contribution to the homes section of the International Exhibition at Halsinborg in June 1955. Electing to base the installation on a flat designed by Eric Lyons for Parkleys Estate, Ham Common, and furnished to designs by Jo Patrick, the intention was to show modern British home planning and furnishing at its best. Designed to suit the taste of a prosperous businessman, wife and thirteen-year-old son, it had details of the 'characteristically British way of life – the bowler hat and umbrella in the hall, the wife's embroidery, the boy's interest in natural history, the early morning tea tray in the bedroom'.[12] It was a cosy Home Counties Contemporary, with its kitchen partitioned from the dining-living room and study, walls decorated in coffee, black and white, and furnished with moulded chairs, oval coffee table, wall unit, and a veneered dining table, set for evening dinner (figure 39).

Products and national identity and values took on an altogether different relationship the following year when on 26 April 1956 the CoID opened the Design Centre in the Haymarket, London, with 1,020 products from 433 firms, selected by its committee of experts, as 'a shopping guide so that people who will buy, will buy better goods, not just more goods'.[13] Not easy to explain, the objects on display were expected to show designers and industry what was considered to be good design (figure 40). A nationalisation of taste, the position of authority was reinforced the following year with the introduction of the Design Centre Awards for outstanding designs, 'component parts of the well furnished home; not designed to be shown off and looked at as collector's pieces, but intended to take their proper place in a setting for everyday life'.[14] Twelve products were selected from about 3,500 shown at the Design Centre during its first year.

In general the pattern was to tell the public what it should like. An interesting exception resulted in the BBC's 'Woman's Hour' House at the 1957 Ideal Home Exhibition. A reflection of the dreams of thousands of

Plan of work for a three-bedroomed house and a family of husband, wife and one baby of 18 months:

7 a.m.	Make early tea and give baby drink.
7.20	Open house. Dress self and baby. (Husband attends to boiler.)
7.45	Cook breakfast and serve it.
8.20	Clear away breakfast, wash up.
8.40	Put baby in pram or play pen. Collect day's washing and put to soak. Make beds. Tidy and dust upstairs, and do daily work in bathroom and lavatory.
9.30	Do daily work downstairs.
10.15	Do daily wash. Make any necessary preparations for lunch.
11	Break for tea or coffee. Attend to baby and put him to rest.
11.30	Special work—see below.
12.30	Get lunch.
1 p.m.	Lunch with baby. Clear away after lunch, wash up and tidy kitchen.
Afternoon:	Attend to baby, shopping, gardening, mending, etc.
4.30	Tea for self and baby.
5.0	Playtime with baby.
5.30	Bath baby and put him to bed.
6.15	Prepare and cook supper.
7.15	Serve supper.
7.45	Clear and wash up supper dishes with tea things. Lay breakfast.

Special Weekly work:

Monday	Washing.
Tuesday	Main bedroom and child's bedroom, alternate weeks.
Wednesday	Bathroom, lavatory, landing and stairs. Spare bedroom when necessary.
Thursday	Sitting-room, and dining-room and hall, alternate weeks.
Friday	Kitchen.
Saturday	Extra baking.

Ironing, silver cleaning, etc., to be fitted in in evenings or afternoons.

Plan of work for four-bedroomed house with a family of three schoolchildren:

6.45 a.m.	Make early morning tea. Wake children.
7.0	Open up house. Draw back curtains, etc. Start preparing breakfast. Husband does solid fuel fire.
7.15	Dress self and supervise children.
7.40	Finish preparing breakfast and serve.
8.0	Get family off to school.
8.15	Clear and wash breakfast.
8.40	Make beds and do daily work upstairs.
9.40	Do daily work downstairs.
10.15	Cooking. Make preparations for evening meal.
11.0	Break for tea.
11.15	Special work (see below).
12.30 p.m.	Prepare and eat snack lunch.
1.15	Tidy kitchen. Finish off special work.
Afternoon:	Shopping, mending, ironing, gardening, etc.
4	Get tea for self and milk and cake for children on their return from school.
5	Put on evening meal.
6	Serve hot meal for whole family.
6.45	Supervise younger children's bedtime.
7.15	Wash up supper dishes. Pack husband's lunch for next day.

Special Work:

Monday	Washing.
Tuesday	Turn out three main bedrooms in rotation. Fourth bedroom when necessary.
Wednesday	Turn out sitting-room and dining-room in alternate weeks.
Thursday	Bathroom, lavatory, hall and stairs.
Friday	Weekend shopping in morning. Extra cleaning of kitchen in afternoon.
Saturday	Extra baking.

38 The housewife's day, *Happy Home*, 1954

its listeners who had taken the trouble to answer the *Radio Times* questionnaire in the autumn of 1956, the outcome was somewhat misleading as the interior design had to be fitted to a Berg detached house, complete with a Palladian entrance and decorative window shutters. Contrasting colours and bold patterns were considered to be the popular choice, as was an open fire in the sitting room. Other notable features were the kitchen that tried to blend the homely with the streamlined, and a teenager's room, complete with wall units and a divan. An unsurprising blend of middle-class taste, it took its place alongside the 'convertible' house that allowed room sizes to be changed according to family needs, the 'open-plan' home, the 'frost-proof' house presented by the Ministry of Housing and Local Government that illustrated a central plumbing system, and a three-storey block of one- and two-bedroom flats. With so much choice now being made available, in the same year the Design and Industries Association as self-appointed guardians of good taste took it on themselves to arrange an exhibition 'Make or Mar', demonstrating how two rooms using the same modern furniture could be spoilt with an over-fussy use of patterns, colours and ornaments.

As retailers of good taste, the CoID also understood that at regular intervals it would be necessary to use room settings to show how new products would impact on the British at home, and to celebrate the first anniversary of the Design Centre, it chose the topical theme of 'Design

39 CoID, British Exhibition at Halsinborg, 1955

40 Design Centre, Haymarket, London, 1956

for Viewing'.[15] Presenting designs for four rooms, two of which were constructed, the intention was to show ideas that would suit families with different incomes and tastes. The preoccupation was with explaining the correct television viewing conditions in terms of height and distance from the screen, and the correct lighting and warmth for the room. Believing that the television would replace the fireplace as the focal point of the room, it was also felt necessary to guide the British public in the necessary rearrangement of their rooms without disrupting the conventions of home-life. Plans of the layout were distributed to the retail trade, and thirty-two stores put on displays to coincide with the London show, with the hope that in the future the nation would be sitting comfortably. It is sometimes difficult to appreciate the seriousness of this debate, but ideas on living space had yet to be resolved, and as television was becoming integral to the home,[16] opinions as to its place varied considerably. In 1958, Wimpey launched its TV house. A three-bedroom semi-detached house, with an integral garage, its selling point was a window behind the sink which looked into the living room and allowed favourite television programmes to be watched while still doing the chores. In contrast *Woman's Journal*, November 1958, collaborated with the Peter Jones team of interior decorators to show how a room need not be dominated by the television set. It could be hidden behind a chair, and the room easily rearranged to accommodate a television supper.[17] First shown at the Sloane Square store, it was later reproduced with some local variations at the other stores in the John Lewis Partnership.

By the end of 1957 the Council of Industrial Design had completed its link with the manufacturers and retail trade with the production of the Design Centre label, available as holed, stringed or gummed, which could be attached to products that had been selected for the Design Centre, confirming to the everyday shopper that the goods were approved and their taste was protected. In September 1958 the Design Centre was taken to Newcastle upon Tyne, where in collaboration with the John Lewis Partnership a selection from the 'Design Index' was put on display at Bainbridges' department store, while a further selection was taken to the Bristol Building Centre.[18] In February 1959, the Design Centre label was launched across the country in the windows of eighty-one shops in fifty-six towns. Taking good taste into the high street, informed choice was promoted as the dominant feature of the consumer culture.[19]

Women's journals were taking a more direct interest in the architecture and furnishing of the home. For example, since January 1953, *Good Housekeeping* had a section on 'Homes Today', and starting in the spring of 1957, *Woman's Journal* had its 'House of the Year'. Initially it had been intended to use a house at Harlow New Town to demonstrate the advantages of the 'Silicone' home,[20] but because of petrol rationing it had been constructed as a series of rooms at Bourne & Hollingsworth in Oxford Street. The following year a similar idea was set out at Bobby's of Eastbourne for an imaginary family of mother, father and two children, offering open-plan living. At the end of the year they took a step closer to using a current house for professional families, featuring the Dormy House, by Wates at Crawley, as the modern approach to house design. It was in March 1959 that the House of the Year became a reality, situated on an estate in Leamington Spa. A four-bedroom detached house, with oil-fired central heating, furnished by Maples to the designs of Gaby Schreiber, it had 'subdued colour schemes giving an overall unity to the house, adding to the feeling of space, and chosen for their enduring virtues – plain fitted carpets emphasising interest in texture rather than design – antique ornaments in a modern setting to show the charm of a subtle combination of old and new'.[21] Cookery demonstrations, fashion shows and a film 'Woman's Journal Home Movie' accompanied the showhouse. The next year, at Liverpool, the programme was even more ambitious with a lecture series by the architects and designers. At a cost of £9,950 the house was expensive middle-class living, but with the blend of natural woods, thermoplastic floor tiles, formica work surfaces, underfloor heating and open fire it was further confirmation of the mainstream mixing of traditional and new materials and services. It was for a family that required 'privacy but also the most free relationship between indoors and outdoors; warmth despite lavish windows; spaciousness for entertaining but a more intimate day-to-day atmosphere; and maximum comfort with minimum drudgery'.[22]

At the 1958 Brussels World Fair, Britain had made great efforts to pull together similar expressions of innovative and traditional design, but the selection and arrangement gave a confused view of national values. Introducing the visitor through a 'Hall of Tradition', with its purple light, regalia and pageantry, dominated by the Annigoni portrait of the Queen, was hardly the most enlightened way into the hall of technology. There was a product range selected by the CoID, five window displays showing the decorative uses of the rose motif from Elizabethan times to the present day, synthetic fibres from Courtaulds and a series of small models showing the uses of formica in the home. A courtyard of Commonwealth flags, and walled gardens with murals that represented the 'British at Home' with a subtle humour that would have bemused an international visitor, compounded the confusion and created a feeling akin to a national bazaar. As the best of British it was a selection that showed a modern Britain wrapped up with its glorious past, escaping into the commercial contemporary world of the Britannia Inn and the Fox and Hounds Pub. It was a self-deprecating image that was uncomfortably close to the reality of a modern Britain, slowly extricating itself from a preoccupation with contemporary styles.

Convenience

While the home was being rearranged, shopping for the family was undergoing an even bigger change, which some saw as a revolution. In 1956 the Coop still held about 60 per cent of a market estimated at 3,100 self-service stores, but its share was steadily reducing as an increasing number of companies were making conversions. From the mid-1950s, it was the food self-service store developed as a supermarket that changed the structure of family shopping, with the pre-packed produce rapidly extending from dry goods and liquids, to fruit and vegetables, and late night opening on Friday evenings.[23] The mobile shop remained a crucial lifeline for families moved to the new housing estates, which had few or no local facilities. There are no precise figures for the trade as a whole, but between 1946 and 1955 the Coop increased its mobile stores from 2,250 to 3,900; this included the expected range of grocers and butchers, and the unexpected such as ladies hairdressing, footwear, drapery and furnishing. By the late 1950s, numbers had doubled and of the 8,000 fully equipped mobile shops, the Cooperative movement was operating over 50 per cent.

Ready-made and pre-packed produce was becoming the dominant trend. 1956 saw the introduction of the aluminium can with a tear strip opener, Colman's 'Instant Desserts', and the Birds Eye frozen chicken pie. The following year Lyons marketed 'Redibrek', and attempts were made to popularise tea-bags.[24] It was the decade when the deep-freezer secured its place in the home, and family meals were being made with quick-frozen foods, 'revolutionising home catering, enabling the housewife to give her family all the year round food that is in prime condition, completely fresh and prepared in a few moments'.[25] It was the new way for the housewife to keep the family well-fed and happy, and when the occasion arose, to be the perfect picture of the 'Cool Hostess'.

As has already been well illustrated, the location, equipping and use of the kitchen played a central role in any repositioning of values and identity of British family life. Out of the necessities of the emergency years it had been radically rethought in terms of its standardisation, and then through the home exhibitions, amongst which the 'Britain Can Make It' of 1946 played a leading role. It was increasingly represented as a living space as well as workshop, and a glimpse into the future for the emancipated family. The social stigma attached to eating in the kitchen was being put under a new attack as yet more middle-class families had to accept fitting themselves into smaller living spaces. At the same time the physical changes being made possible by even more technical improvements in the design of the automatic washing machine were giving greater credibility to the possibility of the family wash being reduced to a background activity, leaving the housewife with more time to play with the children.

It was the kitchen as a core area of family living that marked a radical change in social attitudes. As the multi-purpose living space, with its fitted units and appliances, it was to dominate house design and lifestyle over the next ten years. The basic model was designed for the average household of 4–5 people, taking cooking as the major activity that would require good working surfaces, and well-placed cupboards, cooker and refrigerator. Home laundry, both in terms of washing and ironing, were also accepted as being more likely to be accommodated in the kitchen than a separate utility room, while some provision for meals, certainly informal ones, was becoming commonplace. Overall there was little noticeable change from the ideas that had been developed since the 1930s. Futuristic schemes invariably reworked the labour-saving appliance-based home. For example, the 1955 'Tomorrow's Kitchen' by Fridgidaire, was an open plan with room-divider separating it from the dining area, with the housewife served by and controlling a range of appliances. She had a TV in the kitchen, a closed-circuit system so that she could watch the children in another part of the house, duplicate controls in the kitchen and dining area, and a concealed track system for carrying trays of food and utensils.

The fantasy 'House of the Future' created for two people by Alison and Peter Smithson for the 1956 Ideal Home Exhibition expressed similar ideas. A single-storey rectangular windowless box, with an internal garden patio, its futuristic expression depended on an interior made up of a series of eccentric organic shapes. The surprise of the concept was not so much the attention to the appliance-filled kitchen workshop as gadgets always came first on any list, but that so little attention was attached to its social and practical implications. Internally it had no scope for adaptability, it provided no private space, and the quirky grass patio raised all the obvious questions about where the garden rubbish and tools would be put, and how muddy feet would be dealt with. Externally, there was no consideration of the aesthetic implications of groups of boxes, or the manner in which communities of boxes would interpret neighbourhood values. Intended to be a serious expression of new thinking on factory-made units, obsolescence and new technology, the Smithsons had given little attention to patterns of personal and community behaviour. This was not an unusual occurrence in exhibitions that were devoted to the home and its neighbourhood, but as an opportunity to introduce some radical new thinking to an era that was struggling to resolve its housing and environmental problems, it had trivialised the problem.

The March 1958 Design Centre exhibition 'Design in your Kitchen', concentrated on the problems of standardisation between appliances and kitchen fitments. There was little new to be said in way of ideas. The luxury kitchen was planned as all-electric, costing £1,250, and included every possible kitchen appliance, refrigerator, freezer, washing machine, dishwasher, tumble dryer and cooker; the middle-income kitchen equipped for £375 had a cooker and refrigerator. Formica and vinyl tiles covered most surfaces, introducing colour and pattern, and upsetting the purists with the imitation of natural materials.[26] Despite these minor irritations it was little wonder that the Scottish CoID for its exhibition of design in Glasgow, March 1958, should have chosen to describe the 1950s as 'The Age of Convenience'. Even so the traditional values of the housewife being the good hostess and running the home with efficiency remained in place. Taking a pride in the home the housewife would be nurse, nursemaid, cook, cleaner, laundress and sympathetic companion, as the ideal imagined family was based on the young professional family living in a cosy home.

Concept designs and the planners

The spirit of the post-rationed age was substantially influenced by an increasing interest in the possibilities of creating a technologically improved society. Still hampered by a lack of resources, progress in building a new Britain remained slow, and as seen in the reactions to the new town development, there was little excitement over the new domestic landscapes. With the fun time of the Festival year already history, and the plans of a post-war utopia for Britain long since discounted, the appearance of the first of seven social environmental projects, published between 1955 and 1968 by the Glass Age Development Committee,[27] was well timed. Sponsored by Pilkington Brothers Ltd, the committee of Geoffrey A. Jellicoe, Edward D. Mills and Ove Arup and Partners, was joined by other architects for individual projects. The design briefs were for Britain in the year 2000, but realistic in that they were to make use of technology that was already available. The first project, published in 1955, was for the redevelopment of Soho, an 83-acre site in central London. Retaining buildings of historic interest and existing squares, the residents were to be transferred to six 24-storey residential blocks, offices were to be located in a weatherproof precinct, the existing streets roofed over and the area used for gardens and canals that would have glass bottoms transmitting light to the markets and streets below. Intended to show the role played by glass in creating a future with a controlled clean environment, the central feature was a market, surrounded by shops, cafés, restaurants and offices, with its roof formed by the waved glass underside of the swimming pool. Rooted in modernism, monumental in scale and expression, no attention was given to the social implications of its design. Yet, in its interpretation of covered shopping malls and high-rise flats, it anticipated much of the thinking behind the cityscapes of the 1960s.

More prophetic was the 1956 'High Market' project to serve Birmingham and the surrounding towns. Reworking the American out of town shopping centre, a unified building, 610 m. by 122 m., was intended to restore 'leisure and pleasure to shopping', free from traffic congestion, with parking for 3,500 cars, and served by road, rail and helicopter. Traffic problems by then were dominating city planning, and ideas that seemed to provide any hint of a solution, no matter how fantastic, were treated with some seriousness. The 'Skyport One' project of 1957 was for a series of 500-feet high flight-decks in central London for vertical landing aircraft on inter-city flights in Britain and Europe. Each skyport, with three vertical shafts supporting the deck, rising from the supporting building of hotel, offices and multi-storey car park, would cover an area as large as St Paul's Cathedral and be one-third higher.

The most controversial of the concepts, because of its potential for realisation, was the 1959 project 'Motopia'. This new town plan for 30,000, was based on a grid divided up into rectangles, constructed out of four-storey housing blocks with parking and access at the fourth floor and a dual carriageway on the roof, joined by roundabouts at each intersection. Fifteen of the roundabouts would be connected by the internal public transport waterway, and the areas within each of the thirty-five roundabouts were to be used for community life, theatres, public houses, tea-shops, clubrooms and nursery schools. The 'town centre' was adjacent to the Motopia road system, and the through road network serving the wider regional needs, had linear streets and parking for 3,000 cars. It separated traffic from pedestrians, but demonstrated how little understanding there was of the actual problems of air and sound pollution, the practicalities of car movement and maintenance, car ownership, and the everyday needs of families. Designed for a site between the A30 and A4, near Staines and Heathrow Airport, it was an extreme display of the determination to bring order and control to the motorised city. The debate was not new, but it had attracted increasing attention since the mid-1950s, and in the year that Britain opened its first stretches of motorway, it was a topic that was popular and relevant.[28]

In contrast, the 'Crystal 61' project, that coincided with the 1961 CIAM conference in London, and the 'Crystal Span' of 1963 were much more innovative in design and creative in expression. 'Crystal 61' was a 1,000-feet glass tower exhibition centre, with halls, lecture theatres and restaurants. 'Crystal Span' was a multi-purpose bridge, to replace Vauxhall Bridge next to the Tate Gallery, that would support a seven-floor high glass envelope,

970 feet long containing a hotel, shops, skating rink, exhibition space for the Tate Gallery, and sheltered gardens and open-air performance space on the roof. Blending the concepts of the old London Bridge and the 1851 Crystal Palace, it was a dynamic vision of a revitalised urban landscape.

In the real world, redesigning urban life remained a far more uncertain process, both for the planners and the families caught up in the redevelopment programmes. An incident in the new town landscape well illustrates this problem. Looking at the Henry Moore 'Family Group' at Harlow New Town,[29] with its stable and heroic qualities of the family juxtaposed with the mundane ordinariness of family life, effectively reveals the complexity of accommodating both ideal and everyday values (figure 41). Classical and classless in its interpretation of the family, the protective father and caring mother, it was a monument to a landscape of ordinary life and the beginning of a new social democracy. The question, amongst many, was how well did these planned environments cater for mothers with prams, and children with teddy bears? It was a scene that not only raised questions about new towns, and the values of the concept environment, but also the new phase of urban renewal being taken up by municipal planners

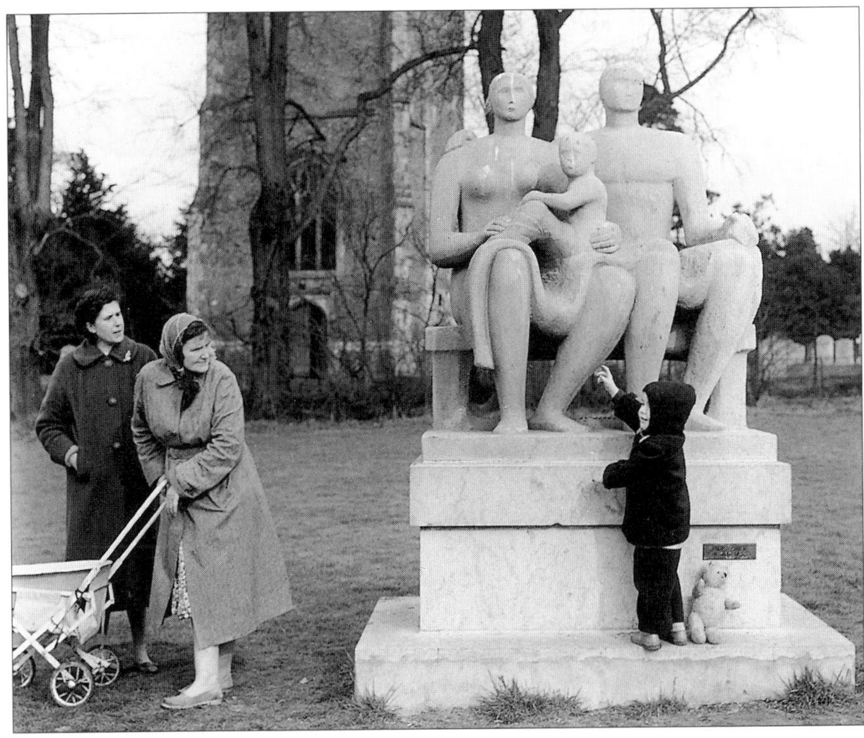

41 Henry Moore, 'Family Group', Harlow New Town, unveiled May 1956

and politicians. Ian Nairn's 'Outrage' articles for *Architectural Review*, published in book form in 1955, set much of the pace of this debate.[30] Describing a horror trip through a wasted landscape from Southampton to Carlisle, unprotected by planners and local authorities, ravished by speculators, it came up with the emotive 'Subtopia', the ailment of modern Britain. This aesthetic excursion did not engage with the broader social issues, but reinforced by the RIBA travelling exhibition,[31] it secured a platform from which to construct arguments for a high-rise, high-density cityscape.[32] The feeling that opportunities to establish new forms of architectural expression were being squandered was reinforced by the Arts Council touring exhibition '45–55, Ten Years of British Architecture' of 1956, for which John Summerson eloquently summarised the dilemma in relation to local authority housing as a reluctance 'to be radical or stylistically positive',[33] in preference to social, middlebrow, cosy ideas. Locating these attitudes within the political left, he recognised the conflict with the emergence of the architectural language defined as 'The New Brutalism'.[34]

Of those authorities about to embrace a radical stance in keeping with their political ambitions Sheffield was to emerge as one of the most enthusiastic converts. As often happens with conversions it can lead to a puritanical ideology taken up with its own sense of rightness. Having already set in motion an inquiry into solutions to what were serious housing problems, Sheffield was to commit itself to a large-scale multi-storey housing project, which resulted in residents occupying the first set of dwellings of Park Hill in November 1959.[35] The scheme largely ignored the 'Living in Flats' report of 1952, and chose to take no notice of lessons learnt from the 1930s, when its own experiences, and any number of local authority reports, had shown that working-class families, like any other section of society, much preferred houses. It was a moment of political and architectural arrogance that not only built Park Hill, but undervalued the social and environmental qualities of the communities it replaced.[36]

While determined to create a traffic free environment, the scheme had failed to comprehend the speed with which car ownership would develop. Although the traffic nightmare haunted the planners, the belief seemed to be that it would be someone else's traffic, so Park Hill with its 2,307 dwellings only had 100 parking spaces, mainly for visitors, and 24 lock-up garages.[37] Advice against using the access balcony system was ignored, and the street deck was made a major feature. It was believed to be ideal for social contact, but its unsuitability as a place for children became immediately apparent. The only break in the uniformity of the design was to paint the front doors different colours. The planning committee was proud of the magnificent views, and of the possibility of the families having meals on their balconies, introducing a touch of middle-class continental living into a heavy industrial town. They were also pleased with the introduction of communal launderettes and their automatic washing machines, but had paid little attention to the complexities of washing and drying the family laundry, particularly for families with young children. Planners, motivated by a desire to build faster and cheaper housing, had undervalued the intricacies of family life.

The core of the problem of Park Hill and other similar schemes was what Michael Young outlined in a concise and stimulating paper, 'The Planners and the Planned, The Family', given to the general meeting of the Town Planning Institute in April 1954.[38] Concerned with the needs of the 'immediate' and 'extended' family, his preference was for redevelopments within towns and cities that retained some level of choice. The argument was for town planning that understood the dynamic of the changing family, similar to the Lansbury model of the Festival of Britain. The urgency for inexpensive and quick solutions to a growing housing problem, and overconfidence in architectural technology, led many local authorities to ignore this social message. In this respect Sheffield was little different from other city councils, whose socialist principles destroyed the cultures of the people they were representing.

Ready-made and adaptable

As already shown by the 'House of the Year' and other exhibition homes, in direct contrast to many of the municipal schemes the middle-class families were being offered ready-made small houses with gardens that emphasised adaptable and flexible living. In the professional debate it was the *Ideal Home*/RIBA 'Small House Competition' announced in November 1958, with the prize-winning designs exhibited at the Building Centre in September 1959, and published as *The Book of Small House Plans,* that captured this trend of popular design for family housing (figure 42). Thirty designs were selected, including detached, semi-detached and terraced houses and bungalows; there were two- and three-bedroom plans, although it was accepted that the three-bedroom house was ideal, its 'flexible planning adapts to a family of any age group and its costs brings it well within range of newly-married couples'.[39] Living space varied from 900 to 1,100 sq. ft., all had a garage or car port, and a great number had patios. The designs were erected as show houses on fourteen residential sites across England, and one in Glasgow.

Not all members of the RIBA were convinced by this popularisation of architectural practice, but it was an important move in introducing to a much wider audience the benefits of working with an architect, even though the potential clients were only buying a set of working drawings for a £15 fee. It was a critical ideological shift by the RIBA, a pragmatic recognition that suburban development provided the bread and butter work of many of its members, and an acceptance that no matter what abuse was directed at suburbia it was expanding. So, if the professional associations could not stop this work, it was imperative that they became more actively involved. Although not intended, it was a move that became part of a more general defence of speculative suburban housing as, in January 1959, *Ideal Home* began a series on 'good ready-made houses', followed up at the spring Ideal Home Exhibition with a 'Village of Ready-Mades'.

In the summer of 1961, a similar collaboration between *Ideal Home*/RIBA resulted in a competition, 'The House Group Design', for the houses and layout of two 4½ acre sites, one at Harlow, the other at Heaton Norris, Stockport. The winning schemes were to be built 'as national models of good estate design – places where middle-income families can invest happily in a new home'.[40] Announcing the prize-winning schemes in May 1962, *Ideal Home* explained to its readers that they would appeal to the youthful in attitude, as they had taken a realistic approach to less private space, more communal gardens, neighbourliness and attractive design.

The new homes had fitted carpets, 'Cosywrap' for the loft, double glazing and central heating. As solid fuel, gas and oil vied for attention there was a renewed campaign to capture the central heating market. Outstanding in bringing together the imagined and real world was the Shell-BP creation of 'Mrs 1970'. Launched on an unsuspecting public in autumn 1959, the campaign brilliantly turned the traditional caring housewife into the vivacious modern mother, living in the luxury of a warm, spotless house, and enjoying much more leisure (figure 43). Making great play of the mother and daughter relationship, it had taken a stage further the images of the jolly happy-go-lucky family, offering the new lifestyle as an attainable dream.[41]

It was a social revolution reinforced by the government's investigation of the family needs in terms of the design and equipment for their home, which after a two-year inquiry resulted in new national guidelines, published in 1961 as *Homes for Today and Tomorrow*. A subject last covered by the 1944 Dudley Report, the new recommendations were based on the principle that people were better off than ever before, with more possessions, secure employment, better education and a more enjoyable home life.

> Housewives now increasingly look to machinery to lighten their household tasks; and the family, and husbands in particular, now expect to help with much of the work that previously the housewife was left to do, so that she

HREE-BEDROOM BUNGALOW *with self-contained sleeping wing* (936 *sq. ft.*).* *Designer: R. F. Smith, A.R.I.B.A., Walsall. Price indication* £3,390-£3,890. *DESIGN* 34.

FIVE-PERSON HOUSE for any aspect (1,100 *sq. ft.*). *Designer: K. Bottomley, A.R.I.B.A., Bradford, Yorks. Price indication* £3,440-£3,940. *DESIGN* 855.

TWO-BEDROOM HOUSE with multi-purpose room (1,080 *sq. ft.*). *Designers: Barber, Bu & Greenfield, F. & A/A.R.I.B.A., Dorking, Surrey. Price indication* £3,760-£4,260. *DESIGN* 622

COURTYARD BUNGALOW (1,100 *sq. ft.*) *and garage for a restricted site. Designer: J. E. Parsons, A.R.I.B.A., London. Price indication* £3,850-£4,350. *DESIGN* 1371.

HOUSE (1,000 *sq. ft.*) *AND GARAGE for a narrow site. Designer: P. J. Ball, A.R.I.B.A., Wickham Bishops, Essex. Price indication* £2,960-£3,460. *DESIGN* 601.

THREE-BEDROOM BUNGALOW in two wings (1,100 *sq. ft.*). *Designer: D. W. Oliver, A.R.I.B.A., Bath, Somerset. Price indication* £4,140-£4,500. *DESIGN* 252.

OPEN-PLAN TERRACE HOUSE with three bedrooms (1,195 *sq. ft.*). *Designer: A. W. Strutt, A.R.I.B.A., Bromley, Kent. Price indication* £3,180-£3,680. *DESIGN* 1470.

TWO-BEDROOM HOUSE for a narrow site (900 *sq. ft.*). *Designer: D. W. Oliver, A.R.I.B.A., Bath, Somerset. Price indication* £3,070-£3,570. *DESIGN* 251.

SPLIT-LEVEL HOUSE (1,296 *sq. ft.*) *with semi-basement garage. Designers: A. F. Benne and R. N. Abadie, A/A.R.I.B.A., London. Price indication* £4,100-£4,600. *DESIGN* 114

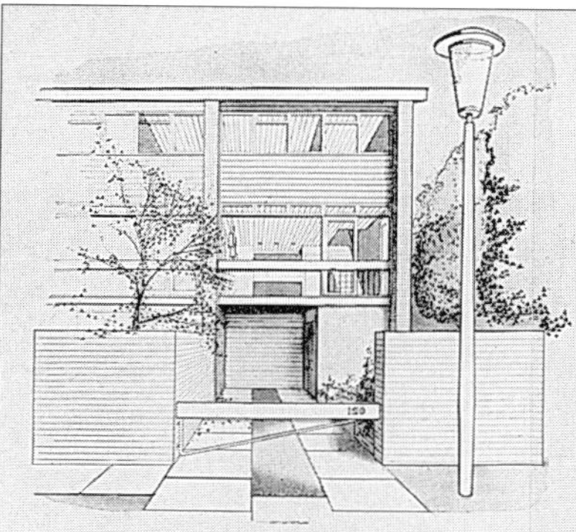

THREE-BEDROOM TERRACE HOUSE (913 *sq. ft.*), *plus garage. Designed by S. R. Sutcliffe, A.R.I.B.A., Crawley, Sussex. Price indication* £2,610-£3,110. *DESIGN* 1216.

SEMI-DETACHED HOUSE (1,000 *sq. ft.*). *with three bedrooms and garage. Designer: R. F. Smith, A.R.I.B.A., Walsall. Price indication* £2,820-£3,320. *DESIGN* 35.

HOUSE (1,000 *sq. ft.*) *AND GARAGE linked by greenhouse. Designer: J. R. Findlay, A.R.I.B.A., Llandaff, Cardiff. Price indication* £3,825-£4,325. *DESIGN* 202.

TWO-BEDROOM BUNGALOW planned to avoid the "small" look (770 *sq. ft.*). *Designer: K. G. West, A.R.I.B.A., Herne Bay, Kent. Price indication* £2,500-£3,000. *DESIGN* 792.

HOUSE THAT IS EXTENDABLE (1,000 *sq. ft.*). *Designers: J. C. Rowell & J. Anderson, A/A.R.I.B.A., Prestwick, Scotland. Price indication* £3,540-£4,040. *DESIGN* 1403.

DETACHED OPEN-PLAN HOUSE with three bedrooms (1,100 *sq. ft.*). *Designer: D. W. Oliver, A.R.I.B.A., Bath, Somerset. Price indication* £4,110-£4,500. *DESIGN* 253.

42 *Ideal Home*/RIBA Small House Scheme, 15 of the 30 published plans, 1959

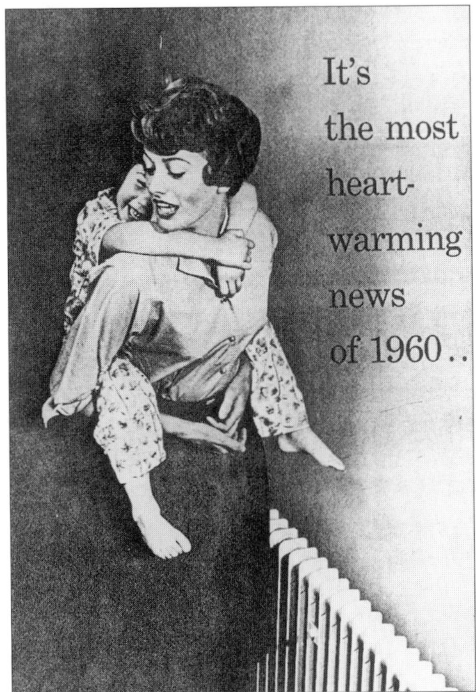
It's
the most
heart-
warming
news
of 1960..

43 'Mrs 1970', BP advertisement, November 1960

> has more free time to live a life of her own. This desire to live their own lives for an increasing part of the time they spend at home is spreading through the family as a whole. Teenagers wanting to listen to records; someone else wanting to watch the television; someone going in for do-it-yourself; all these and homework too mean that the individual members of the family are more and more wanting to be free to move away from the fireside to somewhere else in the home – if only they can keep warm.[42]

To meet these changing needs the report gave priority to two issues, space and heating. Living space had to meet private as well as communal needs, which put increased emphasis on better kitchen design and storage, and heating systems that were adequate for everyday needs throughout the year. The proposition was that architects should begin planning from a better understanding of family needs, keeping a flexible approach, that would, for example, ensure that the positioning of such things as windows and doors would allow furnishings that would make the most effective use of the living space. Minimum standards were set, but as the basis of a house to be proud of, it was hoped that these would not become the maximum.

By the beginning of the 1950s more attention had been given to the children's bedroom as a place to play and grow up in. It had not yet been referred to as the teenager bed-sitting room, but by 1954 that in effect was what it had become, and it was to remain an established part of the ideal home. It was a place to study, take friends, listen to records, ideally with a wash-basin in a cupboard, and as few visible signs as possible that it was a bedroom. Independent living had become an integral part of family homelife. The adaptable house to meet the needs of the growing family was at the core of the thinking. The report left unresolved the question of open-plan space. The living room was seen as needing to take 'two or three easy chairs, a settee, a television set, small tables',[43] and other small possessions. The kitchen-dining room arrangement was recognised as being the most widely used by local authorities, but the report preferred the kitchen with a dining annexe, and ideally the kitchen with separate dining room. Indecisive in its approach to numbers and size of the bedrooms, there was clear support for the use of the bed-sitting room. Space for prams and an adequate size bathroom were included, as were variations for married couples, single persons and the elderly. After all the changes had been taken into account the result was only an additional 60 sq. ft. on the average five-person house, raising the minimum requirement to 960 sq. ft. For most households, there had been an increase in the number of appliances, but few had yet acquired an automatic washing machine, so that water was still accessed and disposed of from the sink rather than through an independent system, and adaptability remained a prime criterion of kitchen design.

Lifts, sound insulation, private balconies and refuse disposal were given some attention in a generalised discussion of flats, but the social problems of families living in them were ignored. The question of the home and its setting was not strictly part of the brief, and although there was an acknowledgement of the needs for play space, car space and landscaping, questions of social, welfare and commercial amenities remained unanswered and the social divide more obvious. At the time it was felt that the differences could be overcome, but this was not to be, and by the end of the decade it was this inability to look beyond the appliance house to the resourced neighbourhood that contributed to the failures of large-scale housing schemes.

Despite these limitations, the concept of adaptable space became the model for family living, allowing for the opening up or closing off spaces as family needs changed. Following on from the *Homes for Today and Tomorrow* report, the Ministry of Housing issued a booklet to accompany two exhibition houses demonstrating the concepts of *The Adaptable House* for the average family.[44] Models for the medium price range, they had 990 sq. ft. of living space, gas warm-air central heating downstairs and secondary heaters upstairs, and were available with or without a garage. They were flat roofed, with single-storey kitchen/dining room, over which was a roof terrace, a cloakroom on the ground floor, and three bedrooms and bathroom on the first floor. Claimed to be easy to run, they were adaptable to the needs of a family of five, following the ageing cycle from bedrooms with bunkbeds and hobby rooms, to study-bedrooms and bed-sitting rooms for teenagers, to the spare room for the married children and a granny room. It was the establishment interpretation of the average dream house for the average British family.

With the house, garden and garage now established as the national dream, the family car completed the image of a new youthful age, and none was more important than the Mini, introduced in 1958. This is not the occasion to repeat again the account of its technical and design innovation, but what should be noted was the way in which its versatility was engineered to meet the social and cultural needs of people who were 'up to the minute ... going places fast – and enjoying every moment'.[45] By 1962 there were eighteen versions of the Mini including one for the 'happy-go-lively', and the family with father, mother, three children and family dog, all set to enjoy the pleasures and freedom of motoring (figure 44). Continuing well established advertising traditions, it was a further reassurance that small could still meet the needs of the new middle-class family without any lowering of social standards and reduction of comfort. In this representation of formal conventions and increased informality, family motoring was matched by the values attached to women drivers as

44 Morris Mini-Minors, 'Great Little Cars' publicity brochure, 1962. Copyright BMIHT/Rover Group

a popular way of conveying the convergence of technical improvement and social change. For example, when the Triumph Herald was launched in April 1959, it came as the new experience in motoring, the car for women's equality. There was plenty of space 'for feminine nick-nacks', it was 'the masculine car that delights women. They can take their corners with greater confidence ... They can master the most difficult manoeuvre ... They can drive well because they drive comfortably'.[46] Introducing the Triumph Vitesse version of the range in 1962, it was the car for the young professional family, about to become parents. Admired by the expectant wife, and yet meeting the needs of the husband parting with the two-seater sports car for a more sedate sporting life of motoring. An inventive expression of modern life, adaptability was responsibility, approved by government and promoted by commerce.

Alternative homes

In 1954, the scale of emergency housing and the continuing need for it was seriously underestimated. An extended debate on caravanning in modern society, in the *Architects' Journal*, was adamant that the non-mobile caravan and residential site should be removed as housing became available, leaving the landscape to be enjoyed by the genuine caravanner, escaping from the town.[47] However, by 1956 it had become increasingly evident that there was a shortfall in the provision of new housing, and a continuing inability to meet slum clearance targets. The 1958 House Purchase and Housing Bill set out partially to remedy this problem by advancing money to building societies to assist with the purchase of pre-1919 houses valued at less than £2,500, and introducing standard grants for improving the amenities of old houses, with the installation of baths, WC and hot water. At the same time Parliament set up an inquiry into the use of caravans as residential accommodation, as it seemed that rather than becoming less, the number of caravans being used as homes had increased.

The subsequent report by Sir Arton Wilson played a critical role in changing attitudes towards the caravan.[48] Since their reintroduction at the 1948 Motor Show the industry had continued to promote the caravan as a permanent home, and with the first Caravan Show at Earls Court in 1959, the concept of the permanently sited caravan as a seaside and country retreat and home took on a whole new profile. Rather than being removed from the landscape caravans were about to be more effectively incorporated into local planning regulations. Arton Wilson found many unsatisfactory sites, and families struggling to survive in minimal living space, but he was quite clear that caravan homes were here to stay and should be treated positively rather than negatively. He had found that there were 150,000 ordinary families in England and Wales using a caravan as a permanent home and that, of the 36,500 caravans manufactured in 1958, 21,800 were potential living-vans and 11,000 of these were intended to be used as homes at the time of purchase. The major groupings of the owners were young married couples, transferred workers, and middle-aged and elderly people whose changed circumstances had necessitated moving from a house. Many families were hoping to obtain a house, but the report considered that the increased demand from the young and old people would more than make up for those moving into conventional dwellings. The outcome was the Caravan Sites and Control of Development Act, 1960, followed by the Ministry of Housing and Local Government 1962 publication, *Caravan Parks, Location, Layout, Landscape,* setting out good practice, emphasising neatness and formality for the design of sites. The mobile home park was now incorporated into the British landscape.

To convince its readers of the quality of life in the new mobile home, *Ideal Home* went to the Pathfinder Village, at Tedburn St Mary, Exeter,[49] to furnish a 'Tenwide' caravan. With oil-fired central heating, double bedroom and living room, bathroom and kitchen it provided 320 sq. ft. of living space, the nearest industrial home unit since the first post-war prefabricated units. *Ideal Home* recommended simple unpatterned carpets, painted walls, unfussy curtains and Ercol furniture. Essentially a home for two people, it was a cheap, pragmatic and attainable home.

Another down-to-earth facet of practical family life, which had been steadily growing from the mid-1950s and established itself as a distinct area at the 1960 Motor Show at Earls Court, was the motorised caravan. Versions had existed since the early 1900s, but by the end of the 1950s it was a major new industry with seventeen firms building conversions, that brought caravan camping within the reach of a new consumer group. In many respects it was unsophisticated motoring, with many of the commercial vans lacking the qualities of steering and power associated with private motoring. Stimulating the expansion of a new interior design industry in minimum living, with foldaway beds, built-in cupboards and cooker, and extending roof, motor caravans were an expression of ingenuity and marketed under wonderful names such as Slumberwagen, Carefree, Land Cruiser, and of course, the Dormobile. In comparative terms they were expensive; on average new ones were selling for between £800 and £1,000.

As the people's motoring of the 1940s had become popular motoring of the 1950s, the democratisation of leisure and the car was taking another turn. While it was possible for the very handy to build their own caravan, the caravan for touring firmly remained a middle-class pleasure, and until there was a serious second-hand market, this was also true of the motorised caravan. But by the end of the 1950s a much wider public was being offered the opportunity to enjoy the freedom of coast and countryside, with previously unrealised home comforts. The spring-loaded steel framed tent, with its awning, plastic window, inner tent and sealed vinyl ground-sheet, now became a realistic alternative. Inspired by the French, and largely dependent on French products, Britain was going continental. Usually referred to as the continental-type tent, it brought in an era of domesticity in camping. It was possible to stand up, there were bedrooms, a living room and kitchen, and the scope for adding sections that were ultimately to lead to the provision of picture windows and a lounge. Colours were introduced, with a two-tone orange and blue the most popular. From some manufacturers you could buy a 'villa' or a 'chalet', that were appropriately given such names as 'Rimini' and 'Riviera'. The marketing of new packaged continental holidays coincided with the camping boom, but the new tents provided the possibility of enjoying being continental in your home field, and for the family who ventured abroad, it gave the extra pleasure of being able to merge into the continental way of life, particularly with the bottle of red wine on the camping table.

A society had emerged that was being offered a trouble-free, appliance-filled, affluent home life, and new horizons for travel, at a time when a great many neighbourhoods lacked basic amenities, and a considerable number of families were surviving in temporary accommodation. The needs of the consumer had acquired greater attention than those of the community. They were not entirely forgotten, the 1960 report of the Wolfenden Committee on Sport had drawn attention to the need for multi-purpose sports centres that could serve the community all year, meeting the demands of minority sports and the needs of the family alongside the established main sports. New towns, such as Harlow and Bracknell, were able to make the first moves, and growing links between the sports centres and schools began to take shape, but they were isolated examples. Rather more attention was being given to commercial competition that included the build-up of the trading stamp wars between grocery chains.

New Britain

Rhetoric and revolution

1963 was National Productivity Year, a time to focus the nation on new efficiency developed out of a greater awareness of consumption and production. The year began unremarkably. The Institute of Directors held a one-day conference on 'Planning Tomorrow's New Products'. The *Ideal Home* allowed itself £850 to furnish an average house with living/dining room and three bedrooms, for a modern-minded young couple with two children, a child of ten and a young baby, who 'would want good looking furniture, some gaiety in colour but everything would need to have simplicity and quality of design so that it would not date and it would need to stand up to the wear and tear of young children'.[50]

At the end of February, the Design Centre opened a major exhibition 'New Design for British Rail'. Presenting good design and a new corporate image, it was a sweetener for the bitterness aroused the following month when Beeching put forward his plan for a reshaping of British Rail, involving a 30 per cent cut and the closure of 2,363 stations out of 4,709, with devastating consequences for rural Britain. Nine months later the Buchanan Report, *Traffic in Towns*, brought public attention to the concerns that had been growing throughout the 1950s, and the apparent contradiction of the car as monster or treasured possession. The Steering Group, under Sir Geoffrey Crowther, was to advise the Minister of Transport on how best to act on the report. This was a defining moment, for it demonstrated establishment acceptance that given the income, every family would want to own a car, whatever the traffic hazards and congestion. The underlying ambition was to reconstruct Britain to keep traffic moving. The key to understanding this objective lies in the fact that the steering group saw the day divided into four activities, work, sleep, leisure, and time spent sitting in vehicles in stationary or slow-moving traffic. The latter had a rising cost in fuel and time, and needed to be reduced. The suggested strategy was to implement a nationally coordinated urban reconstruction for the car, with a big road building programme, and the reorganisation of cities into environmental patchworks, separating network throughways from local roads. The need for a coordinated public transport system for commuters was recognised, but although there was a brief reference to commuters using their cars to get to a suburban station, it was obvious that this could not be taken too seriously when the rail system was about to be axed.

At an international level the Test Ban Treaty was agreed, and Britain's application to join the European common market was rejected. The monument to the new communication age, the Post Office tower, was built, complete with a revolving restaurant. The arts were buoyant,[51] and design happily absorbed Scandinavian influences. But it was the *Guardian* that struck a sombre note in its pamphlet *A New Britain*. Written in anticipation of the General Election, its tone and examples could have been written thirty years earlier. The nineteenth-century inheritance was still being blamed for the contemporary failures, and the inability to give 'to all our people the opportunities for a full life that the twentieth century makes possible'.[52] Slums and old housing, municipal and speculative, were primary topics.

> The people themselves must impress on any Government that a solution means more than providing just a home for every family. It must provide the type of home which is fully in line with the technological revolution and which meets all the demands for a higher standard of living in a modernised Britain.[53]

Policies for transport, industrial relations, education, work, science and leisure were all discussed, with urban renewal figuring as the most intractable problem, town and city centres being squeezed by traffic congestion and ringed by decaying property. With technology firmly linked to social revolution, the question was how more and improved products for consumption could be used for the collective good. It was a case of agreeing a social agenda to put alongside that of economy, as the basis for comprehensive redevelopment schemes.

Harold Wilson saw the 1964 General Election as a mandate for change, an opportunity to build a new kind of society, reacting against materialism and the exploitation of Rachmanism.

> Everywhere I have gone, people have been mainly interested in home affairs – the cost of living, education, pensions, housing. But there is no doubt that the top of the list is housing. It is hard for people to understand that in a civilisation which can talk of landing a man on the moon, we still tolerate 1½ million houses without a bath, 1½ million without internal hot water, and 1½ million with no internal lavatories.[54]

This was Wilson at his electioneering best; the accuracy of his figures could be questioned, but the message was clear. In its simplicity, it gave rise to the feeling that it was a simple problem to answer, and that family needs could be answered by large-scale demolishing programmes and the provision of a new bathroom suite. Unfortunately this was not the case, although many planners and local politicians were happy to follow these lines.[55]

In 1964 and 1965 a series of regional reports introduced plans in which metropolitan areas, new towns and overspill developments were presented as the key to economic planning, claiming to answer the needs of a growing population, while preserving the green belts. Consistently, though, there was the problem of translating theory into a workable reality, as repeatedly plans to reorganise city life or establish new neighbourhoods were thwarted by delays, lack of funding and an over-optimistic belief in the capacity of new materials and services to answer the social needs of communities in general and the family in particular. The twentieth century had gone through its gas, electric, glass, plastic, concrete and stainless steel ages, and was now embracing aluminium and technology. In 1964, Alcan Industries Ltd published five broadsheets which became *A Town called Alcan* booklet, illustrating a theoretical town designed by Gordon Cullen and Richard Matthews, to show the benefits of aluminium in building. With its terraces, town centre malls, cafés and bars it was the place for a good time, raising expectations of life in the comfortable consumer-driven society. At a time when design believed that it was offering more stylistic choice,[56] the perceived fun and self-expression of popular design had little part in the grim determination of the public housing programmes, which lacked visual optimism, and failed to engage with the broader needs of individual families.

This was not how it was seen in 1965. The *Observer Magazine*, 21 February 1965, carried an article 'Town Boss', in which it described the vision and drive of Dan Smith, leader of the Labour-controlled Newcastle City Council, and his determination to push through plans to redevelop the city centre along the lines of the Buchanan Report and replace its 'slumland' with tower blocks. As in other northern cities, the terraced house landscape had been a reminder of the Victorian exploitation, and the failure to remove the hardship and poverty of the inter-war years. Bulldozing the past was a means of clearing the way to build for the twenty-first century. The scheme was criticised for a ruthless autocratic style of planning, but was defended for its efficiency and prestige, and in 1962 given a much-needed establishment lifeline, when a BBC 'Tonight' programme suggested that the principles of Brasilia, the city in the jungle, were being applied in the rebuilding of Newcastle. For a time, the city became 'the Brasilia of the North'. It was an extraordinary notion, yet it brought a touch of romance to a process that was destroying established communities and neighbourhoods.

That this was a key part of the philosophical positioning of these planning schemes, was reinforced by an article, 'Opportunity and Affluence',[57] by two geographers E. M. Rawstron and B. E. Coates. Setting out ideas on the regional economic and employment fortunes of Britain, that would counter the London drift and inequality of opportunity, their proposals suggested the creation of two new metropolitan centres, and other new and expanded towns. These were not particularly radical suggestions, nor was the idea that they should be architecturally pleasing with good communication links. What was significant was their commitment to political intervention to achieve these ends. Committed to a policy of social engineering and land clearance, rooted in 1930s modernism, it was argued that whatever the location of the new settlements, 'all the old, nineteenth-century towns will have to be gutted and rebuilt before AD2000'.[58] A future that they saw blocked by the 'Coronation Street mentality' that clung to an undisturbed neighbourhood, they called on the government to 'act effectively on the scale required and in the time available to dispel it before the damage is too great'.[59] With all the vigour of the post-war onslaught against industrial England, it recalled much of the intensity of Herbert Read's attack against 'that great wilderness of slag-heaps and slums in which half our people live',[60] its towns and people immune to the ugliness of their surroundings, blocking the future of the New Britain. After the limited success of the post-war reconstruction it was surprising that there was still the same level of extreme conviction in planned obsolescence as the basis of social responsibility.

In contrast design for the home took a more adaptable role, for while the market was planned around an obsolescence engineered by innovation and taste, there remained a realisation that established and new values needed to coexist. The *Sunday Times* 'Technique for Living' exhibition at the Central Hall of Harrods, February 1964, arranged by Hugh Casson, introduced the 'push-button age', offering all the technical advantages of a standardised mass-produced pre-packed appliance home. Yet, while representing the latest gadgetry, Casson was careful to explain that even 'the most technically perfect house designed to meet the needs of its owner with the utmost efficiency, economy and grace must be rated as a failure if it is not a home that is lived in with affection and respect throughout its working life'.[61] A reminder of how much designers believed themselves able to provide for the emotional as well as practical needs of a family, qualities of enjoyment and romance, space for personal expression, blossomed in the consumer culture. British families were encouraged to fill their kitchens with stainless steel cooking utensils, enjoy a romantic home dinner party with candles on the table, buy the recently introduced space hopper for their children, and take advantage of the objects for modern living offered by Habitat.[62] The *Woman's Journal* selected the Span town house, designed by Eric Lyons & Partners as its 1965 House of the Year for the young professional couple with two children. With the kitchen, the family room and garden room on the ground floor for noisy activities, a lounge and study on the first floor for quiet activities such as reading and entertaining, and three bedrooms and a bathroom on the second floor, it was a widely accepted model lifestyle associated with the ideal suburban home.[63] Further confirmation of the design taste for this new middle class came in the new Penguin handbook series, that included Diana Rowntree's *Interior Design* and Lena Larsson's *Your Child's Room*, and significantly, *Design to Fit the Family* by Phoebe De Syllas and Dorothy Meade. With their long associations with the Council of Industrial Design, the *Design to Fit the Family* followed on the ideas expressed in the 1945 'Design at Home' Exhibition at the National Gallery, the 1947 CoID 'Furnishing to Fit the Family', and popularised the good design principles rehearsed in the pages of *Design*, which, with an obsessive determination to clear away clutter perceived to be the preferred taste of the ill-informed masses, maintained the ethos of the modernist campaign of the 1940s. Publicised as the guide for

> those who want an attractive home that works – a home that will accommodate them (and their savage children), now and in the future. Examining every corner of the house, from needless old fireplaces to convertible attics, they discuss the pros and cons of such ideas and fittings as open-plan living, floor heating, plastic tiles, tufted carpets, built-in cupboards and kitchen units, oil-fired boilers, and fluorescent lighting.[64]

It was a blueprint for the needs of the young middle-class family, and much time was devoted to the problems of open-plan living, simplicity in decoration and furnishing, and modernisation. Primarily concerned with explaining ideas on taste for the average family, and setting out ideals for those families who wanted to be 'more appreciative of good design',[65] yet its suggestions on buying a dishwasher and having a separate laundry with automatic washer, meant that for the mid-1960s the economics of its aspirations were distinctly for an affluent minority.

While these campaigns were directed at the new homeowners, the adaptable family and the young professional family, the potential of a new phenomena had been perceived, 'Maturityland'.[66] This was the world of the over–45s, married couples with time and money to spend on garden furniture, hobbies, pets and exotic foods, the new pace-setters, who wanted to shop after work, perhaps by telephone or post.

During a period in which houses were settling into an open-plan arrangement, the reduced living space was creating problems. The response was a consumer boom in home extensions and loft conversions. The garage became a store and, where possible, it was often requisitioned into providing additional living space. The RIBA held an exhibition on flexible living, using internal demountable partitioning,[67] and the Design Centre gave its ideas on 'Living in One Room'.[68] Reaching a compromise between new patterns of living and traditional family values was the obvious thinking behind these exhibitions, and was again well illustrated by the 'Living off Trays' Exhibition, October–November 1966. In a collaboration between the Peter Jones store in London and AB Nordiska Kompaniet, Stockholm, the CoID and the Swedish Institute of Cultural Relations, an attempt was made to show popular taste in patterns of eating and entertaining. The trays were set out with the latest designs in a range of materials from the traditional to plastics and stainless steel.[69] A comparison between the British and Swedish ways of life,

> The two trays laid for an executive's office lunch, for example, show the British tray set with Spode dinnerware and EPNS cutlery for a 3-course meal, while the Swedish tray has plate, tankard and coffee cup for a sandwich

lunch. Similarly, the canteen lunch trays make provision for a full lunch for the English employee and a sandwich and coffee for his Swedish counterpart.[70]

In design terms there was little to distinguish the representation of national taste; much more interesting were the lifestyles associated with the products, the presentation of the national values of a good meal.

Britain may have been coming to terms with continental design, but the young family was still being encouraged to begin its day with a really good breakfast, 'First, cereals or porridge, or fruit or fruit juice. Then bacon and eggs and tomatoes, or sausages or fish, and let the hungry ones fill up with all the toast and butter or margarine and marmalade they want' (figure 45).[71] In a decade that had seen the launch of the bright, vivacious housewife, *Nova*, the 'magazine for women who make up their own minds',[72] and Shirley Conran's six-part series, 'The Simple Girl's Guide to Home Design' in the *Observer Colour Magazine*,[73] social order had not changed as much as it might have at first seemed. Calling the housewife 'simple girl' gave a radical flavour, but she was still generally imaged as being responsible for running and furnishing the home for husband and children, and taking care of everything from home safety to the dinner party.

45 'Always begin the day with a really good breakfast', *Family Doctor* special, 1964. Permission BMJ Publishing Group

In a low-key display it was this restrained spirit that represented British family life at Expo '67 in Montreal. With 'Man and his World' as the theme of the World Fair, it had serious concerns but achieved little coherence in the way in which it dealt with Man the Explorer, the Producer, and the Community. Britain's presentation hardly helped for, as at Brussels ten years earlier, it was a mixture of flying the flag, which on this occasion was also painted on a Mini, parading images of past greatness and genius, and in its Britain Today section displaying a self-critical representation of British life. Stereotyping ordinary family life through a series of large photographs brought to an international audience the perceived lifestyles of middle-aged and young married couples living in council flats and suburban houses. It was unlikely that the subtleties of taste and habits would have been fully appreciated but, believable in their details and characteristics, they provided a useful snapshot of the official view of how British homelife was going modern. The differences being made, though, were not between social class, but of the changing taste and attitudes of the generations.

Life in the living-dining room of the council flat provides an effective way of understanding how this had been perceived. The middle-aged couple have finished their evening meal, and they are listening to the wireless with the wife knitting and her husband in his shirtsleeves lying on the settee reading the paper (figure 46). In young Britain, the husband had returned with the shopping and was talking to his wife, who is watering an indoor plant (figure 47). As for the furnishings, the mock chandelier has been replaced by the chinese shade, the portable radio by the hi-fi, the teapot by the decanter, the aspidistra and chrysanthemum pot plant by the large floor-standing evergreen, the carpet by the sheepskin rug. The bureau and settee had gone, the world of beech and stainless steel was in place, and so one could go on listing the before and after, the new for old. A similar story was presented for life in suburbia. The middle-aged wife was making her own curtains, while the husband, still wearing his jacket, was sitting on the settee doing the crossword. Their furnishings were completed with a bookcase, candlesticks, a portable television, daffodils in a vase and a toby jug, providing a deliberate down-beat view of late middle-aged moderate- to low- income Britain. In contrast the young husband and wife were sitting on a black vinyl settee, watching television, and having a cosy cup of tea after baby has been put to bed. Suggesting the beginnings of social change, it remained comfortable and comforting in its representation of the ordinary life of Britain, hinting that a restrained cultural democracy was in place. This was true for some, but others were not so fortunate.

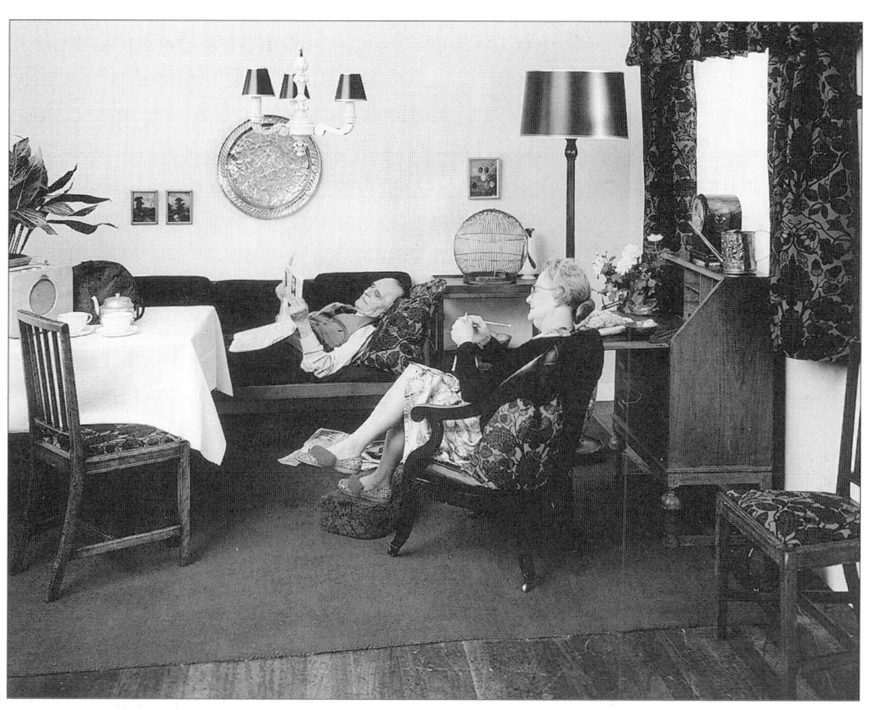

46, 47 Council flats, Expo '67, Montreal

Changes of belief

At a time when the nation began to be alerted to the fact that all was not well with swinging Britain, it seems more than just coincidence that a new caring spirit of architecture followed on from the first showing of the television documentary play 'Cathy Come Home' in 1966, the Shelter's fund-raising campaign of December 1966, and the Salvation Army's 1967 visually radical campaign, that interplayed the slogan 'For God's sake care' with documentary-style photographs of abuse, neglect and poverty, graphically portraying a forgotten Britain. There was still optimism; in January 1967, Milton Keynes had been chosen as the name for the proposed new city, and before the end of the year the first families began to move into the Span urban village at New Ash Green in rural Kent. But the city regeneration programmes were surrounded by uncertainty. Diana Rowntree's review of the Manchester slum clearance programme highlighted these concerns.[74] In the districts of Beswick, Longsight and Harpurhey, 1,730 acres were facing renewal, and it was time to reflect on plans that could take up to twenty years to complete. An opportunity to consider delight as well as convenience, surveying the problems of traffic, pedestrianisation, population densities, community services and architectural style, as the list extended, it was the sense of experimentation that became more apparent and the potential for mistakes more tangible. From this she warned against making assumptions that new buildings would automatically avoid the drabness of the old.

The urge to gut city centres still had its supporters, but more thought was being given to the retention and conversion of city centre properties. Modernisation programmes, run from the mid-1950s, were being extended to embrace preservation of whole areas of decaying grandeur as a means of solving some of the housing problems.[75] By the end of the year these developments had become part of an outright onslaught against the architectural failures of the previous ten years. The *Architectural Review*'s special issue on 'Housing and the Environment' raged against an architectural monumentality that was irrelevant to the needs of the people, having destroyed the fabric of community life, and replaced it with bleak, dingy social ghettoes that satisfied no one. This was not only an attack against the high-rise flats, many of which were badly designed and sited, but also a quest for a policy of rehabilitation.

> A balanced community life depends on the preservation of some continuity between a city's past, present and future and successfully interweaving the old with the new. For these reasons the rehabilitation of sub-standard dwellings is often more desirable than sweeping them away and making a fresh start.[76]

Labour's slogan for its 1964 election campaign had been 'People Matter', but its vision of a New Britain forged out of the technological revolution had foundered as new urban housing schemes swept away the working-class neighbourhoods, and the culture and communities that went with them. Despite the doubts there was still a strong belief that technology could produce totally new urban systems, but the established strategies were under scrutiny. Much of it was futuristic, as had been set out by the Glass Age projects and the Archigram abstract futures of the city as a single building, the computer city, the walking city and underwater city.[77] However, *Architectural Design*, February 1967, devoted to the year 2000+, amongst the imagery of a technological future introduced some astute warnings and predictions. Concerns of fifty years earlier for the personal levels of health and hygiene, and urban pollution and disease, had now become a concern for the world's ecosystems. As the core of John McHale's essay 'The Future of the Future', the issue was presented as an international rather than national problem that was dependent on global organisation. The suggestion was that this could not be achieved solely through technological innovation, but would require new social orders and organisations.[78] Attention was on world institutions, such as the UN. In a similar mood the last of the Glass Age projects, *Sea City*, published in 1968, was a scheme to build a city of about 30,000 population twenty-five miles out in the North Sea, as a response to the growing shortage of building land and contemporary estimates on the inability of Britain's agricultural and ecological systems to support its population (figure 48). The sea, with the increased efficiency of desalination plants, and the discovery of gas fields, was seen as the alternative resource. Taking into account tides, water depth, sea bed, shipping lanes and the need for links with a mainland town the city was envisaged for a site off the coast from Great Yarmouth. Roughly oval in shape the design reinterpreted the concept of a medieval city, using a flexible outer boom to create a moat of calm water, that would protect the city wall. It was to hold sixteen storeys of housing, shops and industries terraced down to the inner lagoon. Floating islands in the lagoon were available for individuals and businesses to construct their own two-storey buildings, providing accommodation for 7,000 people. Great efforts were made to incorporate all the normal recreational and educational facilities, and community services, including a hospital, but it was in its anticipated industries that the project was at its most vulnerable, for while it could expect to have fish farming, dredging, boat building and tourism, it was still dependent on some of the residents commuting to the mainland.

The project caused a stir when presented to the press in 1968 by Anthony Wedgwood Benn, the Minister of Technology.[79] The technological dream was ingenious in its feasibility, an architectural expression of social responsibility, yet as with all such visionary schemes it left unanswered questions of adaptability and the mundane practical logistics of living on a concrete island off the east coast of England. These omissions had been the problem at the heart of planning in post-war Britain, resulting in the construction of domestic islands, whether called villages or estates, that were neither self-sufficient nor adequately linked to neighbouring settlements.

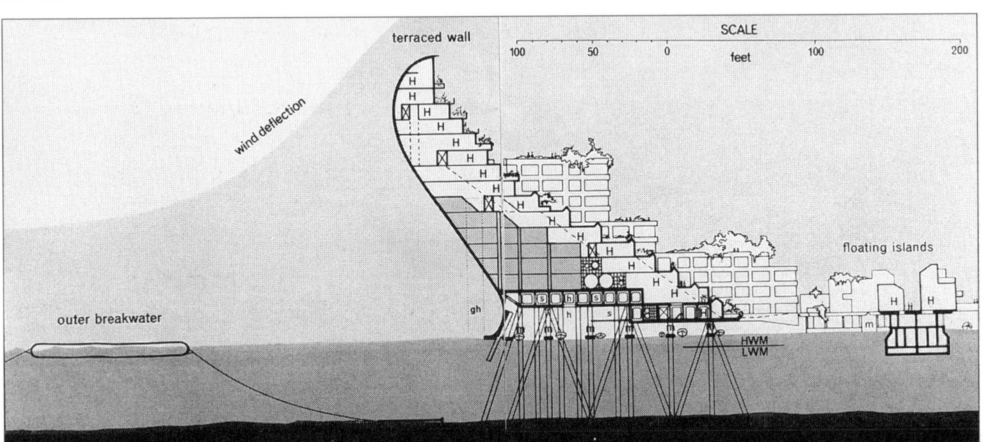

48 Sea City, Glass Age Project, 1968

As the social implications of these schemes faced continuing scrutiny, confidence in architectural technology was challenged in May 1968 with news and pictures of the structural damage caused by the 1968 gas explosion in the Ronan Points high-rise flats.[80] Significantly, though, the position of technology in society continued to be promoted by the government. Wedgwood Benn in a paper to the Royal Society of Arts, 18 November 1968, dismissed student revolutionaries as ineffective, but spoke enthusiastically of the engineers and technologists who were changing society: they 'are the people who are destroying our old society simply by finding better ways of doing things. Every revolution begins by destroying. The constructive part of the revolution starts later'.[81] This was a generalised justification for government intervention in promoting industrial research, but it had little to contribute to an understanding of the social consequences of these changes, or indicate what the constructive part of the revolution would be. At best it was an argument that certain groups, such as politicians, should be more aware of their power and the responsibilities that went with it. A centralist argument, the special issue of *New Society*, March 1969, took an opposing view, with its 'Non-Plan: An Experiment in Freedom'. As an attempt to represent what ordinary people would want, it was a curiously bogus invention of the critics.[82] It was right to be concerned about the oscillating preferences of planners, their interference and failures, but its primary interests were not social responsibility, but taste and free expression, inspired by pop culture, Britain's 'biggest visual explosion for decades'. Issues of resources and pollution were ignored, but as a final self-conscious defence of a philosophy that people should be able to do their own thing, irrespective of any collective responsibility, it suggested that the new-found freedom could potentially allow for more thought to be given to the problems of the poor.

The middle ground was to be occupied by the *Architectural Review* in August 1969, when it introduced its readers to 'Manplan, an Objective for the 1970s'. The suggestion was that Britain as the undefeated Great Power in Europe had been overtaken by the social and economic rebuilding of a defeated Germany, and had become a nation without a role, or at least one against which the *Architectural Review* was opposed. It was stridently against the dehumanising obsession with efficiency and the cost-effective drive of contemporary society, which had pursued the affluence of possessions. It proffered a policy whose philosophy was based on values that had variables, and practice that was adaptable to the needs of society.

> What is wanted now is a new image for the twentieth century in its third phase, which will unearth from beneath the lumber of war, napalm, famine, genocide, concentration camps, conveyor belts, population explosions, sonic

booms and silent springs, a mission – and a determination – to swing the new potential of technology, as revealed in the moonprobes, behind the real objectives of human society.[83]

In the next three months image after image provided a bleak picture of the failure of architecture and planning of the 1960s. Airline engines screamed over suburban rooftops, people were crammed on public transport, and buses and cars jammed the streets and roads, as 'Each Bank holiday the world and his wife destroy what they wish to embrace – beauty, tranquillity, eighteenth century landscape'.[84] A pictorial diary emerged of industrial unrest, militancy, unemployment, educational dissatisfaction, welfare decay, relics of paternalism, overcrowded caravan parks, empty churches, supermarkets that eased life at the expense of customers, commerce that overshadowed the domestic landscape, housing decay and new housing unfinished from industrial strife, while families continued to live in slums.

The blame was no longer being put at the door of the Victorians, but at the decades that had failed to rebuild Britain, and destroyed its humanitarian culture in the process. There was a rediscovery of the value of vernacular qualities of the working-class culture that had been cleared from the British landscape. Posing the Pearly King and Queen in front of the

49 ManPlan, *Architectural Review*, 1969

bleak landscape of a municipal high-rise development, 'The richness of east end life is replaced by monotony and inhumanity' (figure 49). The misuse of technology, and the culture of waiting for something to turn up was attacked, and architects and planners were criticised for their failure to address social needs adequately. Having spent twenty-five years zoning the British landscape, as industrial pollution was diminishing, the new vision was one of an integrated future, the town reinvented as a community established on the reintegration of work, home and leisure.

As part of the growing review of principles behind the urban renewal schemes of the late 1950s and early 1960s, a good example is provided by the change of heart at Newcastle in 1968, where its housing schemes, while still giving notice to the accommodation of a new motorway, placed much greater emphasis on the respect for community spirit in the planning brief. The outcome was Ralph Erskine's 1970 Plan of Intent which included concerns for the traditions and characteristics of the neighbourhood that was to be reconstructed. The result was the immediately famous Byker housing project which, while not without limitations, exemplified a realignment of social priorities, that attempted to counter years of commercial exploitation and municipal insensitivity.

Contradictions

In December 1969 Malcolm Muggeridge wrote a 'Farewell to the Sixties' for the *Observer* reader. Showing his fascination with the social and political framework of popular culture, and awareness of the revolutionary vibrations from the 1968 student protests, his view was of a decade that brought about the breakdown of the power of the upper classes, and introduced new freedoms. Television and tourism had gone global, heart transplants offered new life, literature challenged censorship, and satire made fun of everything. Society was seen as 'Permissive' and 'Affluent', it was the 'Decade of the Pill' and family planning, and the conventions of family life were thought to be under threat. This led Muggeridge to the conclusion that the 1960s had all been a 'foolish dream'.[85] It was not that, any more than any other decade, but there was alarm at its inconsistencies, and impatience at the failure to address social inequalities. Confidence in medical science had been challenged with the thalidomide catastrophe, and the Aberfan landslip that killed a future generation and destroyed the life of a village, had brought attention to the recurring environmental dangers of industrial exploitation.

Certainly any retrospective of the 1960s was going to be affected by the social extremes of 1969. It was a year of contradictions. Enoch Powell was advocating the repatriation of immigrants and the anti-apartheid movement demonstrated against the South African rugby tour; the Direct

Action on London Housing organised its first high-profile squat in London in February highlighting the obscenity of empty properties while homeless families survived the harsh reality of hostel life, and in November the GLC had launched the utopian 'Tomorrow's London'. There were violent protests on the streets of Ulster, widespread industrial unrest symbolised by the rubbish mountains in London from the dustmen's strike, and a growing disenchantment with the performance of the Wilson government. Technology had launched the QE2, produced the first supersonic flight, it was the twenty-first anniversary of the Morris 1000 and the celebration of the production of the two millionth Mini. Practical family motoring was offering improved spaciousness and performance,[86] but the car was under increasing attack for its safety and urban pollution. Britain had a popular culture that was reassured by reminders of its past, and encouraged by fantasies of the future, but enjoyed its dreams on a much more mundane scale. The Birmingham Ideal Home Exhibition, where the ordinary everyday detached house was presented as the 'The house of the century', and conventional house types were given names that reflected the cultural mood, the 'Hathaway' of 1968, became the 'Apollo' of 1969. In a similar mood at the Home Making Exhibition for Wales, 1969, Cardiff, there was the opportunity to have a polaroid picture taken in an exact replica of the Apollo Space Capsule, and enjoy a medieval banquet at Caldicot Castle, where 'every effort to re-create the atmosphere and pageantry of bygone days' had been made. This was an amusing blend of traditional and modern worlds, which could stand alongside the ever popular Scandinavian representation of a modern life for the British family enjoying,

> the new plastic furniture and vinyl surfaces, washable, bright-coloured, the soul of gaiety ... Wood surfaces, pale but warm, suggesting the scent of the forest. Pine and birch, either in their natural light tones or colourfully stained, have an air of intimate warmth which artificial materials lack. A simple pine table or sofa brings the mystery of deep woodlands to the heart of a city. Steel or painted metal is also a favourite in young homes ... No more solid furnishing, but space for living.[87]

These were promotional dreams, a lifestyle effectively marketed by Habitat, and extended round the country through the launch of its mail order catalogue in October 1969. But the representation of the good life coincided with the images of the Shelter 'Face The Facts' campaign 'to rescue thousands of the most desperate families',[88] highlighting again the recurring complexity of the social purposes of architecture and design. Moulded furniture and room dividers, vinyl, laminates, formica, thermoplastic and linoleum tiles, transistor radios and portable televisions encouraged the idea that flexible, easy living was available to all, but for those without a home it was meaningless. The arrival of the automatic environment was accompanied by a growing anxiety that society was losing control of the technology and failing to use it for the benefit of those most in need.

London fashion retained a self-confidence, and art secured the glamour and fun that it had built up over the decade, with the 1969 Pop Art exhibition at the Hayward Gallery.[89] The architects and industrial designers, caught up in this radical mood of creative freedom, had increasingly to question their role in a society where aesthetic expression overshadowed social purpose. Belief in a planned obsolescence as part of social change came even more under question and acceptance that natural resources were not infinite gained support. Since the late 1950s the work of bodies such as the Civic Trust and Victorian Society had done much to bring attention to questions of national heritage, but at the end of the 1960s conservation was taking on a much wider remit. Official reports were published on the future of Britain's historic towns, and in September 1969 the International Congress of the Society of Industrial Designers elected to consider 'Design, Society and the Future' as its theme. Technology cloaked as villain or saviour was on the minds of delegates, as they considered the contemporary landscape.

> Our skies and rivers are polluted; the dwindling open spaces which, with sinking hearts we now call Nature, increasingly desecrated; our cities noisy, perilous, inescapable. We have succeeded in surrounding ourselves by extraordinary ugliness and discomfort: suburbs whence you must travel to work; endless stretches of Levittowns, tracts and rabbit-warren developments; entire countrysides of neon signs, motels, gasoline stations.[90]

The language and images were those of forty years earlier, the ideal was to regain a similar sense of social purpose. Technology, that was considered to have helped to overcome scarcity, now needed to be harnessed to design the future, care for humanity and be used for the needs of a creative society. In November Frank Fraser Darling began his Reith lectures on 'Man and Nature' in which ecology, environment, global changes and conservation were considered as part of a world movement.[91] Leading up to the launch of 1970 as European Conservation Year, the consequences of change had become world issues. Gloom, verging on panic, was spreading, and even *Design*, having championed the interests of British design and industry since its first issue in 1949, was getting caught up by the mood of despair.[92] Celebrating twenty-one years of publication, the January 1970 issue presented a visual resume of the history as a collage of objects, buildings and landscapes, providing a predictable summary of period style and culture. Then, in its concluding remarks, it turned to the contemporary loss of purpose, the failure to accept change and the prospect of a bleak future, 'likely to be terminated by war, pestilence or famine – or all three'.[93] The following month *Life* ran a lead article 'Ecology: A Cause Becomes a Mass Movement' in which images described a world enveloped by the pollution of land, air and water within a decade.[94] Design ethics were turning more to issues of greed and waste, than aesthetics.[95] On a more parochial level Brian Batsford's paper, 'The Face of Britain in the Seventies', to the Royal Society of Arts in March 1970 reminded his audience of the failure to take proper notice of the important and relevant issues raised over forty years earlier by the Design and Industries Association and the writings of Clough Williams-Ellis on the disfigurement of the British landscape.[96] Civic awareness and conservation were projected as a 'Pride in Britain' movement, hopefully catching 'the imagination of the man who takes his family for a drive at the week-end, who would appreciate the object of keeping not only his house and garden tidy, but his street tidy, begin to acquire a civic pride – who could proudly display his PIB badge'.[97] Slightly ludicrous, yet it was a serious concern for collective responsibility and respect, a plea for the importance of the unobtrusive and unpretentious as well as the outstanding and spectacular.

Protests over the failure to deliver a new society that would take care of the interests of future generations were not unique to the late 1960s, but there was a distinctive reappraisal of social issues and the questioning of national identity and values as the failures of the modernist ideology were exposed. The responsible lifestyle was being absorbed into mainstream culture, and was even on show at the 1970 Ideal Home Exhibition, which included modernisation of old houses, a build-it-yourself house, and the geodesic dome solar home. There were still plenty of illustrations of brighter bedrooms, dream kitchens, new colour schemes and notes on home furnishing, but in its first issue of 1970 *Ideal Home* also gave space to an article on the overcrowded, decaying conditions, and exploitation of families sharing kitchens and bathrooms in the multi-tenanted properties of Notting Hill.[98] Drawing attention to the work of the community action group, and its efforts to obtain basic needs, and the rights for a pleasant and healthy neighbourhood, it was further confirmation that while health, comfort and happiness was enjoyed by far more families than at any previous date, the post-war dream of creating a more equitable society had come to an end.

Notes

1 *The Times*, 23 September 1954.

2 *The Economist*, 11 September 1954.

3 It started at Beales in Bournemouth, and then moved to Hull, Norwich, Manchestet; Glasgow, Cardiff and Croydon.

4 *Gazette of the John Lewis Partnership*, 21 August 1954, p. 599.

5 *JL Archive 208/c/49*.

6 There had been a handicrafts exhibition at Olympia in October 1953. The first 'Do-It-Yourself' programme with Barry Bucknell was broadcast on 5 January 1960.

7 *Design*, April 1957, p. 39.

8 *Design*, March 1955, p. 9.

9 For example in 1956, one exhibition was taken from Cardiff to Portsmouth, Carlisle, Leeds and Torquay; two years later it was to go from Cardiff to Cheltenham, Carlisle, Bristol, Bradford, and Bolton.

10 Good Housekeeping Institute, *The Happy Home*, London, 1954.

11 P. L. Garbutt, 'Homemaking – The New Art', *Good Housekeeping*, July 1954, p. 81.

12 *Design*, June 1955, p. 11.

13 *Gazette of the John Lewis Partnership*, 9 June 1956, p. 415.

14 *Design*, June 1957, p. 21.

15 Exhibition was held from 11 March–27 April 1957.

16 There was a growing popularity for portable televisions, but equally increasing demand for televisions to be a piece of furniture and fitted into a Queen Anne bureau or Tudor chest. With the expansion of TV rental schemes by the end of the decade licences had reached 10,469,753, but although the BBC television service had extended to 98.8 per cent of the population, it still meant that the remote hill and mountain areas of Britain were without provision.

17 The Design Centre came back to the issue in 1960 with a 'Room for Viewing'.

18 A Design Centre Exhibition at the Bluecoat Chambers, Liverpool, opened on 11 May 1960.

19 Autumn 1957 saw the formation of the Consumers' Association. The first issue of *Which* came out in 1957, four were issued in 1958, and from October 1959 it was issued monthly. In November 1965 the Consumer Council introduced its 'Teltag' label, to be attached to product listing technical and performance details.

20 Fabrics were treated with 'Dri-Sil', furniture protected by silicone polish, and brickwork given a silicone finish.

21 *Woman's Journal*, March 1959, p. 53.

22 *Woman's Journal*, March 1960, p. 21. The house at Beaconsfield Road, Woolton, Liverpool, was furnished by George Henry Lee's of the John Lewis Partnership.

23 August 1956, estimated at fifty stores.

24 In January 1958 Bendix announced the opening of its thousandth self-service launderette in West Hartlepool, and drip-dry fabrics increased in popularity.

25 Good Housekeeping's *Family Meals with Quick-Frozen Foods*, London, 1958, p. 2.

26 Formica had been introduced to Britain in 1948, but it was very much the functional material of the 1950s.

27 First established in 1937.

28 M. MacEwan, 'Metropolis-Can We Get Out of the Jam', *Architects' Journal*, 1 October 1959.

29 Unveiled on 17 May 1956.

30 I. Naim, *Outrage*, London 1955.

31 July 1957 RIBA 'Subtopia' exhibition, with pamphlet by Ian Nairn.

32 The Living Town, Symposium and Exhibition, RIBA, May 1959, was a further response to the failure to rebuild cities and towns in an imaginative way, and the continuing spread of 'subtopia', but did little to resolve the general confusion.

33 John Summers on, 'Introduction', *'45–'55. Ten Years of British Architecture*, Arts Council Catalogue, London, 1956, p. 8.

34 See Reyner Banham, *The New Brutalism*, London, 1966.

35 Sheffield Housing Committee had sent a delegation to several European sites in September 1954, and returned with great enthusiasm and commitment. Work commenced building Park Hill in April 1957.

36 An unconvincing defence of the these schemes has been presented. See Roy Hattersley, 'Time to Knock Them Down', *Independent on Sunday*, 4 September 1996, p. 19; Roy Hattersley, 'A Farewell to Slums', *Guardian*, 10 August 1998, p. 14.

37 In 'Housing the Motor-Car', *Journal of the Town Planning Institute*, September–October 1961, J. L. Womersley outlined how rapidly this position had been revised.

38 *Journal of the Town Planning Institute*, May 1954, p. 134.

39 *Ideal Home*, April 1960, p. 63.

40 *Ideal Home*, May 1962, p. 49.

41 Richard Hamilton, 'Persuading Image', *Design*, February 1960, recognised the importance of these developments of mass-marketing and mass-consumption, and the need for industrial design to exercise greater control over the consumer. It aroused much professional criticism, yet the CoID had been exercising this role since its foundation.

42 Department of Environment, *Homes for Today and Tomorrow*, London, December 1961, p. 2.

43 *Ibid.*, p. 10.

44 London, 1962.

45 *Advertisement*, 1962.

46 *Publicity Leaflet*, June 1959.

47 *Architects' Journal*, 4 November 1954, pp. 545–66.

48 Sir Arton Wilson, *Caravans as Homes A Report*, London, 1959.

49 First established in 1934.

50 All the items were selected from John Lewis, who displayed the results in its Holles Street windows. *Gazette of the John Lewis Parnership*, 2 February 1963, p. 9.

51 The Beatles secured international status; you could have watched 'The Avengers' and 'That Was the Week That Was' on television; British Art and London were taking centre stage; David Hockney, Allen Jones and Alan Davie had won international art prizes.

52 *Guardian, A New Britain*, Manchester, 1963, p. 4.

53 *Ibid.*, p. 17.

54 *Guardian*, 22 September 1964, p. 10

55 General agreement that 500,000 new houses should be the target every year.

56 'Today there are many types or styles worth supporting: the Heal manner (or craft tradition), International, and of course Danish' (Christopher Heal, interview, *Design*, July 1965, p. 43–4). This, Christopher Heal believed, marked the end of the revolutionary period of design.

57 *Guardian*, 26 July 1965, p. 5.

58 *Ibid.*

59 *Ibid.*

60 H. Read (ed.), *The Practice of Design*, London, 1946, p. 10.

61 *Sunday Times*, 2 February 1964, p. 15.

62 Opened in London, May 1964.

63 *Design*, July 1965, commented on the value of 'The House of the Year', in the case of the Span 'Town House' which, because of additional space, cost 30 per cent more than the other four in the block: 1 Foxes Dale, London, SE3.

64 P. De Syllas and D. Meade, *Design to Fit the Family*, Harmondsworth, 1965, back cover.

65 *Ibid.*, p. 129.

66 *Gazette of the John Lewis Partnership*, 7 November 1964, reference to pamphlet of the same name published by the London advertising agency, Garland–Compton.

67 March 1965.

68 May 1965.

69 There were twenty-four trays in all, twelve from each country, with the British contribution selected by Robin and Lucienne Day, the design consultants to the John Lewis Partnership.

70 CoID, Press Release, IDG 1226, 17 October 1966, p. 2. The other trays were for coffee, children, cocktails, picnic, afternoon tea, breakfast, television supper, buffet supper, eating in the garden, and hotel room service.

71 British Medical Association, *Doctors' Orders*, London, 1964, p. 11.

72 *Nova*, March 1965.

73 *Observer*, 7 March 1965, p. 34.

74 *Guardian*, 21 January 1967, p. 7.

75 'Liverpool', report, *Guardian*, 6 February 1967.

76 T. Rock, 'Rehabilitation', *Architectural Review*, November 1967, p. 371. N. Taylor reworked his attack on tower blocks and estate development that he had first made in the *Architectural Review* in 1967, published as *The Village in the City*, London, 1973.

77 Archigram 5 Metropolis, March 1965.

78 *Architectural Design*, February 1967, pp. 65–6. Other articles dealt with microcommunication, ocean resources, the advances of bio-engineering, and genetic engineering. On a rather more mundane level the Ministry of Transport published the report *Cars for Cities*. By the end of 1967 there was the anticipation of microwave cooking.

79 The Ministry of Technology had been set up in 1964.

80 In the exhibition and book, *How to Play the Environment Game* (London, 1973,

p. 85), Theo Crosby took the 1968 gas explosion in the Ronan Points high-rise flats as the 'best thing that ever happened to British Architecture'.

81 A. Wedgwood Benn, 'Government and Technology', *Journal of the Royal Society of Arts*, vol. CXVII, February 1969, p. 164.

82 'Non-Plan: An Experiment in Freedom'. *New Society*, March 1969, pp. 435–42. Also see P. Barker, 'Non-Plan Revisited: Or the Real Way Cities Grow', *Journal of Design History*, vol. 12, no. 2 1999, pp. 95–110.

83 'Manplan', *Architectural Review*, August 1969, p. 90.

84 *Architectural Review*, September 1969, p. 169.

85 *Observer*, 21 December 1969, pp. 22–42.

86 It was the decade of the Rover 2000, Hillman Imp and the Cortina, the new Anglia, and the 1968 Ford Escort, advertised as 'a new concept in small-medium mass-market saloon'.

87 M. H. Wiberg, 'Keep the Home Young', *Designed in Finland*, Helsinki, 1969, p. 48.

88 *Advertisement*, 11 September 1969.

89 At the same time there was professional confusion in art and design which, while confident of its international status, felt that its own sense of value and identity was under threat with changes to an art education system that had been put in place in the 1850s. Those art schools that had largely benefited from new structures implemented in the early 1960s, were at the end of the decade struggling to come to terms with a loss of identity through relocation into the new polytechnics. The arts and crafts ethos had ended, its concepts of unity of practice discarded in the rush to establish separate subject identities, and the panic to get on board the technology raft.

90 H. Ozbekhan, 'Feasibility is no Criterion', *Design*, October 1969, p. 56.

91 Frank Fraser Darling, 'Man and Nature', *The Listener*, 13 November 1969, p. 656.

92 Editorial, *Design*, September 1965, in reference to the 4th International Congress of the International Council of Societies of Industrial Design, had noted the emerging concern for social responsibilities in the face of the fading post-war technological dream. But two years later, when the Design Centre Awards had been renamed The Council of Industrial Design Awards to signal a wider range of interests, the principles of Prizes for Elegant Design, first introduced in 1959, had remained the same.

93 *Design*, January 1970, p. 103.

94 *Life*, 16 February 1970, pp. 12–20.

95 Note the launch of the British group of Friends of the Earth in May 1971, followed shortly afterwards by its highly successful publicity campaign to return 'non-returnable' bottles to Schweppes.

96 Brian Batsford, 'The Face of Britain in the Seventies', *Journal of the Royal Society of Arts*, vol. CXVIII, June 1970, pp. 379–89.

97 *Ibid.*, p. 387.

98 T. Wardle, 'When Houses Cease to be Homes', *Ideal Home*, January 1970, pp. 70–3.

✧ Conclusion

SETTING out the concepts of a better and improved life, raising expectations, then frequently failing to deliver, has been a recurring cycle of this history. It is not a history of failure, but it is a reminder of the complex and important relationship between the ideal and the commonplace in the social values attached to products, homes and neighbourhoods, and of the difficulties of dealing with the concepts of reconstruction. As an introduction to key stages in which national and commercial influences constructed ideal models of family lifestyles, it has drawn attention to the extent to which practical and humanitarian needs associated with family life, such as privacy and community, efficiency and adaptability, health and pleasure, were identified with architectural and design strategies and schemes.

In considering patterns of influence the study has balanced the popular with the official, periodicals with reports, trade with policy, and has shown the persistent importance of exhibitions and showhouses in the redefining of taste and lifestyles. Encouraging the public imagination to bridge the gap between 'today' and 'tomorrow', many of the events referenced are well known, others less so. In some instances the importance of their contributions has been undervalued, and this has certainly been the case with the Ideal Home Exhibitions. As a synthesis of new and popular ideas and products, able at any one time to accommodate projects that the government believed were of national importance, give space to concepts of tomorrow's world, and embrace the luxury and practical models of the modern home, these exhibitions played a major role in cultivating a national belief in progress. Popularising ideas on what was good for the nation, regional exhibitions have been shown to be of similar importance. Outstanding amongst these, and deserving more attention, were the municipal exhibitions such as the Housing and Health Exhibitions held in Glasgow throughout the 1920s and 1930s, and the provincial Ideal and Better Home exhibitions of the inter- and post-war years.

Through the work of the Design and Industries Association and municipal authorities, and then the CoID and retail trade, moderate and tasteful, simple and economic, became the key principles of design that were put forward as universal values of a new society. The problem was that while these could just about be realised in the home, the potential of a new social democracy was undermined by the inability to sustain the same values in the urban and neighbourhood schemes. The RIBA made some important contributions through its touring exhibitions, but remained uncertain over its association with popular taste, so that while it entered into a successful collaboration with *Ideal Home* on designs for small houses, it continued to add its voice to the opponents of suburbia.

During the fifty years that forms the bulk of this study, raising living standards was matched by a determination to raise standards of taste. What has been shown is that in both instances there was a professional acceptance that true and lasting values were not restrained by social class. The concept and expression of 'contemporary' was the unexpected consequence of these ideals, making it possible to represent a middle class lifestyle that could be accessed by a wider social group. By the early 1960s this had made a major contribution to the emergence of a new middle-class that readily adapted to less living space, while retaining traditional patterns of organisation and responsibility.

The nineteenth-century legacy played a critical part in developing a greater awareness of the need for economic design, and placing health as the central objective of the social purpose of architecture and design. During the 1920s and 1930s this was formulated into a clear set of principles, with a general acceptance that the clean healthy life was a right and not just a dream for every family. Gas and electric appliances, a ready supply of hot water and good sanitation, new glass products and wipe clean surfaces, freedom in green fields, and healthy diets of fresh vegetables, were accepted as the basics of everyday life rather than luxuries. By the end of the 1920s an inclusive ideology on the rights of all families to have a comfortable home had gained credibility, and the concept of 'the people' had been extended to include those who had nothing, therefore creating a greater need for subsidies and municipal involvement.

What distinguished the phases of recovery from two world wars was that in the first period of reconstruction the new society was expected to be created from building new homes in the cottage style, whereas the second time it was a more ambitious brief, absorbing modernist ideals of clearing away, and building a society of social equality. Based on the 1930s concept of 'New for Old', reinforced by the modernists' visual interpretation of yesterday and tomorrow in terms of grey and white, with the nineteenth-century industrial towns seen through a grainy filter, blocking the way of the planned sunswept tower block landscape of the new world, it was an idealism that could not be sustained. Ultimately leading to the frustrations and disappointments of the 1960s, the demise of modernism owed most to the social failings of its aesthetic and technology. In its disregard for the family as an institution, and the needs of the housewife, it had failed to think in terms of future generations, providing no scope for adaptability, or for freedom of expression. It did not build for children or grandchildren, and showed no respect for the cultures that it demolished. This need not have been so, but the possibility of a middle road as outlined in the summary and conclusion of Elizabeth Denby's *Europe Re-housed*, and expressed in the Lansbury development for the 'Festival of Britain' had been ignored. Instead, the modernists had looked towards a time when obsolescence would be an integral part of architectural and design planning for society and the concept of homelife based on the cottage model would be replaced by neighbourhoods arranged into well-ordered blocks. It was as this architectural expression of social revolution became associated with landscapes of social inequality that its dogma was directly challenged. In retrospect it had become possible to see that a more effective revolution would have been to accept the popular dream, which remained what the Mass Observation's *An Enquiry into Peoples' Homes* (1943) had identified as the 'small modern suburban house, preferably possessing all modern conveniences'.[1] This was the popular choice of an architecture of social equality.

The vision of a well-ordered society as a model for a new Britain had failed to take account of the vernacular traditions of British culture. Rightly dismissive of an over-romanticised concept of village life, insufficient attention was given to the importance of adhoc developments, the inherent values in the scale of the English landscape and the qualitative relationship between home and landscape. Arthur Bryant in 1933, in a radio talk series on 'The National Character', had spoken of it as the outcome of a love of the countryside and nonconformist puritanism, that saw utopia as 'a rose garden and a cottage in the country'.[2] It was to remain a popular stereotype of national identity that J. B. Priestley had described as 'cosy'. Families loved it, not just for the romance, but for its practicalities. In this respect I have probably given insufficient attention to the cultural significance of the garden, from the kitchen garden and allotments for the working classes, to the increasing emphasis on its use for recreation and leisure, spawning a nation of amateur gardeners.[3]

Perfection was village scale with urban resources. This, though, was an unattainable dream, as the social purpose of architectural and design planning for the family fell apart when there was no work and the national economy was unable to sustain the ideals drawn out on the planners' maps. Local initiatives offered stop-gap solutions, but there was a general failure to learn of the need for incremental development, and almost inevitably large-scale reconstruction programmes and new town developments suffered from similar problems. More significant was the unwillingness to embrace the lessons of prefabrication, and Do-It-Yourself conversions of buses and railway carriages, in meeting the housing shortage, although the 'parkhomes' developments of the recent past have shown that the recognition of the potential benefits of the manufactured homes have not been completely lost.

The inability to accommodate the motor car effectively in contemporary life was not simply a result of the failure to recognise the planning implications of the increasing volume of traffic, but a consequence of the initial antipathy towards the car, which was perceived as a threat to the established order of life, first disturbing the peace of rural lanes and then clogging the city high streets. From the 1930s road safety and highway codes widened the debate on the ethics of motoring, but it was fear of death on the roads, which reached new levels of anxiety in 1956 when the *Illustrated London News* pictured crowd scenes symbolising the thousands killed and injured on British roads in one year, that held public attention. In terms of family motoring, the critical failure was the inability to anticipate the scale of the expanding market, and incorporate adequate space for parking and garaging in new housing schemes. That the initial garden suburbs had underprovided for this need was understandable, but for the same mistakes to be made in the 1950s showed an unwillingness to accept that from the family of six getting the car ready for the new season, to the images of trouble-free motoring of the early 1960s, car ownership remained the popular dream.

As the setting of minimum living standards became a central issue, the arguments that had been used to justify the limited living space of those dependent on municipal and company housing schemes, were subsequently adapted to convince the middle-class house owners in the 1950s and 1960s of the merits of open-plan living and contemporary design styles. These values were already evident in the 1946 'Britain Can Make It' exhibition, sustained in the 1950s in the CoID open-plan room, and consolidated by the adaptable homes of the 1960s. Conventions of homelife had crossed class barriers. Crucial to these changes was the introduction of a wide range of appliances and services. For example, without a flexible or central heating system, the development of the bedroom into the bedsitting room would have been impossible, and similarly the possibility of cooking by gas or electricity allowed a much great flexibility in interior layout. In redefining homelife individual pieces of furniture were given symbolic functions: the table could accommodate homework, be laid for dinner, set with a vase of flowers when not in use, or folded away; likewise the room divider, the kitchen cabinet and divan could have multiple uses, while the television, initially seen as a challenge to the established routines, functioned as the focus of family entertainment, replacing the piano and radio. Of all the indicators of both social change and division, the equipping and space of the kitchen has been the most precise measure of attitudes and prejudice. For the British Pavilion at the Paris Exhibition, 1937, Mrs Darcy Braddell had designed a kitchen with maid's sitting room, as the national model. At Halsinborg, 1955, it was the kitchen of the small family home.

As these changes unfolded, the representation of the housewife was critical as a reassuring note of social improvement and stability. Once the role of the housewife had been established as manager and worker, whose efficiency would allow her to spend more time with the children and run a happy home, the pattern of expectation and provision remained substantially unchanged.[4] Fashions changed, informality became the norm, but from the attractive mother of the 'Sunlight' soap advertisement to the fun-loving spirit of 'Mrs 1970', the social conventions had been modified rather than replaced. Whether it was modernisation or modernism, architecture and design did little to challenge the traditions of homelife. The position taken by Anthony Bertram in *The House*, his 1945 revised edition of *Machine for Living In*, was typical: 'The housewife who cooks and polishes with pride, who creates a home out of a shell, is probably a happier person than the one whose chief interest in her home is to get out of it'.[5]

Visual reminders of the unresolved social problems of poverty, homelessness and abuse were important to the appreciation of the actual progress made in terms of the health and welfare of the family. The stoicism of Luke Fildes' working man's family in the face of tragedy, the brave entry into the cultured world of the museum, the pioneer settlers of the government landschemes, all had the same determined spirit that was embodied in Henry Moore's 'Family Group', the father's protective arm round the mother, as together they confidently look to new horizons. Stoicism had given way to the heroic, and although it is easy to dismiss this as misplaced idealism, it is just as possible to undervalue the heroism born of desperation that moved families into new settlements. Critically, though, in this pattern of representation, there was an important difference in the purposes behind the imaging of the destitute families in Victorian England and the inter-war years, and those constructed by the Salvation Army and Shelter on the streets of Swinging Britain of the 1960s. In the earlier instances the social problems had been seen as the inherited failures of previous generations, while those of the 1960s were perceived as an expression of the failures of its own systems and values. Malcolm Muggeridge had identified the funeral of Winston Churchill in 1965 as a marking of the old social order passing away. The steady break-up of the Empire, and the critical mood generated by the 'Angry Young Men' of the 1950s,[6] added to the social frustrations over the failure to build a new Britain. The world of sunshine visualised in the 1930s had given way to that of technology, but both had shown that it was one thing to dream of the perfect life of AD2000, and rather a different matter to deal with the basics and ordinary matters of everyday family life.

At the beginning of the century the interests in children and the welfare of the family were strongly nationalistic, with architecture and design recruited to work for the good of the Empire. If all other arguments failed to convince a sceptical audience, claims that planning was for the good of the children could be expected to undermine the most determined opposition. The boy and girl stepping out of the flats on the new White City estate, standing in the doorway of a worker's cottage, or looking out of the rear window of a Mini, were the images not just of 'today', but of the future of Britain. In an edited account of a lecture 'The Year 2000' by R. Buckminster Fuller, he was reported as saying, 'In looking forward to the year 2000, it is not the 'Buck Rogers' details which are important but whether the world will be a good place for our children and grandchildren'.[7] The problem of conserving and using world resources wisely had been personalised through an association with the concept of 'our family'. The redefining of social responsibility in terms of ecology and world resources was an important change of mood, for while industry and the retail trade continued to provide the trappings for family life, questions of the needs of future generations were being reshaped by concerns over resources, rather than products.

The inquiry has confirmed that health, comfort and happiness were useful premises on which to base an investigation of the social purpose of architecture and design for the family. The events and ideas that have been drawn together suggest that the long-term successes were dependent on a balanced provision of living space, services and neighbourhood resources; a flexibility and adaptability that allowed for changing needs and expectations; a place for dreams and self-expression; and allowance for continuity and durability as well as obsolescence. They show that architecture and design were at their most effective when the needs of the family were fully understood, the collaboration between tradition and new exploited, and the resource implications properly accounted for. The enduring impression is of a design culture that valued principles of modesty and order, and in practice muddled through.

Having visited and revisited many sites, trawled journals and archives I am aware of material still to be assimilated into this history, but I believe that it will round off rather than change the pattern that I have set out. There are of course many subjects caught up in this account that justify study in their own right. The representation of architecture and design in women's journals, the municipal role in the construction of civic Britain, and the images of family in defining patterns of social change, are just some of the most obvious topics that would extend the understanding of the social purpose and place of architecture and design in everyday life.

Notes

1 Mass Observation, *An Enquiry into People's Homes*, London, 1943, p. 226.

2 Arthur Bryant, 'The National Character', *The Listener*, 11 October 1933, p. 531.

3 By the 1950s it was claimed that there were 19 million amateur gardeners: *The Economist*, 21 June 1958.

4 Shirley Conran's *Superwoman*, 1975, is a good example of how little the culture and language had changed. Introduced in the *Observer Magazine*, 15 June, as 'how to become your own home help', all the reviews likened it to a twentieth century Mrs Beeton. Twenty years later in celebration of the Good Housekeeping Institute's 70th anniversary, the journal ran a feature based on a Gallup survey on 'The secret life of the modern housewife' little had changed (*Good Housekeeping*, July 1994, p. 56). There is much research needed into how the publications on housework and management redefined and reflected the changing role of the housewife.

5 A. Bertram, *The House. A Summary of the Art and Science of Domestic Architecture*, London, 1945, p. 109.

6 D. Wilson, 'Are Young Men Angry?', *The Listener*, 6 June 1957. p. 908–9.

7 *Architectural Design*, February 1967, p. 63.

✧ Bibliography

Books

Abercrombie P. (ed.), *The Book of the Modern House*, London, 1939.

Adams A., *Architecture in the Family Way. Doctors, Houses and Women 1870–1900*, Quebec, 1996.

Aitken P., Cunningham C. and McCutcheon B., *The Homesteads Stirling's Garden Suburb*, Stirling, 1984.

Aldous T., *Goodbye Britain?*, London, 1975.

Aldridge M., *The British New Towns*, London, 1979.

Allen G., *The Cheap Cottage and Small House*, London, 1919 (1st ed. 1912).

Allwood S., *The Great Exhibitions*, London, 1977.

Arts Council, *'45–'55, Ten Years of British Architecture*, catalogue, London, 1956.

Arts Council, *Thirties, Exhibition Catalogue*, London, 1979.

Ascot Gas, *Houses into Flats*, London, 1947.

Ashbee C. R., *Craftsmanship in Competitive Industry*, London, 1908.

Ashworth W., *The Genesis of Modern British Town Planning*. London, 1954 (reprint 1968).

Association of Teachers of Domestic Subjects, Foreword by R. B. Parker, *Architecture and Home Organisation*, London, 1926.

Atfield J. and Kirkham P., *A View from the Interior. Women and Design*, London, 1989.

Baillie Scott M. H., *Houses and Gardens*, London, 1906.

Ballantyne A., *Choose Your Kitchen*, London, 1944.

Banham M. and Hillier B., *A Tonic to the Nation*, London, 1976.

Banham, R., *The New Brutalism*, London, 1966.

Barnes H., *Housing: The Facts and the Future*, London 1923.

Barton J. E., *The Changing World. Vol. 6 Modern Art*, London, 1932.

Beattie S., *A Revolution in London Housing: LCC Housing Architects and Their Work 1893–1914*, London, 1980.

Beckett J. and Cherry D. (ed.), *The Edwardian Era*, London, 1987.

Bertram A., *The House: A Machine for Living In*, London, 1935 (reissued 1945 as *The House*).

Bertram A., *Design in Everyday Things*, London, 1937.

Bertram A., *Design*, London, 1938.

Birchall J., *Coop: the people's business*, Manchester, 1994.

Bondfield M., *Our Towns, a Close-Up*, London, 1943.

Boulton, E. H. B., *Timber Houses*, London, 1937.

Bowley M., *Housing and the State, 1919–1944*, London, 1945.
Boxshall J., *Good Housekeeping. Every Home Should Have One*, London, 1997.
Boyd A. and Penn C., *Homes for the People*, London, 1946.
Briggs A., *Victorian Things*, London, 1988.
Brown W. E., *Changing Britain*, Bourneville, 1943.
Burgess Wise D., *The Motor Car*, London, 1979.
Burnett J., *A Social History of Housing 1815–1985*, London, 2nd ed. 1986.
Cardiff Worker's Cooperative Garden Village Society, *Prospectus*, Cardiff, 1913.
Carrington N., *Design in the Home*, London, 1933.
Carrington N., *Design and a Changing Civilisation*, London, 1935.
Carrington N. and Harris M., *British Achievement in Design*, London, 1946.
Carruthers A., *The Scottish Home*, Edinburgh, 1996.
Carter E., *Seaside Houses and Bungalows*, London, 1937.
Central Housing Advisory Committee, *Houses We Live In*, London, 1939.
Central Housing Advisory Committee, *Design of Dwellings*, London, 1944.
Central Housing Advisory Committee, *Living in Flats*, London, 1952.
Clarke P., *Hope and Glory, Britain 1900–1990*, London, 1996.
Cooperative Building Society, *Design for Britain*. First series 1941–42; second series 1942–44. John Mansbridge, *Here Comes Tomorrow*, special issue 1942.
Council for Art and Industry, *The Working Class Home, Its Furnishing and Equipment*, London, 1937.
Council of Industrial Design, *Design '46*, London, 1946.
Council of Industrial Design, *Britain Can Make It, Exhibition Catalogue*, London, 1946.
Council of Industrial Design, *Furnishing to Fit the Family*, London, 1947.
Council of Industrial Design, *How to Buy Things for the Kitchen*, London, 1948.
Council of Industrial Design, *Ideas for Your Home*, London, 1950.
Council of Industrial Design, *Design in the Festival*, London, 1951.
Cowling D., *An Essay for Today. The Scottish New Towns 1947–1997*, Edinburgh, 1997.
Cox I., *Guide, South Bank Exhibition, London, Festival of Britain*, London, 1951.
Crafts Council, *The Omega Workshops 1913–19*, London, 1984.
Crittall Mr and Mrs F. H., *Fifty Years of Work and Play*, London, 1934.
Crosby T., *How to Play the Environment Game*, London 1973.
Cullen G., *A Town called Alcan*, Banbury, 1964.
Daily Express, *The Housewife's Book*, London, n.d. (*c.* 1938).
Daily Mail, *Designs for Ideal (Workers') Homes*, London, 1919.
Daily Mail, *Ideal Home Book*, London, 1946–47 (first of the annuals published through into the 1950s).
Daily Mirror, *The Perfect Home and How to Furnish It*, London, 1913.
Darling C. R., *Modern Domestic Scientific Appliances*, London, 1932.
Daunton M. J., *House and Home in Victorian City: Working-class Housing 1850–1914*, London, 1983.
Davison T. R., *Port Sunlight*, London, 1916.
Dean D., *The Thirties: Recalling the English Architectural Scene*, London, 1983.
Denby E., *Europe Re-housed*, London, 1938 (2nd ed. 1944).
Department of the Environment, *Homes for Today and Tomorrow*, London, 1961.
Departmental Committee on the Royal College of Art, *Report*, London, 1911.
Design and Industries Association, *A New Body with New Aims*, London, 1915.
Design and Industries Association, *Design in Everyday Life and Things, Year Book 1926–27*, London, 1927.

Design and Industries Association, *The Face of the Land, Year Book 1929–30*, London, 1930.
Design and Industries Association, *Furnishing A Small House*, Birmingham, 1937.
De Syllas P. and Meade D., *Design to Fit the Family*, Harmondsworth, 1965.
Dick S. and Allingham H. *The Cottage Homes of England, London, 1909*
Eastlake C. L., *Hints on Household Taste*, London, 1868.
Edwards A., *The Design of Suburbia*, London, 1981.
Edwards A. T., *A Hundred New Towns for Britain*, London, 1933.
Edwards E. E., *Electricity in Working Class Homes*, London, 1935.
Egan M., *The All Electric Home*, London, 1931.
Electrical Association for Women, *Housing Digest*, London, 1946.
Fairbrother N., *New Lives, New Landscapes*, London, 1970.
Farr M., *Design in British Industry*, Cambridge, 1955.
Forty A., *Objects of Desire: Design and Society 1750–1980*, London, 1986.
Frederick C., *Scientific Management in the Home*, London, 1920.
Friedman B., *Flats, Municipal and Private Enterprise*, London, 1938.
Gaskell S. M., *Model Housing. From the Great Exhibition to the Festival of Britain*, London, 1987.
Geddes P., *City Development*, Bourneville, 1904.
Geffrye Museum, *Utility Furniture and Fashion, 1941–1951*, London, 1974.
Girouard M., *Sweetness and Light, The Queen Anne Movement*, Oxford, 1977.
Girouard M., *Life in the English Country House*, New Haven, 1978.
Glasgow Corporation, *Housing & Health Exhibition*, catalogue, Glasgow, 1919 (exhibition runs through 1920s and 1930s).
Glass Age News, nos 18, 19, 23, 25, 27, 32; *Glass Age Projects*, 1957–68.
Glendinning M., *Rebuilding Scotland*, East Linton, 1997.
Glendinning M. and Muthesius S., *Tower Blocks*, New Haven, 1994.
Gloag, J., Introduction in *The Face of the Land*, DIA Year Book, London, 1929/30.
Gloag J. (ed.), *Design in Modern Life*, London, 1934.
Gloag J. and Mansfield L., *The House We Ought to Live In*, Edinburgh, 1923.
Gloag J. and Wornum G., *House Out of Factory*, London, 1946.
Goldfinger E. and Carter E. J., *County of London Plan*, London, 1945.
Good Housekeeping Institute, *The Happy Home*, London, 1954.
Gould J., *Modern Houses in Britain 1919–1939*, London, 1977.
Gover G., *Exploring English Character*, London, 1955.
Gregory, E. W., *The Art and Craft of Home-Making*, London, 1913.
Greenhalgh P., *Ephemeral Vistas: The Expositions universelles, Great Exhibitions and World Fairs, 1851–1939*, Manchester, 1988.
Guardian, *A New Britain*, Manchester, 1963.
Halford L., *Colour Rules Your Home*, London, 1958.
Hardy D., *From Garden Cities to New Towns*, London, 1991.
Harris J. *Private Lives-Public Spirit, Oxford, 1993.*
Harris J., Hyde S. and Smith G., *1966 and All That. Design and the Consumer in Britain 1960–1969*, London, 1986.
Haywood W., *Birmingham Civic Society 1918–1946*, Birmingham, *c.* 1946.
Health and Hygiene, *Exhibition Catalogue*, Edinburgh, 1930.
Herbert G., *Land Settlement Report*, York, 1934 (unpublished Homestead).
Heskett J., *Industrial Design*, London, 1980.

Hopkins H., *The New Look. A Social History of the Forties and Fifties in Britain*, London, 1963.
House-Building Industries' Standing Committee, *Your New Home*, London, 1946.
Howard E., *Garden Cities of Tomorrow*, reprint London, 1965 (1st pub. 1902).
Huxley J., *TVA Adventure in Planning*, London, 1943.
ICI, *Furnishing Your Home*, Northwich, 1952.
Ideal Home/RIBA, *The Book of Small House Plans*, London, 1959.
Jackson A. A., *Semi-Detached London*, London, 1973.
Jackson F., *Where Shall I Live? The Building of the First Garden City at Letchworth*, Nottingham, 1978.
Jackson L., *The New Look. Design in the Fifties*, London, 1991.
Jackson L., *Contemporary Architecture and Interiors of the 1950s*, London, 1994.
Jarvis A., *The Things We See – Indoors and Out*, Harmondsworth, 1947. The first in a series that included Brett A., *Houses* (no. 2) and Russell G., *Furniture* (no. 3).
Jencks C., *Modern Movements in Architecture*, Harmondsworth, 1973.
Jones B., *The Unsophisticated Arts*, London, 1951.
Jones S. R., *The Village Homes of England*, London, 1912.
Joyce P., *Visions of the People*, Cambridge, 1991.
Kinchin P. and Kinchin J., *Glasgow's Great Exhibitions*, Bicester, 1988.
Lancaster O., *Pillar to Post*, London, 1938.
Larsson, L., *Your Child's Room*, Harmondworth, 1965.
Le Corbusier, *Towards a New Architecture*, London, 1927.
Le Corbusier, *The City of Tomorrow*, London, 1929.
Local Government Board, Committee Report, *Provision of Dwellings for the Working Classes in England and Wales, and Scotland (Tudor Walters Report)*, London, 1918.
Long H., *The Edwardian House*, Manchester, 1993.
MacCarthy F., *A History of British Design 1830–1970*, London, 1979.
McCready K. J., *The Land Settlement Association: Its History and Present Form*, Occasional papers No. 37, The Plunkett Foundation, 1974.
McGrath R., *Twentieth Century Houses*, London, 1934.
McGrath R. and Frost A. C., *Glass in Architecture and Decoration*, London, 1937.
McKibbin R., *Classes and Cultures, England 1918–1951*, Oxford, 1998.
Maguire P. J. and Woodham J. M., *Design and Cultural Politics in Post-War Britain*, London, 1997.
Mannin E., *Castles in the Street*, London, 1942.
Mansbridge, A., *Wise for Thy Houses*, London, 1942.
Martin J. L., and Speight S., *The Flat Book*, London, 1939.
Marwick A., *British Society Since 1945*, London, 1996.
Mass Observation, *An Enquiry into Peoples' Homes*, London, 1943.
Merivale M., *Furnishing the Small Home*, London, 1938 (revised edn 1943).
Metropolitan Railway, *Country Homes, Official Guide*, Watford, 1910.
Ministry of Health, *Fitter Britain*, London, 1938.
Ministry of Health, *Management of Municipal Housing Estates*, London, 1945.
Ministry of Health, *Conversion of Existing Houses*, London, 1945.
Ministry of Health, *Housing Progress*, London,1948.
Ministry of Health, *Our Gardens*, London, 1948.
Ministry of Health, *Housing Manual*, London, 1949.
Ministry of Housing and Local Government, *Design in Town and Village*, London, 1953.

Ministry of Housing and Local Government, *The Adaptable House*, London, 1962.
Ministry of Information, *Make Do and Mend*, London, 1943.
Ministry of Local Government and Planning, *Housing for Special Purposes*, London, 1951.
Ministry of Transport, *Buchanan Report, Traffic in Towns*, London, 1964.
Ministry of Works, *Demonstration Houses*, London, 1944.
Morris E. S., *British Town Planning and Urban Design*, London, 1997.
Morris L., *The Working of the Household*, Oxford, 1990.
Morris W. F., *The Future Citizen and His Surroundings*, London, 1945.
Movable Dwelling Conference, *Movable Dwellings*, London, 1950.
Murray P. and Trombley S., *Modern British Architecture since 1945*, London, 1984.
Muthesius H. *The English House, London, 1979 (based on 2nd edn 1908–11).*
Nairn I., *Outrage*, London, 1955.
National Health Exhibition, *Official Guide*, London, 1913.
Naylor G., *The Arts and Crafts Movement*, London, 1990.
Nettleford J. S., *Slum Reform and Town Planning*, Birmingham, 1910.
North A. E., *The Book of the Trailer Caravan*, London, 1959 (1st edn 1952).
Oakley A., *The Sociology of Housework*, London, 1974.
Oliver P., *Dunroamin: The Suburban Semi and its Enemies*, London, 1981.
Open University, *History of Architecture and Design 1890–1939, Units 19 & 20*, Milton Keynes, 1975.
Parker, R. B., *Our Homes*, Buxton, 1895.
Patmore D., *Modern Furnishing and Decoration*, London, 1936.
Peel D. C., *The Labour Saving House*, London, 1917.
Peel D. C., *The Art of Modern Housekeeping*, London, 1935.
Political and Economic Planning, *Planning Broadsheets*, London, from 1933.
Political Economic Planning, *Housing England*, London, 1934.
Political Economic Planning, *The Market for Household Appliances*, London 1945
Pevsner N., *Pioneers of the Modern Movement*, London, 1936.
Pevsner N., *An Inquiry into Industrial Art in England*, Cambridge, 1937.
Pevsner N., *Visual Pleasures from Everyday Things*, London, 1946.
Pevsner N., *Studies in Art, Architecture and Design, Volume 1 & 2*, London, 1968.
Phillips R. R., *The Servantless House and How to Equip It*, London, 1920.
Phillips R. R., *The Modern House and its Equipment*, London, 1937.
Physick J., *The Victoria and Albert Museum*, London, 1982.
Pleydell-Bouverie M., *Daily Mail Book of Post-War Homes*, London, 1944.
Rayner C., *For Children: Equipping a Home for a Growing Family*, London, 1967.
Read H. (ed.), *The Practice of Design*, London, 1946.
Reilly C., *Architecture as a Communal Art*, London, 1946.
RIBA, *Health, Sport and Fitness*, exhibition catalogue, London, 1938.
RIBA, *Towards a New Britain*, London, 1943.
RIBA Reconstruction Committee, *Housing*, London, 1944.
Richards J. M., *An Introduction to Modern Architecture*, London, 1940.
Rowetz A. and Turkington R., *The Place of Home. English Domestic Environments 1914–2000*, London, 1995.
Rowntree B. S., *Poverty. A Study in Town Life*, London, 1901.
Rowntree B. S. and Lavers G. R., *English Life and Leisure*, London, 1951.
Rowntree D., *Interior Design*, Harmondsworth, 1965.
Royal Society of Arts, *The Post-War Home: Its Interior and Equipment*, London, 1942.

Russell G., *How to Buy Furniture*, London, 1947.
Ryan D. S., *The Ideal Home. Through the 20th Century*, London, 1997.
Schaffer F., *The New Town Story*, London, 1970.
Scottish Housing Advisory Committee, *Report, Planning Our New Homes*, London, 1944.
Scottish Housing Advisory Committee, *Report, Modernising our Homes*, London, 1947.
Seddon J. and Worden S., *Women Designing. Redefining Design in Britain between the Wars*, Brighton, 1994.
Sharp T., *Exeter Phoenix, a Plan for Rebuilding*, London, 1946.
Sharp T., *The Anatomy of the Village*, Harmondsworth, 1946.
Shaw F., *The Homes and Homeless of Post-War Britain*, Carnforth, 1985.
Silk G., *Automobile and Culture*, New York, 1984.
Simon E. D., *How to Abolish the Slums*, London, 1929.
Simon E. D., *The Anti-Slum Campaign*, London, 1933.
Smithells R., *Better Homes Book*, London *c.* 1955.
Sparke P., *Design in Context*, London, 1987.
Sparke P., *A Century of Design*, London, 1998.
Sparke P. (ed.), *Did Britain Make It? British Design in Context 1946–86*, London, 1986.
Sparke P. (ed.), *The Plastics Age. From Modernity to Post-Modernity*, London, 1990.
Stamp G., *Britain in the Thirties*. AD Profiles 24. London, n.d.
Stamp L. D., *The Land of Britain. Its Use and Misuse*, London, 1948 (3rd ed. 1962).
Stevenson J., *British Society 1914–1945*, London, 1984.
Swenarton M., *Homes Fit for Heroes*, London, 1981.
Taylor N., *The Village in the City*, London, 1973.
Thane P., *Foundations of the Welfare State*, London, 1996.
Thorns D., *Suburbia*, St Albans, 1972.
Timmers M., *The Way We Live Now*, catalogue, London, 1978.
Todd D. and Mortimer R., *The New Interior Decoration*, London, 1929.
Tormley C. G., *Furnishing Your Home*, London, 1940.
Tubbs R., *Living in Cities*, London, 1942.
Tubbs R., *The Englishman Builds*, London, 1945.
Tudor Walters J., *The Building of Twelve Thousand Houses*, London, 1927.
Turner M., *The Decoration of the Suburban Villa*, exhibition catalogue, London, 1983.
Unwin R. and Baillie Scott M. H., *Town Planning and Modern Architecture at the Hampstead Garden Suburb*, London, 1909.
Waldermar Leverton, Mrs, *Small Homes and How to Furnish them*, London, 1903.
Ward. C. *Goodnight Campers. History of British Holiday Camps, London, 1986.*
Weaver L., *The House and its Equipment*, London, 1912.
Weaver L., *The Country Life Book of Cottages*, London, 1913.
Weaver L., *Cottages*, London, 1926.
White R. B., *Prefabrication. A History of Its Development in Great Britain*, London, 1965.
Whitechapel Art Gallery, *Setting Up Home for Bill and Betty*, London, 1952.
Whiteley N., *Pop Design: Modernism to Mod*, London, 1987.
Whiteley N., *Design for Society*, reprint London, 1998 (1st edn, 1993).
Whiteman W. H., *The History of the Caravan*, London, 1973.
Whittick A., *The Small House: Today and Tomorrow*, London, 1947.
Williams-Ellis C., *England and the Octopus*, London, 1928.
Williams-Ellis C. and Williams-Ellis E., *The Pleasures of Architecture*, London, 1924.
Wilson A., *Caravans as Homes, A Report*, London, 1959.

Woodham J. M., *Twentieth Century Design*, Oxford, 1997.

Yorke F. R. S., *The Modern House in England*, London, 1937.

Yorke F. R. S. and Penn C., *A Key to Modern Architecture*, London, 1939.

Yorkshire and North Midlands Model Cottage Exhibition, *Official Illustrated Catalogue*, Sheffield, 1907.

Periodicals/journals

Extensive use has been made of the following sources: *Architects' Journal, Architectural Review, Builder, Ideal Home, Design*; company and trade publications that include *Gazette of John Lewis Partnership*; CWS publications including *The Producer, Coop Review* and *Weekly Press Digest*; *Thousand and One Uses for Gas*; *The Electrical Age*.

Occasional but essential use has been made of: *Architect & Building News; Builders Journal & Architectural Record; Design & Construction; Design for Today; Studio; Autocar; Motor; Country Life; Homes & Gardens; Good Housekeeping; Womans Journal; Illustrated London News; The Listener; Municipal Journal; Picture Post; Journals of Design History, RIBA, RSA, Town Planning Institute.*

✧ Index